T0190457

IFIP Advances in Information and Communication Technology

638

Editor-in-Chief

Kai Rannenberg, Goethe University Frankfurt, Germany

Editorial Board Members

TC 1 – Foundations of Computer Science
Luís Soares Barbosa⑩, University of Minho, Braga, Portugal

TC 2 – Software: Theory and Practice
Michael Goedicke, University of Duisburg-Essen, Germany

TC 3 – Education
Arthur Tatnall⑩, Victoria University, Melbourne, Australia

TC 5 – Information Technology Applications
Erich J. Neuhold, University of Vienna, Austria

TC 6 – Communication Systems
Burkhard Stiller, University of Zurich, Zürich, Switzerland

TC 7 – System Modeling and Optimization
Fredi Tröltzsch, TU Berlin, Germany

TC 8 – Information Systems
Jan Pries-Heje, Roskilde University, Denmark

TC 9 – ICT and Society
David Kreps⑩, National University of Ireland, Galway, Ireland

TC 10 – Computer Systems Technology
Ricardo Reis⑩, Federal University of Rio Grande do Sul, Porto Alegre, Brazil

TC 11 – Security and Privacy Protection in Information Processing Systems
Steven Furnell⑩, Plymouth University, UK

TC 12 – Artificial Intelligence
Eunika Mercier-Laurent⑩, University of Reims Champagne-Ardenne, Reims, France

TC 13 – Human-Computer Interaction
Marco Winckler⑩, University of Nice Sophia Antipolis, France

TC 14 – Entertainment Computing
Rainer Malaka, University of Bremen, Germany

IFIP – The International Federation for Information Processing

IFIP was founded in 1960 under the auspices of UNESCO, following the first World Computer Congress held in Paris the previous year. A federation for societies working in information processing, IFIP's aim is two-fold: to support information processing in the countries of its members and to encourage technology transfer to developing nations. As its mission statement clearly states:

> IFIP is the global non-profit federation of societies of ICT professionals that aims at achieving a worldwide professional and socially responsible development and application of information and communication technologies.

IFIP is a non-profit-making organization, run almost solely by 2500 volunteers. It operates through a number of technical committees and working groups, which organize events and publications. IFIP's events range from large international open conferences to working conferences and local seminars.

The flagship event is the IFIP World Computer Congress, at which both invited and contributed papers are presented. Contributed papers are rigorously refereed and the rejection rate is high.

As with the Congress, participation in the open conferences is open to all and papers may be invited or submitted. Again, submitted papers are stringently refereed.

The working conferences are structured differently. They are usually run by a working group and attendance is generally smaller and occasionally by invitation only. Their purpose is to create an atmosphere conducive to innovation and development. Refereeing is also rigorous and papers are subjected to extensive group discussion.

Publications arising from IFIP events vary. The papers presented at the IFIP World Computer Congress and at open conferences are published as conference proceedings, while the results of the working conferences are often published as collections of selected and edited papers.

IFIP distinguishes three types of institutional membership: Country Representative Members, Members at Large, and Associate Members. The type of organization that can apply for membership is a wide variety and includes national or international societies of individual computer scientists/ICT professionals, associations or federations of such societies, government institutions/government related organizations, national or international research institutes or consortia, universities, academies of sciences, companies, national or international associations or federations of companies.

More information about this series at https://link.springer.com/bookseries/6102

Jun Sasaki · Yuko Murayama ·
Dimiter Velev · Plamena Zlateva (Eds.)

Information Technology in Disaster Risk Reduction

6th IFIP WG 5.15 International Conference, ITDRR 2021
Morioka, Japan, October 25–27, 2021
Revised Selected Papers

Springer

Editors
Jun Sasaki
Iwate Prefectural University
Takizawa, Iwate, Japan

Yuko Murayama 🔟
Tsuda University
Tokyo, Japan

Dimiter Velev
University of National and World Economy
Sofia, Grad Sofiya, Bulgaria

Plamena Zlateva
Bulgarian Academy of Sciences
Sofia, Bulgaria

ISSN 1868-4238 ISSN 1868-422X (electronic)
IFIP Advances in Information and Communication Technology
ISBN 978-3-031-04172-3 ISBN 978-3-031-04170-9 (eBook)
https://doi.org/10.1007/978-3-031-04170-9

This Springer imprint is published by the registered company Springer Nature Switzerland AG
The registered company address is: Gewerbestrasse 11, 6330 Cham, Switzerland

Preface

It has been ten years since the Great East Japan Earthquake and Tsunami struck a large coastal area of the northern part of the main island of Japan, including the coast of the Iwate prefecture, on the afternoon of Friday, March 11, 2011. This anniversary provided the incentive for us to have our IFIP WG 5.15 annual conference, the 6th International Conference on Information Technology in Disaster Risk Reduction (ITDRR 2021), in Morioka, Iwate, Japan.

The experience of the crisis response ten years ago was, indeed, the motivation for us to look into the research domain of Information Technology in Disaster Risk Reduction (ITDRR). When we introduced the research domain at the IFIP General Assembly in 2014 in Vienna, the idea was highly applauded by Acad. Blagovest Hristov Sendov (February 8, 1932 – January 19, 2020) who was IFIP President from 1989 to 1992 and an Honorary Member. The idea of using IT for disaster response and management was new to him. Previously, traditional research topics for IT and disaster were limited to technical aspects of networking, simulation, and risk evaluation and management. We set up a Domain Committee on ITDRR within IFIP in 2016, which was later transformed into a working group within Technical Committee 5, WG 5.15, in 2020.

Due to the recent global environmental changes, we have observed an increasing number of natural disasters, such as floods, tornadoes, wildfires, and earthquakes. Given current trends there are unfortunately more to come in the future.

The Sixth IFIP WG 5.15 Conference on Information Technology in Disaster Risk Reduction (ITDRR 2021), was held during October 25–27, 2021, at the Aiina Campus of Iwate Prefectural University, Morioka, Japan. Due to the COVID-19 pandemic, ITDRR 2021 was held in hybrid format.

The conference focused on various ICT aspects and the challenges of disaster risk reduction. The main topics included areas such as information analysis for situation awareness, evacuation, rescue, COVID-19 issues, risk assessment, and disaster management.

ITDRR 2021 invited experts, researchers, practitioners, academics, and all others who were interested in disseminating their work. The conference established an environment that fostered the discussion and exchange of ideas among different academic, research, business, and public communities.

The Program Committee received 18 paper submissions, out of which 11 research papers were finally accepted. The volume editors would like to express their special gratitude to the members of the Program Committee, and to the many reviewers of the papers, for their dedication in helping produce this volume.

For this conference, we started two awards: the Best Paper Award and the Best Student Paper Award. The following winners were selected based on the review results:

- The ITDRR 2021 Best Paper Award — Keisuke Utsu, Natsumi Yagi, Airi Fukushima, Yuma Takemori, Atsushi Okazaki, and Osamu Uchida: Analysis of Quote Retweets for COVID-19 State of Emergency Related Tweets Posted from Prefectural Governors' Accounts in Japan.
- The ITDRR 2021 Best Student Paper Award — Shono Fujita and Michinori Hatayama: Development of Automatic Method to Calculate Damage Rate of Roof by dividing Roof Image into Sections by Image Segmentation.

We hope that these awards encourage the winners and future candidates in deploying their research and inspire new submissions to our future conferences.

December 2021

Jun Sasaki
Yuko Murayama
Dimiter Velev
Plamena Zlateva

Organization

Honorable Chair

Atsuto Suzuki   Iwate Prefectural University, Japan

General Chair

Jun Sasaki   Iwate Prefectural University, Japan

Program Committee Co-chairs

Yuko Murayama   Tsuda University, Japan
Dimiter Velev   University of National and World Economy, Bulgaria

Publicity Chairs

Plamena Zlateva   Bulgarian Academy of Sciences, Bulgaria
Osamu Uchida   Tokai University, Japan
Benny B. Nasution   Politeknik Negeri Medan, Indonesia

Steering Committee

Diane Whitehouse   The Castlegate Consultancy, UK
Erich Neuhold   University of Vienna, Austria
Jose G. Gonzalez   University of Agder, Norway
A Min Tjoa   TU Wien, Austria
Igor Grebennik   Kharkiv National University of Radio Electronics, Ukraine

Program Committee

Orhan Altan   Istanbul Technical University, Turkey
Liz Bacon   Abertay University, UK
Frederick Benaben   IMT Mines Albi, France
Marcos R. S. Borges   Universidad de Navarra, Spain
Madhu Chandra   Technische Universität Chemnitz, Germany
Tadeusz Czachorski   Institute of Theoretical and Applied Informatics – PAS, Poland
Julie Dugdale   Université Grenoble Alpes, France
Terje Gjøsæter   University of Agder, Norway
Igor Grebennik   Kharkiv National University of Radio Electronics, Ukraine

Wei-Sen Li	National Science and Technology Center for Disaster Reduction, Taiwan
Kenny Meesters	Tilburg University, The Netherlands
Tilo Mentler	Trier University of Applied Sciences, Germany
Yuko Murayama	Tsuda University, Japan
Erich Neuhold	University of Vienna, Austria
Benny B. Nasution	Politeknik Negeri Medan, Indonesia
Jaziar Radianti	University of Agder, Norway
Caroline Rizza	Telecom Paris/I3 CNRS, France
Jun Sasaki	Iwate Prefectural University, Japan
Hans Jochen Scholl	University of Washington, USA
Walter Seböck	University for Continuing Education Krems, Austria
Tullio Joseph Tanzi	Telecom Paris/Institut Polytechnique de Paris, France
A Min Tjoa	TU Wien, Austria
Denis Trcek	University of Ljubljana, Slovenia
Osamu Uchida	Tokai University, Japan
Keisuke Utsu	Tokai University, Japan
Dimiter Velev	University of National and World Economy, Bulgaria
Kayoko Yamamoto	University of Electro-Communications, Japan
Plamena Zlateva	Bulgarian Academy of Sciences, Bulgaria

Local Organizing Committee

Kayoko Yamamoto	University of Electro-Communications, Japan
Masaki Nagata	Shizuoka University, Japan
Keisuke Utsu	Tokai University, Japan
Jiahong Wang	Iwate Prefectural University, Japan
Bhed B. Bista	Iwate Prefectural University, Japan
Katsumasa Ohor	Iwate Prefectural University, Japan

Contents

IT Use for Risk and Disaster Management

-

Information Analysis for Situation Awareness

Automatic Calculation of Damage Rate of Roofs Based on Image Segmentation

Shono Fujita[1][✉] and Michinori Hatayama[2]

[1] Graduate School of Informatics, Kyoto University, Sakyo-Ku, Kyoto, Japan
fujita.shono.32x@st.kyoto-u.ac.jp
[2] Disaster Prevention Research Institute, Kyoto University, Uji-City, Kyoto, Japan
hatayama@dimsis.dpri.kyoto-u.ac.jp

Abstract. In the event of a natural disaster, Japanese local governments investigate the level of damage of the buildings and issue damage certificates to the victims. The damage certificate is used to determine the contents of support provided to the victims; hence, they must be issued rapidly and accurately. However, in the past, the investigation of damage was time consuming, thus delaying the support provided to the victims. Additionally, while investigating the roof of the damaged building, it was difficult for the investigators to look at the entire roof and calculate the damage rate accurately. To address this issue, we have developed an image processing model to automatically calculate the rate of damage on a roof through image recognition from aerial photos. To circumvent the problem of lack of training data reported in our previous study [1], in this study, roof images were divided into roof surfaces based on image segmentation by deep learning, and the number of training data was increased. Our model calculated the rate of damage for up to 80% of roof data more accurately than the conventional assessment by a field investigator.

Keywords: Deep learning · Instance segmentation · Roof damage · Earthquake

1 Introduction

1.1 Problem in Building Damage Investigation

In the event of natural disasters, such as earthquakes, storms, and flood, the Japanese local government investigated the level of damage of each building and a damage certificate was issued to the victims to prove that the buildings were damaged by the disaster. This certificate is used to determine the content of their support and is necessary for reconstruction of life. Hence, they must be issued accurately and rapidly [2]. After the earthquake in Great East Japan, the Basic Act on Disaster Control Measures was revised and local governments were instructed to issue the damage certificate without delay [3]. However, in the past, the process of building damage investigation and issuing damage certificates was time consuming and delayed the support provided to the victims.

© IFIP International Federation for Information Processing 2022
Published by Springer Nature Switzerland AG 2022
J. Sasaki et al. (Eds.): ITDRR 2021, IFIP AICT 638, pp. 3–22, 2022.
https://doi.org/10.1007/978-3-031-04170-9_1

In the roof damage investigation, the investigators cannot look at the whole part of the roof. They look at the roof from a distance and investigate within range of vision from the ground. Additionally, they must calculate damage degree by each roof surface and need advanced expert knowledge. Considering the above investigation way they look at the roof from the ground, it is difficult for the investigator who doesn't have expert knowledge to investigate the roof damage accurately.

1.2 Usage of Aerial Photos Images During Disaster

After the April 2016 Kumamoto earthquake, the Japanese Cabinet Office revised the manual on investigating damaged buildings and specified that an investigator can assess complete collapse from aerial photos [4]. During a disaster, various public or research organizations take aerial photos using air crafts or drones. The Geospatial Information Authority of Japan takes aerial photos of the damage area as important data for initial response, capturing the state of damage or rehabilitation [5]. Crisis Mappers Japan, a Non-Profit Organization, provides the disaster rescue teams with "DRONE BIRD", to capture the aerial photos needed for support activities such as rescue [6]. Thus, we can use these aerial photos from these organizations during a disaster.

1.3 Study Purpose

Considering the above background, the purpose of this study is to develop an image processing model to calculate the rate of damage on roofs based on aerial photos, more accurately than the conventional assessment by field investigators, to facilitate a more rapid and accurate investigation.

2 Previous Study

Vetrivel et al. developed a damage building detection model using deep learning, 3D point cloud features, and multiple-kernel learning [7]. They used high-resolution oblique aerial photos as the input for the model. Tu et al. developed a detection model to identify the damaged regions using the bag-of-words model and support vector machine [8]. They used multi-temporal high-resolution remote sensing images to detect changes in the building due to damage. This study uses aerial photos that are obtained by drones or aircraft at a low price. This provides easy access to training and estimated data during disasters.

Fujita et al. [9] developed a detection system of damage building by tsunami using convolutional neural network (CNN) deep learning from aerial photos. Inoguchi et al. [10] developed a buildings detection system with blue sheet using convolutional neural network (CNN) deep learning from aerial photos from drones. They used data of roof images extracted by human hands one by one from aerial photos. However, their method to obtain data manually is time-consuming during disaster. We obtain image data using an original trimming algorithm that uses the geospatial information from the location information of building polygon.

Ji et al. estimated damaged buildings using texture analysis and convolutional neural network (CNN) from differences in post-disaster and pre-disaster aerial photos [11]. In addition, Fujita et al. used the information on differences in post-disaster and pre-disaster aerial photos to detect damage of the building by tsunami using CNN [9]. However, the pre-disaster aerial images may be old, and the information of the building may be significantly different from the post-disaster images. Such buildings not only include damaged buildings but also new buildings or demolished buildings. This problem has been addressed in this study because it uses only post-disaster aerial photos.

Radhika et al. [12] determined the rate of damage on roofs caused by wind using remote sensing and a texture wavelet analysis. Lucks et al. [13] assessed roof damage from aerial photos using random forest after segmentation. They [7, 12, 13] calculated the rate of damage by looking at the damage area proportions in respect to the whole roof area. This study calculates the rate of damage not only in terms of the damage region area but also the damage degree of each damage region. This study's model also reproduces the calculation method of the Japanese building damage investigation for disasters.

3 Development of Automatic Method to Calculate the Rate of Damage on Roof

3.1 The Method to Calculate the Rate of Damage on the Roof in the Building Damage Investigation

During the investigation, the investigator calculates the damage rate of certain parts of the building, such as wall, foundation, and roof and determines the level of damage of the building from the total amount of damage. The damage rate of the roof is calculated by multiplying the rate of damage degree with area rate of the roof surface. These values are then added as in (1) where S_i is the area of the roof i, S^w is the area of the entire roof, *and D_i is the damage degree of roof i*. This damage degree is represented as a percentage based on the damage type and damage position. If one roof surface has a different degree of damage, then the degree of damage is calculated by the average weight of these areas.

$$Damage\ rate = \sum_i \frac{S_i}{S^w} \times D_i \tag{1}$$

3.2 The Method to Calculate Damage Rate of Roof in This Study

Figure 1 shows the flow of our method. Our study automatically calculated the rate of damage on a roof in four steps. First, we automatically made the image data of the roof using a trimming algorithm. Next, we divided the roof image into roof surfaces using a dividing model. Then classified the degree of damage for each roof surface using a classification model. Finally, we multiplied the degree of damage by area rate and summed up these values in all the roof surfaces.

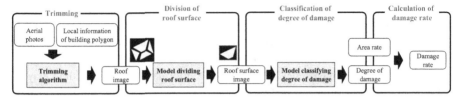

Fig. 1. Flow of the proposed method to calculate damage rate of the roof

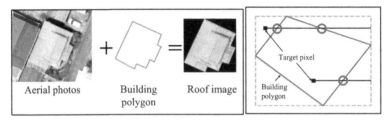

Aerial photos   Building   Roof image   Building
                   polygon   polygon

Fig. 2. Left: example of trimming algorithm, right: Judging pixel inside of building polygon

3.3 Trimming Algorithm

The trimming algorithm automatically makes the image data of a roof using aerial photos and the location information of the building polygon vertex, which is geospatial information, as shown in the Fig. 2 (left). First, the trimming algorithm assesses whether each image pixel is in the building polygon or not. Then, the pixels captured in the building polygon are colored while the pixels outside the building polygon are colored black. We assessed if pixels were inside or outside by counting the number of intersection points on the building polygon and a half line drawn from a target pixel in right direction as shown in the Fig. 2 (right). If the number is even, the target pixel is inside of the building polygons.

Because this trimming can extract each building image from aerial photos, this model can reduce time to make image data and estimate rapidly during disaster. Additionally, this trimming can make a lot of training data for deep learning. Moreover, because this uses building polygons, our model can estimate damage by not area but building and obtain more detailed information. Some previous studies such as Miura et al. [14] also made image data from building polygons. However, because their goal was to estimate damage on the whole building, they used a circumscribed quadrangle of the building polygon and included information outside of the polygon. Our study removes the parts outside of building polygon as they were unnecessary for the calculation of the roof's rate of damage and this will increase our study's accuracy.

3.4 Shortcomings of this Study

Our previous study [1] estimated the damaged roof and roof covered with a blue sheet using deep learning from trimming roof data. Because many victims cover the damaged part of the roof with a blue sheet to prevent wind and rainwater, we identified the roof covered with blue sheet as a damaged roof. As a result, the accuracy of estimation of the damaged roof was lower than that of the roof covered with blue sheet. Based on this result, we concluded that the challenges to be addressed were: difficulty in extracting the features of the damaged part and lower resolution of the aerial photos captured by the aircraft. To improve the accuracy of deep learning models, it is necessary to use abundant training data. However, there are no sufficient aerial photos of high resolution that include roofs damaged by earthquakes. The reasons for this are: low frequency of earthquake, short time since the development of drones that can capture aerial photos with high resolution, and time limitation, which forces us to take aerial photos of the roof covered with a blue sheet. Thus, we concluded that the problem in estimation from aerial photos during disasters in our study was limited training data, which is necessary for the improvement of accuracy.

3.5 Increase of Data by Division of Roof Surface

Based on the above problem, the trimming of roof images is divided into roof surfaces, thus increasing the number of training data as shown in Fig. 1. Generating multiple roof images from one trimming roof image enables us to obtain training data several times.

Ise et al. suggested a deep learning method using finely divided image data obtained from images as training data to classify moss and obtain high accuracy [15]. This shows that the division method generates a large amount of training data from one image to improve on accuracy and classify the object whose shape is irregular by deep learning. Moreover, the division expands the damaged parts in the image data and makes detection easier. Additionally, because the data size of the divided image reduces, the division method will reduce the number of necessary parameters of the next classifying damage degree model.

4 Division of Roof Surface

4.1 Previous Study About Roof Surface

Some studies [7, 12, 13, 16] divided the target roof into roof surfaces based on information on color or texture. They may wrongly divide roofs with irregular regions such as damaged or dirty part. Therefore, our study divided the roof not using information on color or texture but a deep learning segmentation model, which can extract roof surfaces with even more complicated features.

4.2 Segmentation Model

There are two types of segmentation models; semantic segmentation models and instance segmentation models. Both classify each pixel in an image into classes and extract the object region. While semantic segmentation model can't recognize objects of the same class individually, an instance segmentation model can. At first, this study used DeepLabv3+ [17], which is one of semantic segmentation models, to divide roof. As a result, each roof surface was connected to each other and became one roof surface (Fig. 3).

Fig. 3. Result of division by DeepLabv3 + [17]

Our study used Mask R-CNN [18], an instance segmentation models using deep learning. This model won in three sections (instance segmentation, bounding-box object detection and person key point detection) of the COCO challenge in 2016, an international image recognition competition. Figure 4 shows the structure of Mask R-CNN. This model first extracts image features from the convolutional backbone layer and gets a feature map. Second, a circumscribed quadrangle of the region of interest (RoI), which is likely to be region of object, is extracted from the region proposal network (RPN) of the convolutional layer. Next, the extracted feature of RoI from the feature map is changed to a fixed size. Then, the model inputs this extracted feature to the mask branch of the convolutional layer and classifies each pixel as an object or background. Simultaneously, the model inputs this extracted feature to the fully connected layer and gets an error of estimated circumscribed quadrangle of object and a classification result. Finally, the model extracts the object region in the image from the result of classification in the fully connected layer and pixels estimated as object in the mask branch. This model therefore decreases the calculation volume and increases accuracy by separating the classification task from the segmentation task.

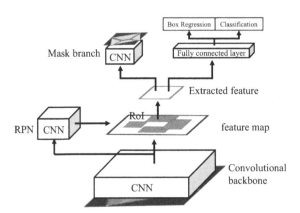

Fig. 4. Structure of mask R-CNN [18]

4.3 Used Data

We have generated images of the roof using a trimming algorithm and aerial photos taken in Mashiki town of Kumamoto prefecture after the 2016 Kumamoto Earthquake. The location information of building polygons was taken from the Fundamental Geospatial Data of Geospatial Information Authority of Japan. These aerial photos were taken by an aircraft rather than drones, and the resolution was 20 cm. This annotation took approximately 1 min for one roof image and a total of 8–9 h. In this study, 2400 (300 × 8) images were used as training data for updating parameters, 800 (100 × 8) images as validation data to confirm overfitting, and 800 (100 × 8) images as test data to evaluate the accuracy of the model. The number of data points was increased by eight times with horizontal flipping and rotation of each image. Because there is a gap between the location of the building polygon and actual building, we excluded the roof image whose gap was large or the roof surface could not be judged by observation from these datasets.

4.4 Training Method

Fine tuning was performed in the proposed study. This means that the model trained by the COCO dataset beforehand was trained by the trimming roof images and label of roof surface again. We confirmed the loss function of the validation data to prevent overfitting. When this value increased, we considered the increase to be overfitting and stopped training. In this study, the classification classes were set to 2 (roof and background), size of input image to 256 × 256, batch size to 2, number of iterations in one epoch to 100, and number of iterations in the calculation of the loss function of validation data to 5. We have used Tesla K40c and GeoForce GTX 1060 6 GB of NVIDIA as GPU in this experiment.

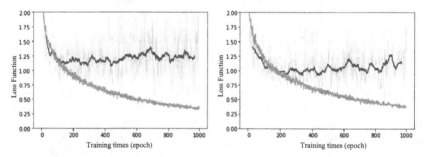

Fig. 5. Transition of the loss function. Left side shows the first experiment, and right side shows one of the additional experiments. The orange line represents one of the training data and blue line represents one of the validation data.

4.5 Result of Division in the First Experiment

The training of 1000 epochs took approximately 16 h. The left side of Fig. 5 shows the transition of the loss function of training and validation data. Because an increase in the loss function appeared in epoch 500, the training was stopped at epoch 500 with the proposed model. The average intersection of union (IoU) by image in the first experiment is 0.7580 and average of average precision (AP) is 0.6670 as shown in Table 1 . IoU indicates the degree of overlap between the correct and estimated regions. AP indicates the degree of recall and precision of the regions estimated by image. Figure 6 (left side) shows images that have a high average of AP and IoU, while Fig. 6 (right side) shows images with a low average of AP and IoU. The images with high average of AP and IoU tended to have large and few regions of roof surfaces in each image. Conversely, the ones with a low average of AP and IoU tended to have small and many regions of roof surfaces in each image. Additionally, in these images, the color difference between adjacent roof surfaces tended to be small, and the boundary line tended to be thin. Moreover, there were many overlapping regions with multiple estimated regions and overlooked regions that were not estimated as roof surfaces.

Table 1. Result of division in the first experiment

The first experiment	All images	Images with damage regions in roof surface	Images with damage regions in boundary	Images with leaf
Average of IoU	0.7580	0. 7341	0. 6874	0.7237
Average of AP	0. 6670	0. 6846	0. 5752	0. 3979

Fig. 6. Right side: roof image with high IoU and AP, left side: roof image with low IoU and AP

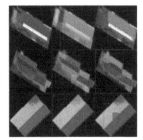

Fig. 7. Left: images of the roof with damage in roof surface, center: images of the roof with damage in boundary, and right: images of the roof with leaf. Each row shows original image, correct region, and estimated region from left to right

4.6   Roof Image with Some Features

For the roof images with damaged regions as shown Fig. 7 (left and center), there was a difference in the accuracy in the division of roof surfaces between roof images with damaged regions on the roof surfaces (Fig. 7 Left) and roof images with damaged regions in the boundaries of the roof surfaces (Fig. 7 Center). Because the IoU of these 40 images (5 original images) with the damaged regions in the roof surfaces was lower by 0.0239 and the AP was higher by 0.0176 than the average of all the images as shown in Table 1, the model accurately divided the roof surfaces of these images into all the other roof images. Therefore, even if color or texture in roof surface was discontinuous or damaged, the model divided the roof surface accurately.

This result suggests that instance segmentation using deep learning is effective for division in this study. Because the IoU of these 40 images (5 original images) with damaged regions in the boundaries was lower by 0.0706 and the AP was lower by 0.0918 than the average of all the images, the model could not accurately divide roof surface of these images with the same accuracy as the other roof images. It was also observed that roof images with a low average of IoU and AP included roof images with leaf as shown in Fig. 7 (right) other than images with the above features. The IoU of these 24 images (3 original images) with leaf was lower by 0.0343, and the AP was lower by 0.2691 than the average of all images. This implies the leaf hid the roof's regions, and the model miscalculated the region around the leaf as not part of the roof region but as an outside ground such as a garden or road. The miscalculation is likely caused by a gap between the building polygon and the actual building and reflecting outside ground part other than the roof with leaf in image of training data.

4.7   Result of Division in Additional Experiment

To handle images with the above-mentioned features, we have added 160 images with damage regions in the boundary (20 original images) and 160 images with leaf (20 original images) to train the data. The proposed model is trained with 2720 training data, 800 validation data, and 800 test data. The right side of Fig. 5 shows the transition of the loss function of training and validation data. Because an increase in the loss function appeared in epoch 600, the training was stopped at epoch 600 with the proposed model. As a result, the average IoU of roof images with damage regions in the boundary was lower by 0.0016 and average AP was higher by 0.0342 compared to that in the first experiment as shown in Table 2. The average IoU of roof images with leaves was lower by 0.0163 and average AP was higher by 0.0649 compared to that in the first experiment. In both roof images with damage region in boundary and with leaf, both IoU and AP did not increase. However, the difference between the increase and decrease in both these values indicates that the accuracy of the division of these images improved to some extent.

4.8   Image Processing After Division

To prevent duplicated extraction and overestimating the area rate, the model needs to eliminate overlapping regions in multiple estimated regions. The model can eliminate

Table 2. Result of division in the additional experiment

The additional experiment	All images	Images with damage regions in boundary	Images with leaf
The average of IoU	0. 7672	0. 6858	0. 7074
The average of AP	0. 6934	0. 6094	0.4628

the overlapping regions by selecting the correct estimated region and excluding all others. From the roof images with overlapping regions as shown in Fig. 8 left, many regions whose area were largely expanded to regions whose area were small. Therefore, we selected the smallest region on the overlapping regions and excluded the rest to eliminate the overlaps. To prevent overlooked damaged regions and underestimating the area rate, the model needed to remove roof regions not included in any estimated regions. Therefore, we compensated overlooked regions by expanding estimated regions as shown in Fig. 8 right after eliminating overlapping regions. In this expansion of estimated regions, we made an algorithm (Fig. 9) for the estimated regions and expanded the images equally on all sides.

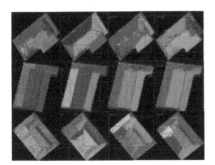 

Fig. 8. (Left): Roof images with overlapping regions, (Right): Roof images with overlooked regions. Each row shows the original image, correct region, estimated region and estimated region after eliminating the overlapping or overlooked region ordered from left to right.

We made the image data of the roof surfaces after the division by instance segmentation, eliminating overlapping and eliminating overlooked regions as shown in Fig. 10. The model painted regions except for roof regions in black as well as the trimming algorithm.

5   Classification of Damage Degree

5.1   Classification Model

We used ResNet50 [19], a deep learning model, to classify the degree of damage on each roof surface. This ResNet won an ILSVRC in 2015, which is an international image recognition competition, and is known for the high accuracies in image classification.

Algorithm 1 Delete Overlooked Region

1: **while** overlooked region exist in building polygon region of image **do**
2:     **for** $R_i \in$ all estimated regions **do**
3:         $R' \leftarrow R_i$
4:         **for** $P_j \in$ all pixels in R_i **do**
5:             **for** $P'_k \in$ pixels adjacent to top, bottom, left and right of P_j **do**
6:                 **if** P'_k is in building polygon **and** P'_k is not in any estimated regions **then**
7:                     P'_k is added to R'
8:                 **end if**
9:             **end for**
10:         **end for**
11:         $R_i \leftarrow R'$
12:     **end for**
13: **end while**

Fig. 9. Algorithm to remove overlooked region

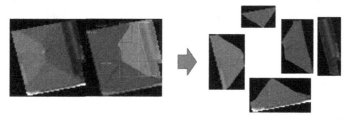

Fig. 10. Example of divided roof surface data image.

Because the competition had 1000 classes for the image classification, ResNet is a model with high versatility. In general, a multi-layered deep learning model can have complex expressiveness. However, if the layers are too many, the model cannot transmit the gradient of loss function to the lower layers in back propagation to update parameters. This is referred to as the vanishing gradient problem. ResNet can transmit gradient to lower layers by a residual module even if this adds several layers without introducing the vanishing gradient problem. Keras Applications, which is a deep learning API, offers some types of ResNet with varying numbers of layers. We used the ResNet50, with the fewest layers, because the classification task in this study is restricted by the degree of damage and the size of the image data, which is decreased by the division of the roof surfaces.

5.2 Data Used

Roof surface image data created by division of roof surface has a low resolution because the image of the roof from which the roof surface is divided has a resolution of 20 cm. Therefore, it is difficult to determine the degree of damage of these images in detail. Thus, we have constructed a model that classifies five classes of roof surfaces: no damage, damage (-25%), damage (25–50%), damage (50–75%), and damage (75%). The corresponding image data was generated as shown in Fig. 11.

In this study, we have used 30 roof images each for with and without damage as test data. In 30 roof images with damage, we have selected roof images with different degrees of damage to obtain various damage types. Then, we have divided the images with damage using the division model described in Sect. 4, and requested the staff in the Department of Crisis Management of Shimanto-cho, Kochi prefecture who have an experience of building damage investigation to input the correct label of damage degree to 208 divided images. To input this, he assessed the degree of damage from three image types; the roof surfaces image, whole roof image painting the roof surfaces and whole roof image, as shown in Fig. 12. In this study, 684 roof images with damage and 500 roof images without damage were used as training and validation data. A total of 4,392 roof surface images were divided from the roof images with damage. These were fed as input label of degree of damage in reference to the label of test data and investigation manual. As a result, this model could generate 2,171 roof surface images with damage from 684 roof images with damage indicating that the training data could be increased by 3.174 times. In this study, the number of data points of each class in the training and validation data are equal by horizontal flip and rotation. Additionally, in roof images without damage, we selected one roof surface from one roof to obtain various types of roof data.

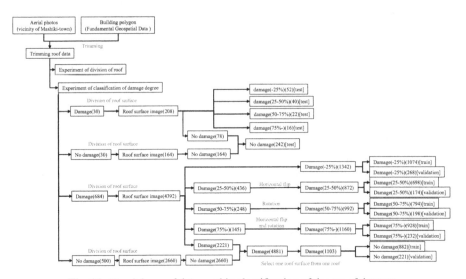

Fig. 11. Breakdown of data used in classification of degree of damage

To make the training and validation data, it took about 10 h to extract 684 roof images with damage from about 24,000 roof images. It also took about 12 h to input the degree of damage labels to 4,392 roof images picked from these images. For the local government staff to make the test data and input the degree of damage labels to 208 roof surfaces images, it took about 2 h.

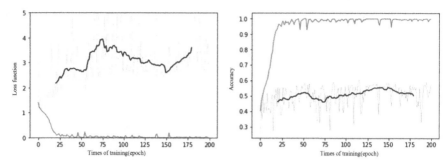

Fig. 12. Image used for judgement in inputting

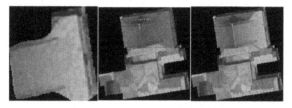

Fig. 13. Left: loss function and right: accuracy. Orange line: transition of training data and blue line: transition of validation data (moving filter)

5.3 Training Method

We trained ResNet50 using the data given in the previous subsection. For this study, we fine-tuned the trained data by making the ResNet50 retrain the data after the ImageNet, which is large data set. The batch size is set to 16, size of the input image to 256 × 256, and loss function to cross entropy loss. It took 5 h and 56 m in to train this model using the GPU GeoForce GTX 1060 6 GB of NVIDIA for 200 epochs. Figure 12 shows the transition between the loss function and accuracy. 1 epoch represents 274 times of training. This represents the total number of times training was provided to all the data at once. Figure 13 indicates that the training was stopped at epoch 500 when accuracy was high and loss function increased.

5.4 Classification Result

Table 3 shows the confusion matrix of estimation result of test data. As a result, the recall of no damage was 0.7479, damage (−25%) was 0.5577, damage (25–50%) was 0.1250, damage (50–75%) was 0.1364, and damage (75%) was 0.2500. The recall of image data with damage particularly for damage (25–50%), damage (50–75%), and damage (75%), were lower than image data without damage. Additionally, Table 4 shows the percentage dividing each value of confusion matrix by the number of data of each actual class, which means which class each data is estimated as. From this Table. 4, degree of damage of image data with large damage, such as damage (25–50%), damage (50–75%), and damage (75%) were underestimated.

Table 3. Confusion matrix of classification of damage degree

		True label					
		No damage	Damage (-25%)	Damage (25-50%)	Damage (50-75%)	Damage (75-%)	
Estimated label	No damage	181	15	9	4	0	
	Damage(-25%)	42	29	19	6	6	
	Damage(25-50%)	8	5	5	5	5	
	Damage(50-75%)	6	1	3	3	1	
	Damage(75%-)	5	2	4	4	4	Average Recall
	Recall	0.7479	0.5577	0.1250	0.1364	0.2500	0.3634

Table 4. Matrix of tendency of estimation by our model

		True label				
		No damage	Damage (-25%)	Damage (25-50%)	Damage (50-75%)	Damage (75-%)
Estimated label	No damage	0.7479	0.2885	0.2250	0.1818	0.0000
	Damage(-25%)	0.1736	0.5577	0.4750	0.2727	0.3750
	Damage(25-50%)	0.0331	0.0962	0.1250	0.2273	0.3125
	Damage(50-75%)	0.0248	0.0019	0.0750	0.1364	0.0625
	Damage(75%-)	0.0207	0.0380	0.1000	0.1818	0.2500

Left of Fig. 14 shows some examples of underestimated image data. In these under-estimated image data, there were many roof surfaces that reflected a little damage in the image but collapsed overall or reflected only the damaged part. These examples suggest that the data were judged from not only the roof surface of the target but also from other roof surfaces when the label of the damage degree of the test data was fed as input. Therefore, the model underestimated the degree of damage because, it was trained and estimated based on the information from only the roof surface of the target. Addition-ally, using aerial photos with low resolution as inputs to the label of degree of damage probably resulted in the mixing of individual subjects in the judgment criterion. This implies that the difference in judgment criterion between the staff of the local govern-ment inputting labels of test data and training data caused low recall of image data with large damage.

Moreover, Fig. 14 (right) shows data for the "no damage" estimated as damaged. From these images, the model wrongly estimated rough surface of the tiled roof by reflection of light, ground, outside object and some materials in the border of the roof surfaces as damaged parts. Because various parts appeared damaged such as the above examples, for accuracy the model needs to add various roof image data without damage as training data.

Each row shows the original roof surfaces image, whole roof image painting the roof surface and whole roof image ordered from left to right.

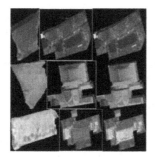

Fig. 14. (Left): Underestimated roof image with extensive damage. The correct label of the upper row images was damage (75%), estimated label of upper row was damage (−25%), true label of middle row was damage (50–75%), estimated label of middle row was no damage, true label of lower row was damage (25–50%), estimated label of lower row was no damage. (Right): Roof image without damage estimated as damaged. True label of upper row was no damage, estimated label of upper row was damage (−25%), true label of middle row was no damage, estimated label of middle row was damage (−25%), true label of lower row was no damage, estimated label of lower row was damage (25–50%).

6   Calculation of Damage Rate

6.1   Calculation Method of Estimated Damage Rate

In this study, the value of degree of damage was assigned to each class classified in Sect. 5. The value of no damage was set to 0, damage (−25%) to 0.125, damage (25–50%) to 0.375, damage (50–75%) to 0.625, and damage (−75%) to 0.875 as degree of damage. Then, the model multiplied these degrees of damage by area rate and summed the values of every roof surface to calculate the damage rate of the roof. The area rate of the roof surface is calculated by dividing the number of pixels of each roof surface by the number of pixels of the entire roof. These the roof surfaces pixels and the whole roof pixels show the pixels except for the pixels in black which aren't considered as part of the roof after trimming.

6.2   Error of Correct Answer

To get the correct damage rate label for the roofs, we asked the same staff we asked for Sect. 5 to input the damage rate of 30 roof images with the test data damage shown in Fig. 10 as well as the damage degree label. On the other hand, we calculated the rate of damage with the correct degree of damage of these 30 roof images got in Sect. 5 using the abovementioned calculation method.

The average of error between these 2 types of damage rates was −9.482 and the average of the absolute value error was 9.681. This study defines the absolute value error between these 2 damage rates as a "correct error". This "correct error" indicates that the model in this study tended to underestimate the damage rates. The cocfficient of the correlation between this "correct error" for the 30 roof images and IoU of these roof images was 0.0356, and the coefficient of correlation between this correct error and AP was −0.0409. This suggests that there is no correlation between accuracy of division of roof and error caused by the calculation method of this study. Therefore, this indicates that "correct error" or underestimate arise even if the model divides the roof accurately. This suggests that the reason our calculation method tends to underestimate damage rate is the underestimate of the damage degree in the inputting label. It was probably difficult for the staff to input the accurate label when the damaged parts were on the edge of the roof surfaces image of the target or an assessment of the degree of damage from the information around the target image. On the contrary, the no correlation indicates that the wrong division of the roof does not result in a "correct error" or underestimate. We determined the reason is constantly keeping the degree of damage and area rate as a whole by preventing overlapping and overlooking of the damaged region and roof in Sect. 4.8. However, to construct an explainable model for the victims, the model needs to accurately capture the damaged part of the roof and approach the actual calculation method of damage rate. Therefore, the model needs high accuracy in the division of the roof.

6.3 Comparison of Correct Damage Rate and Estimated Damage Rate

The model estimated the damage rate of 30 images of the roof with damage and 30 images without damage of the test data using the above calculation method from the degree of damage of each roof surface estimated in Sect. 5. The coefficient of determination between the correct and estimated damage rates was 0.3445. The coefficient of correlation was 0.6486, average error was −5.401, and average absolute value error was 11.07. Figure 15 shows a scatter diagram of the correct and estimated damage rates. For the roof images with damage, the mean of error was −13.44 and the histogram of the error was Fig. 16 (left). For the roof images without damage, the mean of error was 2.461 and the histogram of the error was Fig. 16 (right).

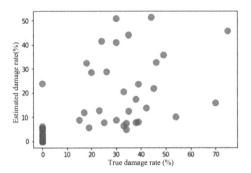

Fig. 15. Scatter diagram of correct damage rate and estimated damage rate

For images of the roof with damage, the histogram and the average error indicated that the model underestimated the damage rate. This was due to an underestimation of the classification of the degree of damage in Sect. 5.4 and input label in Sect. 6.2. Similarly, for the images of the roof without damage, the histogram and the average error indicated that the model estimated multiple data as little damage and only 12 of 30 images as no damage. This is because, the model incorrectly calculates damage as a whole if the classification model estimates even one roof surface without damage as damage. Therefore, the model needs to increase the recall of no damage in the classification of the degree of damage.

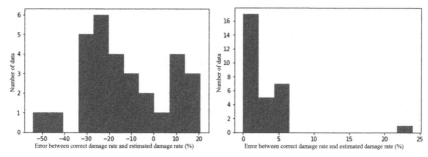

Fig. 16. Histogram of error between correct damage rate and estimated damage rate. Left side: roof data with damage, right side: roof data without damage

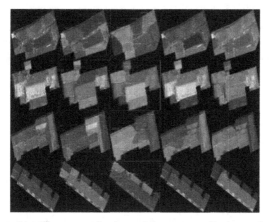

Fig. 17. Roof image with a large error of estimated damage rate. Each row shows the original roof image, whole roof image painting true roof surfaces, whole roof image painting estimated roof surfaces, whole roof image painting true damage degree and whole roof image painting estimated damage degree ordered from left to right. (Color figure online)

Figure 17 shows roof data with a large error. In the image visualizing estimated damage degree and true damage degree of Fig. 16, we colored the roof surfaces of damage (-25%) in yellow green, damage (25–50%) in yellow, damage (50–75%) in orange and damage (-75%) in red. Several roof image data had large errors when the errors of their roof surface degree of damage accumulated. Additionally, when the roof data had error in the damage degree of the roof surface which was a large area or was wrongly estimated as a large area in the division of the roof, the data had large error of damage rate.

6.4   Evaluation of Model Accuracy

We asked the staff who input the labels in the previous experiment to evaluate the accuracy of the 60 test data this estimated model. In the evaluation of this model, it is desirable to quantitatively compare the accuracy of this model with the accuracy of the investigation by an investigator who looks at the roof from the ground or from the ground and aerial photos. However, these data are difficult to obtain. Thus, the staff were advised to classify estimated accuracy of each roof data into four classes, such as "equal to investigators who look at the roof from ground and aerial photos," "(lower than the above and) higher than the investigator who looks at the roof from ground," "(lower than the above and) equal to the investigator who looks at the roof from ground," and "lower than the investigator who looks at the roof from ground" to evaluate accuracy qualitatively. Table 5 shows the evaluation result. This indicates that the proposed model can calculate the damage rate of 30% of roof data more accurately than the investigators who look from the ground, which is a conventional judgment method, and that of 80% of roof data is the same accurately or more than the investigators who look from the ground.

Table 5. Result of accuracy evaluation of the model

Answer choices	It is as accurate as investigator judging from aerial photos and the ground.	It is more accurate than investigator judging from the ground.	It is as accurate as investigator judging from the ground.	It is more inaccurate than investigator judging from the ground.	total
How accurate is it?	15(25.00%)	3(5.000%)	30(50.00%)	12(20.00%)	60

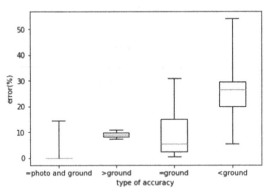

Fig. 18. Box plots of error of estimated damage rate of each class. This shows box plots of "equal to investigators who looks at roof from ground and aerial photos", "(lower than the above and) higher than the investigator who looks at roof from ground", "(lower than the above and) equal to the investigator who looks at roof from ground" and "lower than the investigator who looks at roof from ground" ordered from left to right.

Figure 18 shows the box plot of the absolute value error of the estimated rate of damage for each answer. This indicate that error of "equal to investigators who looks at roof from ground and aerial photos" and "(lower than the above and) higher than the investigator who looks at roof from ground" was lower than approximately 10%, error of "(lower than the above and) equal to the investigator who looks at roof from ground" was lower than about 20%, and error of the "lower than the investigator who looks at roof from ground" was higher than approximately 20%. We identified reason some values or averages in the box plot, don't increase in proportion to the four answer class of accuracy as changing accuracy of the investigator assessed from the ground, which is the comparison object by conditions around target building or structure of roof.

7 Discussion and Future Tasks

We developed an image processing model consisting of four processes; that is, trimming, division of roof, classification of the degree of damage, and calculation of the rate of damage on buildings from photographic aerial photos. This study increased the training data by the division of the roof surfaces using instance segmentation to handle the lack of training data during a disaster, which was the problem with our previous study [1]. In the division of the roof surfaces, this study showed that instance segmentation using deep learning is more effective in representing the damage on the roof surfaces as previous models inaccurately divided the roof surface based on discontinuous color or texture. Additionally, the accuracy of division increased to some extent by adding data that tended to be mistaken for training data. However, we needed to find more data, which was mistaken by the model to increase the quantity and quality of training data for increased IoU and AP. In the classification of the degree of damage, we faced several problems because the average recall was 0.3634. The model needed to not only use roof surfaces information but also whole roof information as input to prevent underestimates and make training data by multiple inputting person to construct a more general model. In the calculation of the rate of damage, this study showed that the degree of damage underestimates in inputting labels arose, and the model needed a more devised input method. These underestimates caused an underestimate of the damage rates. Moreover, we suggested that the model increase the recall of the degree of damage of roof surfaces images without damage to accurately estimate damage rates of the "no damage roof" label. In the evaluation of the accuracy by the staff who investigated damage, this study showed that this model could calculate the rate of damage of 30% of roof data more accurately than the conventional assessment and that of 80% of the roof data was equally accurate or greater than the conventional assessment. This proved that the model automatically calculated the rate of damage on roofs from aerial photos more accurately than conventional assessment by a field investigator.

In the future, in addition to the abovementioned shortcomings, the model needs to accurately handle roof images excluded because of a gap in the building polygon or low resolution for a higher estimation accuracy.

References

1. Fujita, S., Hatayama M.: Estimation method for roof-damaged buildings from aero-photo images during earthquakes using deep learning. Inf. Syst. Front. (2021)

2. Disaster Management, Cabinet Office in Japan: Guidelines of the Operation of Criteria for Building Damage Investigation in Disasters (2020). (in Japanese)
3. Disaster Management, Cabinet Office in Japan: Guidance of the Implementation System for Building Damage Investigation in Disasters (2020). (in Japanese)
4. Cabinet Office in Japan: Outline of the March 2018 Revision. http://www.bousai.go.jp/tai saku/pdf/h3003kaitei.pdf. Accessed 10 May 2021. (in Japanese)
5. Geospatial Information Authority of Japan: Aerial Photograph. http://www.gsi.go.jp/gazoch osa/gazochosa41006.html. Accessed 10 May 2021. (in Japanese)
6. DRONEBIRD: Drone Rescue Team of Disaster, DRONEBIRD. https://dronebird.org/. Accessed 10 May 2021. (in Japanese)
7. Vetrivel, A., Gerke, M., Kerle, N., Nex, F., Vosselman, G.: Disaster damage detection through synergistic use of deep learning and 3D point cloud features derived from very high resolution oblique aerial images, and multiple-kernel-learning. ISPRS J. Photogram. Remote Sens. **140,** 45–59 (2018)
8. Tu, J., Li, D., Feng, W., Han, O., Sui, H.: Detecting damaged building regions based on semantic scene change from multi-temporal high-resolution remote sensing images. Int. J. Geo-Inf. **6**(5) (2017)
9. Fujita, A., Sakurada, K., Imaizumi, T., Ito, R., Hikosaka, S., Nakamura, R.: Damage detection from aerial images via convolutional neural networks. In: 2017 Fifteenth IAPR International Conference on Machine Vision Applications (MVA) (2017)
10. Inoguchi, M., Tamura, K., Hamamoto, R.: Establishment of work-flow for roof damage detection utilizing drones, human and AI based on human-in-the-loop framework. In: 2019 IEEE International Conference on Big Data (Big Data), pp. 4618–4623 (2019)
11. Ji, M., Liu, L., Du, R., Buchroithner, M.F.: A comparative study of texture and convolutional neural network features for detecting collapsed buildings after earthquakes using pre- and post- event satellite imagery, Remote Sens. **11**, 1202 (2019)
12. Radhika, S., Tamura, Y., Matsui, M.: Determination of degree of damage on building roofs due to wind disaster from close range remote sensing images using texture wavelet analysis. In: IEEE International Symposium on Geoscience and Remote Sensing (IGARSS) (2018)
13. Lucks, L., Bulatov, D., Thonnessen, U., Boge, M.: Superpixel-wise assessment of building damage from aerial images. In 14th International Joint Conference on Computer Vision, Imaging and Computer Graphics Theory and Applications (VISAPP) (2019)
14. Miura, H., Aridome, T., Matsuoka, M.: Deep learning-based identification of collapsed, non-collapsed and blue tarp-covered buildings from post-disaster aerial images. Remote Sens. **12**, 1924 (2020)
15. Ise, T., Minagawa, M., Onishi, M.: Classifying 3 Moss species by deep learning, using the "chopped picture" method. Open J. Ecol. **2018**(8), 166–173 (2018)
16. Susaki, J.: Segmentation of shadowed buildings in dense urban areas from aerial photographs. Remote Sens. **4**, 911–933 (2012)
17. Chen, L.-C., Zhu, Y., Papandreou, G., Schroff, F., Ada, H.: Encoder-decoder with atrous separable convolution for semantic image segmentation. In: ECCV (2018)
18. He, K., Gkioxari, G., Dollar, P., Girshick, R.: Mask R-CNN. arXiv:1703.06870 (2017)
19. He, K., Zhang, X., Ren, S., Sun, J: Deep residual learning for image recognition. arXiv preprint arXiv:1512.03385 (2015)

Flood Disaster Mitigation System Adopting Meteorological Data and Geographic Information Systems

Haruki Kanai[✉] and Kayoko Yamamoto

The University of Electro-Communications, Chofugaoka, Chofu, Tokyo, Japan
{haruki.kanai,kayoko.yamamoto}@uec.ac.jp

Abstract. Recently climate change causes greater disaster than before, and the conventional measures especially against flood disaster are not enough at present. Integrated measures of facilities and Information systems are reinforced to cope with these situations. This study describes a solution to the issues. Flood disaster mitigation system is designed and developed to mitigate the damages caused by flood disaster adopting meteorological data and geographic information systems (GIS). In the phase of requirements analysis, system dynamics (SD) techniques, such as Iceberg Model and causal loop diagram (CLD), were applied to clarify three leverage points (precipitation data observation, river level forecast, and evacuation/alarming issuing). Precipitation information was derived from MesoScale Model (MSM) data provided by the Japan Meteorological Agency, and river level forecast was conducted based on Urban Tank Model. Swiss Cheese Model, basin hydraulic control, necessity of information (software) and facilities (hardware) were adopted into the structure of the Iceberg Model. The test site of the system is planned in the basins of the Nogawa and Tama Rivers in Tama Area, Tokyo, Japan. This study relates to the 9th "Industry, Innovation and Infrastructure" and the 13th "Climate Action" of the sustainable development goals (SDGs) proposed by the United Nation (UN).

Keywords: Flood disaster mitigation system · Iceberg Model · Causal loop diagram · Climate change · Precipitation · River level forecast · Alarm · Evacuation

1 Introduction

In recent years, because the occurrence frequency of meteorological disasters such as typhoon, local heavy rain and heavy snow in addition to earthquake and volcanic eruption tremendously increased, it is the most important issue to adopt the effective measures for disaster prevention and reduction around the world. This research targets flood disaster, because the occurrence frequency recently increased by climate change and the amount of damages are the most expensive comparing other disasters. The final purpose of this research is to provide proper information by the integrated systems to minimize the

© IFIP International Federation for Information Processing 2022
Published by Springer Nature Switzerland AG 2022
J. Sasaki et al. (Eds.): ITDRR 2021, IFIP AICT 638, pp. 23–34, 2022.
https://doi.org/10.1007/978-3-031-04170-9_2

damages by flood disasters in Tokyo metropolis, Japan. The system aims to mitigate flood disaster with a series of information processing. Specifically, the system monitors the amount of precipitation and the water level of river to forecast the latter, and gives the alarm to urge residents living in the nearby area to evacuate to safety places at the times when flood disaster is judged to occur. The stakeholders are public organizations (the Ministry of Land, Infrastructure, Transport and Tourism, the Japan Meteorological Agency, and central and local governments) and common residents living in the nearby area.

Figure 1 shows the relationship between this research and the sustainable development goals (SDGs) of the United Nation (UN). Among 17 goals, this research has close relationship with the 9th goal (Industry, Innovation and Infrastructure) and the 13th goal (Climate Action).

This research consists of three steps. In the first step, a feasibility study will be conducted to grasp the achievements and subject of the previous researches, and examine how the system will be design and developed with the piece of structural elements. In the second step, a requirement analysis of the system will be conducted for the basic design of the system, the development of the prototype adopting meteorological data and geographic information systems (GIS), and the evaluation. Finally, in the third step, these results will be sorted out.

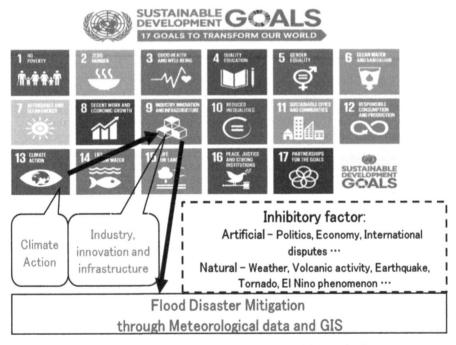

Fig. 1. Relationship between this research and the UN SDGs

2 Related Work

In the related academic areas with this research, the previous researches have clarified many facts until now. The results of Hirata et al. (2007) [1], Yaginuma et al. (2014) [2], Yoshimi et al. (2019) [3] and Susumu et al. (2019) [4] in the industry world showed that the experts in the academic fields of meteorological radar, power demand and public facilities collaborated to prevent and mitigate disasters. In the academic area of meteorological administration, in order to prevent and mitigate disasters, the coordination committee for weather forecast research (2011) [5], Sato (2018) [6], Uno et al. (2018) [7], Tsuboi et al. (2019) [8] showed that the necessity of collaboration with the industry world in addition to each research related to meteorological model, typhoon and flood to prevent and mitigate disasters.

In the academic area of system dynamics (SD), Medrilzam et al. (2020) [9] and Phan et al. (2020) [10] conducted current analyses of the disaster measures of national and local governments, and discussed what we should do against the candidates of forecastable future results. The above previous researches adopted the causal loop diagrams (CLD) and showed important points (we call "leverage points" in this research) to show a route to solve the issues.

In the academic area of information processing, Usuta (2020) [11] and Tai (2020) [12] mentioned that though there were currently many disaster mitigation systems, governments as ordering destinations could not derive enough requirements, and the tasks were instructed to system integrator in many cases. Additionally, they also pointed out the necessity of IT education for the planning department of governments.

Rossi et al. (2017) [13] introduced the i-REACT (improving resilience to emergencies through advanced cyber technologies) provided by the United Nation International strategy for Disaster Reduction (UNISDR) that is mostly composed of European members, and the system covers a wide area of disasters including earthquake, forest fire and flood etc. It is a large-scale system that forms an eco-system, and it could conduct information processing as a data bank. It has specific database in response to three measure stages (prevention, preparedness and post action) against various kinds of disasters. However, as the system aims to provide the measures against various kinds of disasters, it had not applied to any cases yet.

Based on the result of the above previous researches, targeting flood disasters, this researches uniquely develop a flood disaster mitigation system (FDMS) adopting meteorological data and GIS. Additionally, comparing the above previous researches, the originality of this research is to develop a series of system that monitors the amount of precipitation and the water level of river to forecast the latter, and gives the alarm to urge residents living in the nearby area to evacuate to safety places at the time when flood disaster is judged to occur.

3 System Design Requirement Analysis of FDMS Using SD

3.1 Outlines of SD

Referring to Sterman (2000) [14] and Sheffield et al. (2012) [15], SD methods including Iceberg Model and causal loop diagram (CLD) etc. are applied to the system of this research. First, an analysis of the current status and the issues concerning the research target was conducted, and both visible and non-visible objects were sorted out.

Next, based on these, the relationship between various elements was clarified to propose the measures to solve the above issues and examine the feasibility. Specifically, Iceberg Model is used and element relationship was expanded in multi causal loop diagrams, deeper analysis was conducted and the leverage points are clarified.

3.2   Iceberg Model Analysis

Figure 2 shows the Iceberg Model that were developed in response to the purpose of this research sorting out considerable elements. Iceberg Model compares to the iceberg floating in the sea water. The upper part of iceberg floating in the sea water, which is visible to us, is assigned as "event (phenomenon)". The lower parts of iceberg, which are not visible to us, are assigned as "pattern (behavior)", "structure" and "mental model" from top to bottom.

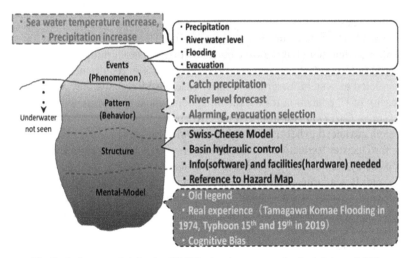

Fig.2. Iceberg model for the FDMS adopting meteorological data and GIS

Due to sea surface temperature raise and precipitation increase caused by climate change, we can observe precipitation, river level, flood disaster and evacuation as visible "event (phenomenon)". Moreover, it is necessary for us to deeply consider the above two issues as the "pattern (behavior)" of Iceberg Model, grasp precipitation, forecast river level, give the alarm, and select evacuation behavior. As a necessary "structure" to realize these behaviors, Swiss Cheese Model proposed by Reason (1997) [16], necessity of flood control in basins, and necessity of both information provision (software) and facilities (hardware), and reference to hazard map are proposed. "Mental model" as the lowest part of Iceberg Model includes old legend, real experience and cognitive bias. Next, the relationship between the considerable elements in multiple CLDs will be developed and analyzed in the following sections.

3.3   Causal Loop Diagram Analysis

Figure 3 shows the CLD that denotes the relationship between the elements described as "event (phenomenon)" in the upper level of Iceberg Model in Fig. 2. According to the left part of the loop, as climate change and global warming affect sea surface temperature, increase of vapor in the air, rain cloud, rain-fall, river level. Precipitation causes river level rise, flooding and disaster. Based on the data concerning past disasters, evacuation shelter and disaster prevention database are enriched. These contribute to mitigate flood disaster caused by river level changes. Thus, this CLD is balanced feedback loop.

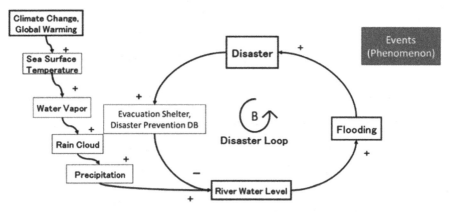

Fig. 3. CLD at event level

Next, the elements described in the "pattern (behavior)" and "structure" of Iceberg Model in Fig. 2 as well as those in Fig. 3 are examined. Figure 4 shows the CLD that includes disaster mitigation loop to forecast future flood disaster occurrences added to the CLD in Fig. 3, using both current and forecast values of river level. The CLD shows the disaster mitigation status, by setting hardware of flood disaster measure facility (rain water shelter storage pond) so as to make the time delay of flood disaster and minimize the damages. The mitigation loop (B1) shows that the river level is forecasted. If the level is judged to reach the warning river level, flood disaster is mitigated by giving the alarm to residents living in the nearby area. The mitigation loop (B2) shows the smarter disaster mitigation comparing the one in B1, those are planning of disaster mitigation, selection of the most appropriate mitigation plan from the candidates, alarming and urge of evacuation.

3.4   Leverage Points

In order to realize these relationships, it is essential to examine what the leverage points are. Figure 5 shows the CLD at pattern level. This CLD shows three leverage points. First one is to grasp the amount of real-time precipitation, second one is to grasp the actual situation and forecasted simulation of river level, and third one is planning of disaster mitigation.

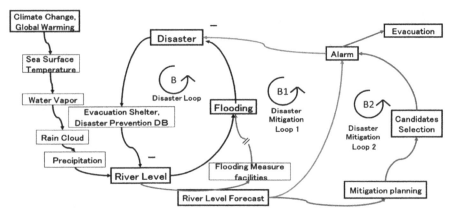

Fig. 4. CLD at event level adding disaster mitigation loops (B1 and B2)

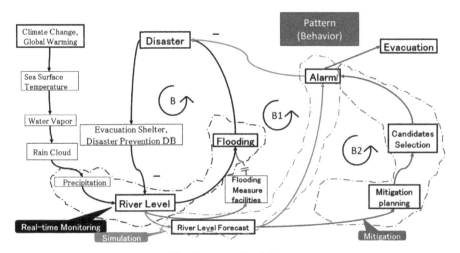

Fig. 5. Pattern level CLD

3.5   Observed Data Examples at River

Figure 6 shows the observed data examples concerning actual river. If the river flows from right side to left side, the river level meter is set at the important point to measure the current river level. The amount of current precipitation is measured by precipitation meter. In order to adjust the appropriate river level, the rain water shelter storage pond has the special function that is set to intake the river water into it, when the river level is going to reach the dangerous water level so as to delay the increasing river level in lower basin. Also, in order to visualize the river level that is dangerous to residents living in the nearby area, the digital display of river level and arrowed marking to show dangerous river level in visual confirmation.

Thus, the FDMS developed in this research is composed of two elements, one is observed data (digital data) measured by online software, and the other is flood disaster prevention facilities (hardware). The system gives the first-responders the alarm to clearly understand what is going to happen. Thus, integrating and managing multiple systems into single system, it enables to mitigate flood disaster and minimize the damages.

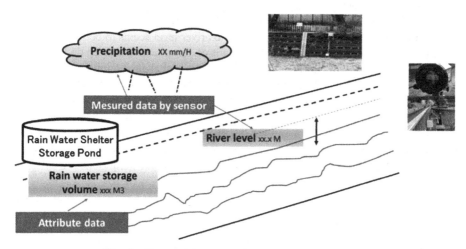

Fig. 6. Observed data examples concerning actual river

3.6 System Concept

Figure 7 shows the system concept of the FDMS. Necessary data are saved into the database using data collection logic and the decision logic including human decision. As the result of information processing is displayed on the digital map of GIS, the FDMS can provide necessary information for the stakeholders (first-responders and residents living in the nearby area) in easy-to-understand manner.

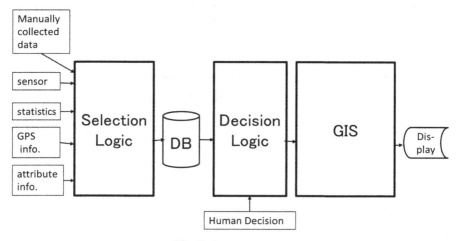

Fig. 7. System concept

4 Basic Design and Integration of System

4.1 Basic Design of System

According to the Iceberg Model, the whole of basin is considered as one system. Using precipitation data, the river level is forecasted taking river level and rain water shelter storage pond into consideration. If the forecasted river level seems to be abnormal, the alarm is given to the stakeholders. Online data is collected and displayed on the digital map of Web-GIS. Applying the location information of global positioning system (GPS), current position that shows the abnormal status is shown on the digital map.

If stakeholder (first responder and residents living in the nearby area) ask for information about something by means of smartphones, the FDMS displays the evacuation site candidates that are the nearest to the questioner's current location and the shortest route to these. In response to this, it is necessary to refer to the hazard maps and adopt 70 m/min as the walking speed for older people, not 80 m/min for normal adults.

4.2 Integration of System

4.2.1 Real-Time Monitoring

For the real-time monitoring, the amount of precipitation in the unit of mesh is decided. For the purpose, wgrib2 module, which is provided by the National Oceanic and Atmospheric Administration (NOAA) in the U.S. and adopted in the Japan Meteorological Agency, is used. Additionally, MesoScale Model (MSM) and the data provided by the real-time precipitation monitoring system of Japan and called AMEDAS are also applied. The current river level is measured by a water level gauge sensor. These data are displayed on the digital map of GIS included into the FDMS.

4.2.2 Simulation

Using Urban Tank Model, the river level is forecasted based on the amount of precipitation and current river level. If the forecasted river level is going to exceed the warning water-level, the alarm will be given to the first-responders and the residents living in the nearby area.

4.2.3 Proposal for the Flood Disaster Mitigation Measure

With the operation of the system, the flood disaster mitigation measure is proposed. From the precipitation monitoring to give the alarm when flood disaster occurs, the system can collect and process data, notice the importance of the alarm, and respond to the tense situation considering residents' personal conditions.

5 System Verification

The targets of the verification for the system are planned in the suburb of Tokyo Metropolitan area in Japan. Figure 8 shows the relationship of Japan, Tokyo Metropolitan area, and its suburb named Tama District.

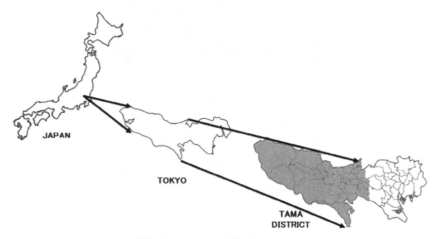

Fig. 8. Map of verification area

The reasons why the Nogawa River and Tama River are selected as the first and second verification target are denoted in Table 1. The Nogawa River is one of the branches of the Tama River. In the case of the Nogawa River and Tama River, if a flood disaster occurs seriously, its basin suffered damage.

Table 1. Details of verification target river

Name of river	River class	Channel length (KM)	Managed by	Managed as
Nogawa	First	20.2	Tokyo Metropolitan Government	Flood Disaster Forecasted River
Tama River	First	183	Ministry of Land, Infrastructure, Transport and Tourism	Flood Disaster Forecasted River

Tokyo Metropolitan Government formulated the "Flood Control Plan" [17], the "Improvement Plan in the Nogawa River Basin" [18], and the "Countermeasures Plan against Heavy Rain in the Nogawa River Basin" [19]. The Nogawa River is regarded as one of the most important rivers. A large-scale expansion of rain water shelter storage pond near Oosawa-Ikegami Area of Nogawa is under construction at present, and have double capability in November, 2021.

Figure 9 shows the actual situation concerning the basin of the Nogawa River when the alarm at level 3 was given. The river gauges are set in parallel in left position for human-recognizable one and in right position for digital device so as to collect river level automatically.

Fig. 9. Nogawa under level 3 alarm

Figure 10 shows the current situation of large-scale expansion of rain water shelter storage pond. This corresponds to the hardware of flood disaster measure facility in the CLD shown in Fig. 4.

Fig. 10. Rainwater shelter storage pond under expanding construction

Figure 11 shows the middle basin of the Tama River near Komae City. Around this part, a large-scale flooding over the levee occurred and many houses were washed away in 1974. After this flooding, the measures against flood disasters had been proposed and executed in the basin of the Tama River.

Fig. 11. Tama River near Komae City

6   Conclusion

In this research, a flood disaster mitigation system (FDMS) is uniquely developed and designed. The system is composed of the observed data, forecast data, personal position data (software), and the flood disaster prevention facilities (hardware). The system gives the first-responders the alarm to clearly understand what is going to happen in proper timing. Thus, integrating and managing multiple systems into single system, it enables to mitigate flood disaster and minimize the damages. Additionally, in this research, SD method is applied to the phase of system design requirement analysis. The requirements were clearly expressed as three leverage points and integrated into the functions so as to alarm issuing toward the flooding via river water level forecast. Therefore, the FDMS is an advanced system rather than the ones that just monitor the present status.

This research described a part of example situation when flood disasters occurred in Tokyo Metropolis. However, we confirmed many patterns of flooding, as Swiss Cheese Model explains. Accordingly, it is necessary to cover various cases of flood disasters to raise the usability of the FDMS.

References

1. Hirata, Y., Ono, Y., Wada, M.: Technology for long term prediction of water volume inflow to sewerage facilities using information from fine grid weather simulations. Toshiba Review **62**(4), 38–41 (2007)
2. Yaginuma, R., Ando, Y., Kawano, S.: Weather disaster reduction and mitigation solutions contributing to realization of safe and secure society. Toshiba Review **69**(12), 2–6 (2014)
3. Yoshimi, K., Mizutani, F.: Approaches to meteorological disaster mitigation using 3D observation data of multi-parameter phased array weather radar. Toshiba Review **74**(6), 67–70 (2019)
4. Susumu, H., Shiga, Y., Ichikawa, R.: High-precision electricity demand forecasting method using weather prediction data and deep learning. Toshiba Rev. **74**(5), 22–25 (2019)
5. Coordination Committee for Weather Forecast Research: Report on the 7th Research Meeting of Weather Forecast. Tenki **58**(9), 63–70 (2011)
6. Sato, T.: Report on the 48th meteorological research meeting and the research meeting of meteorological disaster committee. Tenki **65**(8), 91–95 (2018)
7. Uno, F., Otake, H., Yoshida, K., Udagawa, Y., Shimada, T.: Report on the specialist committee in autumn of FY 2017 "utilization of meteorological observation and prediction information including renewable energy into meteorological business. Tenki **65**(2), 55–59 (2018)
8. Tsuboi, K., Sato, K.: Report on the symposium in spring of FY 2018 "future of observation for disaster prevention and reduction and short-time prediction technology." Tenki **66**(10), 3–4 (2019)
9. Medrilzam, H.B.I., Faruk, M., Ahmad, F., Tasrif, M., Suarga, E.B.: Integration of system dynamics and spatial dynamics modeling to predicted changes in environmental carrying capacity in Indonesia. In: Proceedings of the 3rd Asia Pacific System Dynamics Conference, 10p. Brisbane, Queensland, Australia (2020)
10. Phan, T., et al.: Assessing the vulnerability of an island water system subject to climate change and tourism development: a system dynamics approach. In: Proceedings of the 3rd Asia Pacific System Dynamics Conference, 7p. Brisbane, Queensland, Australia (2020)
11. Usuta, Y.: Information and disaster prevention perspective on the future of disaster information systems by researchers: 2. Information platform for disaster resilience and expectations for the future. IPSJ J. **61**(12), e8–e11 (2020)
12. Tai, Y.: Information and disaster prevention perspective on the future of disaster information systems by researchers: 3 why do not information systems for disaster management work well in Japan? IPSJ J. **61**(12), e12–e16 (2020)
13. Rossi, C., Garza, P., Yasukawa, S., Poletto, D., Baker. J.: Advanced Cyber Technologies to Improve Resilience to Emergencies. 28p. United Nations Office for Disaster Risk Reduction (2017)
14. Sterman, J.D.: Business Dynamics: Systems Thinking and Modeling for a Complex World. Irwin Professional Pub, 982p. United States, Burr Ridge (2000)
15. Sheffield, J., Sankaran, S., Haslett, T.: Systems thinking: taming complexity in project management. On the Horizon **20**(2), 126–136 (2012)
16. Reason, J.: Managing the Risks of Organizational Accidents. Ashgate Publishing Limited, London (1997)
17. Tokyo Metropolitan Government: Flood Control Plan in Tokyo Metropolis. 138p. (2021)
18. Tokyo Metropolitan Government: Improvement Plan in the Nogawa River Basin. 38p. (2017)
19. Tokyo Metropolitan Government: Countermeasures Plan against Heavy Rain in the Nogawa River Basin. 60p (2019)

Flood Disaster Management System for Situation Awareness and Response Using Twitter Data

Manzu Gerald$^{(\boxtimes)}$ and Kayoko Yamamoto

The University of Electro-Communications, Chofugaoka, Chofu, Tokyo, Japan
k2030044@edu.cc.uec.ac.jp, kayoko.yamamoto@uec.ac.jp

Abstract. Social media has increasingly become a convenient tool for sharing and consuming information during emergencies and disasters such as floods. The annual floods of the River Nile in South Sudan devastates lives and property, leaving towns and villages submerged. The present study focuses on utilizing data from Twitter to develop a Flood Disaster Management System for Situation Awareness. Tweets about flooding are gathered and filtered from Twitter. Tweet location or mentions of locations or hashtags are important in getting the relevant content on flooding in South Sudan. Towns with reported flooding are represented on a web application with GIS functionalities. Information for Situation Awareness is generated and shared with flood victims, potential victims and humanitarian organizations, governmental and non-governmental organizations concerned with disaster response. The data collected during the half of the 2021 rainy season was experimentally used to evaluate this research and two of the areas reported to have had severe flooding in July and August 2021 based on Twitter data were also featured in an information report released by the United Nations Office for Coordination of Humanitarian Affairs (OCHA) in the first week of August 2021. The study aims to fully operationalize the Flood Disaster Management System for Situation Awareness and Response using Twitter in the next rainy season in 2022. This study shows that social media, particularly twitter is vital for gathering user generated flood related data and generating information for situation awareness which in turn can improve awareness and disaster response by partners concerned with disasters.

Keywords: Flooding · Twitter · Disaster management · Disaster response

1 Introduction

Flooding is the worst natural disaster affecting parts of South Sudan almost each and every year. The country has two seasons: The wet or rainy season which runs from April to October and the dry season which runs from November to March. In recent years, the country has experienced devastating floods in towns situated along the White Nile and its tributaries, most especially in central and eastern South Sudan as reported by the United Nations Office for the Coordination of Humanitarian Affairs (OCHA) [1], herein

© IFIP International Federation for Information Processing 2022
Published by Springer Nature Switzerland AG 2022
J. Sasaki et al. (Eds.): ITDRR 2021, IFIP AICT 638, pp. 35–48, 2022.
https://doi.org/10.1007/978-3-031-04170-9_3

referred to as 'UNOCHA'. According to a November 23rd 2020 weekly review by the Sudd Institute which is a South Sudanese Research Think-tank, heavy rainfall in 2019 and 2020 led to accumulation and an unprecedented rise of water levels in Lake Victoria, where the Nile starts its journey from [2]. A November 2020 report by UNOCHA termed flooding mainly in Central and Eastern parts of South Sudan as 'abnormal', following the overflow of the Nile, Sobat, Pibor, Lol and other rivers during the rainy season in 2020 [1].

This in turn led to flooding in eight (8) out of ten (10) states in South Sudan in 2019. In October 2020, preceded by a declaration of a state of emergency in the country, almost the whole town of Bor was submerged in what became as the worst floods in over a century [2]. Efforts from Humanitarian and Government agencies were overwhelmed by the magnitude of the floods.

UNOCHA reportedly estimated that in the 2020 floods in South Sudan, up to one million people (1,034,000) were directly affected, with flood response activities very much constrained by persistent heavy rains, infrastructure damage and physical accessibility, as well as insecurity and limited resources [1]. With this, it is imperative to consider other mechanisms of positively contributing towards disaster risk mitigation or reduction.

For that matter, Information Technology has since been used to support disaster risk reduction, with Palen et al. [3] suggesting the role of Information and Communication Technology in generating warnings and planning for response activities during the course of a natural disaster. In the past decade, coupled with citizen participation during disasters to publish, communicate, share and disseminate information, thereby helping in the response efforts of government authorities and partners [4–6]. To be particular, the role of social media networks in shaping disaster response and risk mitigation has grown ever since the devastating wild fires of San Diego in California, where Twitter was notably used to coordinate disaster response [7, 8].

The research questions (2) for this paper are: How can data on annual flooding in South Sudan, posted on Twitter be useful in Situation Awareness? How can the affected communities get information generated for Situation Awareness at times of flooding in South Sudan?

Affected populations, citizen journalists, humanitarian Organizations and others are increasingly utilizing social media during disasters by posting not only textual information, but also images and videos related to the incident. It is extremely useful for humanitarian organizations to gain situational awareness and plan relief operations supporting decision making and coordinating emergency response actions [6–8].

For the case of Flooding in South Sudan, utilizing data from twitter would aid in supplementing risk mitigation and response efforts of governmental and humanitarian organizations involved in the flood disaster cycle. In this case, it would act as an alternative source of information for Situation Awareness during floods.

2 Related Work

The present study develops a flood disaster management system for situation awareness and response using Twitter data, which aims at providing situation awareness to victims, potential victims and organizations involved in disaster management. The field of Situation Awareness and the usage of social media particularly Twitter for situation awareness are both central to the current study. Therefore the current study explores both of these.

2.1 Situation Awareness

Situation awareness can be defined differently, in relation to the context and underlying paradigms. In the late 1980s, how pilots maintained awareness of the very many dynamic, yet complex events occurring simultaneously in a flight and how such information was used became such a growing interest. The term Situation Awareness (SA) was adopted to describe the process of attention, perception, and decision making that together form a pilot's mental model of the current situation [11, 12, 19].

One of the most common definitions of Situation Awareness (SA), is that agreed upon by The Enhanced Safety through Situation Awareness Integration in Training consortium as "the perception of the elements in the environment within a volume of time and space, the comprehension of their meaning, and the projection of their status in the near future" [11]. This definition was further expanded into 3 phases of situation awareness namely [12]:

Level 1: Perception of the elements in the environment

The status, attributes and dynamics of the relevant elements in the environment have to be perceived in this level. In short, it is all about equipping oneself with the available information.

Level 2: Comprehension of the current situation. Based on the familiarity grasped in level one, level 2 situation awareness involves understanding the significance of the elements in level 1, leading to a holistic view of the environment.

Level 3: Projection of future status. The 3rd level makes it easier to project the future actions of the environments, given the knowledge of levels 1 and 2.

Hence Situation Awareness is not just limited to air traffic control but also used in many other fields like military operation systems and tactical areas such as firefighting and also spanning into fields like medicine.

Therefore, Situation Awareness in the context of Natural Disasters can be defined as "the ability to identify, process and comprehend the critical information about an incident", Federal Emergency Management Agency (FEMA) [10].

This research focuses on addressing Level 1 and Level 2 phases above.

2.2 Usage of Social Media for Situation Awareness During Disasters

Social Media Network sites such as Twitter are currently by no doubt active communication channels during disasters. Research has shown that usage of Social media dramatically increases when natural disasters occur, with communities affected by disasters, first responders, citizen journalists and news-seekers all trying to find useful information or to provide help and support where necessary. One of the biggest notable social media events followed the destructive Hurricane Sandy in 2012. Twitter reported that the terms "sandy", and "hurricane" were massively used and on the 3rd of November 2012, Twitter posted a tweet that said "People sent more than 20 million Tweets about the storm between October 27th and November 1st" (Twitter) [13].

2.3   Disaster Response and Relief

In the event of a disaster like a flood, potential victims need information as much as the first relief responders. In the event of a pre-disaster, during or after a disaster - potential victims, victims, Government agencies and humanitarian organizations are likely to become direct or indirect contributors of information via social media. The information from all actors posted on social media, if made into use for planning and or responding to a disaster, can provide alternative situation awareness information, secondary to that locally provided by the authorities.

Kumar et al. (2011) [14] worked on a tool that provided analytical and visualization functionalities that served as near real-time, data reduction and historical review.

Funayama et al. (2017) [15] extracted useful information from tweets by analyzing, and performing visualizations and developed a web application for extracting & searching effective information, which can be used in the time of disasters.

Ashktorab et al. (2014) [16] presented Tweedr as a Twitter-mining tool for extracting actionable information for disaster relief workers during natural disasters, - thereby enabling the extraction of relevant information for first responders from tweets generated during disasters in real time as well as enable analysis after the disaster has occurred. Tweedr consists of three main parts: classification, clustering and extraction [16]. The authors [16] extracted actionable information for disaster relief workers during natural disasters, validated with tweets collected from 12 different crises in the United States since 2006, demonstrating that "it is possible to extract nuggets of information from heterogeneous Twitter data using a relatively small set of labeled data".

Using a number of classification methods such as sparse linear discriminant analysis (sLDA), support vector machines (SVM) and logistic regression, the authors classified whether a tweet reported a disaster damage or casualty information. Whereas during the clustering phase, filters were used to merge tweets that looked similar to one another. In the extraction phase, the authors used tokens and phrases that reported specific information about different classes of infrastructure damage, damage types and casualties [16].

Following the great East Japan Earthquake and Tsunami in 2011, Yuko Murayama et al., researched on the possibility of the usage of IT for disaster response and recovery in Japan [17]. One of the systems they implemented is the Recovery watcher, which is an information sharing system to keep people aware of the process of recovery in a disaster area by reporting images from the disaster area. According to the authors, the original idea of the Recovery watcher was to keep people aware of what was happening at the recovery stage after the disaster. They used cameras placed at multiple places in the disaster area with images uploaded to the server. After the images were processed, the people in need would then browse through the images for current situations. The information sharing space was also presented on an open street map (OSM) for lookups. To include emergency response for the actors on the scene of a disaster, they opened and implemented a functionality for people on the scene of a disaster to upload images via social network sites (SNS) which would be managed by the information manager [17].

2.4   Originality of the Present Study

Flooding in South Sudan happens annually, making the areas in Central and Eastern South Sudan special in terms of socio-technical view.

The present study focuses on addressing level 1 and level 2 of Situation Awareness discussed earlier, by continuously streaming Twitter for data that can be used for Situation Awareness in areas that face severe flooding. So far, there are no studies that have utilized twitter for Flood Disaster Management and Response in South Sudan, hence the novelty of this research.

Technically, primary focus is almost always emphasized on sentiment analysis of tweets [15, 18]. In cases where the data posted on social media, Twitter in particular is too small, it presents a potential technical difficulty in sentiment analysis. South Sudan still has very low internet penetration [21] and limits the overall interactivity which is vital for sentiment analysis. This study therefore does not make use of sentiment analysis and only focuses on the main texts/messages being tweeted.

The study pursues collaboration with local sources of information, so as to share the messages generated for situation awareness with victims and potential victims as well as humanitarian organizations. Much of South Sudan is remote and exploiting other ways of sharing information other than using the internet alone is imperative in reaching the masses. This is necessary for communities that may rely much more on traditional sources of information sharing like community radio stations. Hence, the study's contribution to flood disaster management.

3   System Design

3.1   System Configuration

Individual tweets about flooding are gathered and filtered from Twitter. Tweet location or mentions of locations or hashtags are important in getting the relevant content on flooding in South Sudan. Towns with reported flooding are represented on a web application with functionalities of generating information on Situation Awareness which is relayed back to flood victims and potential victims, humanitarian organizations, governmental and non-governmental organizations concerned with disaster response.

3.2   Data Collection

Data about flooding is collected from Twitter with the help of the Twitter API (Tweepy). We created a Twitter bot account and developed a script that streams twitter for any content related to our hashtags or search terms. The script was coded to retweet any content that meets our criteria and the bot acted as an archive for flood related data (Figs. 1 and 2).

To capture random tweets might not include any of the hashtags, we also streamed tweets that mentioned any of the flood prone counties (23) in Eastern and Central South Sudan, which contained the words flooding or floods. Otherwise a tweet is ignored (Table 1).

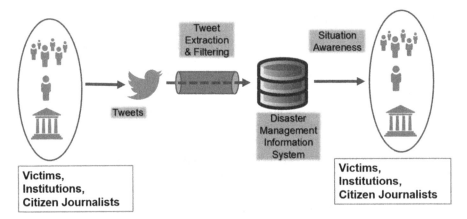

Fig. 1. System design

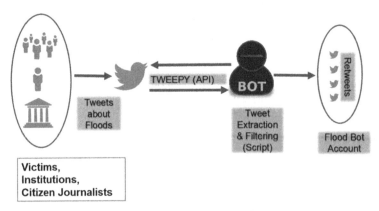

Fig. 2. Data collection overview

Table 1. Streamed hashtags, words and towns

Streaming Criteria [Hashtags, words, county-names]	
Hashtags	#floodsSouthSudan, #floodingSouthSudan, #SouthSudanFloods, #SSD-Floods, #FloodsSSD
Words	South Sudan Floods, South Sudan Flooding
Counties / Towns	Akobo, Ayod, Bor, Bor South, Pibor, Fangak, Duk, Nyirol, Pochalla, Twic East, Uror, Nasir, Maban, Maiwut, Malakal, Manyo, Melut, Ulang, Mangala, Bentiu, Rubkona, Aweil East, Aweil West

3.3 Extraction of Information Location

We filtered the data from the flood bot and looked for location matches, by comparing the location name(s) with flood prone locations in Northern, Eastern and Central South Sudan. The criteria of obtaining the name(s) of locations in the tweet data included:

1. Location mentions in the hashtags.
2. Location mentions in the tweet text if not included in the hashtag.
3. Tweet location, based on the location parameters of the original tweet author, if location settings were enabled by the tweet author.

3.4 Web Application

Flood locations plotted on a web map are based on the extracted location of the tweets from the flood bot data. A location has to be mentioned at least ten (10) times in different tweets by different tweet authors, in a period of at least fourteen (14) days. Every fourteen (14) days, the dataset is refreshed and only tweets that are within the period get plotted or refreshed. A list of affected locations is also generated and displayed (Fig. 3).

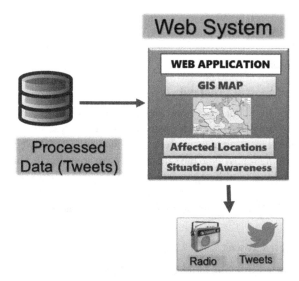

Fig. 3. Presentation on the web app

3.5 Situation Awareness

Information about flooded towns, current flooding, and Situation Awareness are displayed on the Web app. The same information is also twitted by the Flood bot account (SSD Flood Bot). Population data of South Sudan's towns is separately stored in a database and linked to the data of the affected locations. Information for Situation Awareness includes the following: the name of the location, the population of the location and the number of tweets per the location (Fig. 4).

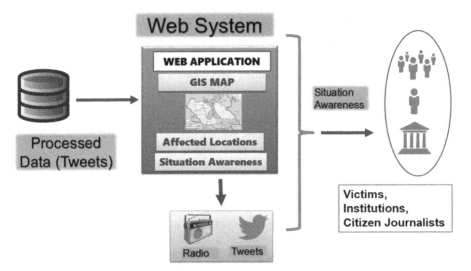

Fig. 4. Situation awareness flow

4   System Development

4.1   System Frontend

4.1.1   Overview of System Frontend

Data obtained by the flood bot is accessed and automatic tweet locations are represented on the web map, so long as the criteria for consideration of representing the data on a map are met. For a random location to be plotted on the map, at least 10 tweets posted by different users mentioning referring to the said location are considered. This is important in reducing the possibilities of utilizing tweets that are possible sources of misinformation. The number of tweets mentioning the same location and the town population information are ingredients for generating information for Situation Awareness.

4.1.2   Flood Affected Towns

From the data extracted from the flood bot, a list of the affected areas is constructed and displayed on the web application.

4.1.3   Map Visualization of Flood Affected Towns

The web app utilizes Python's Folium library to automatically generate a map visualizing the areas/towns that are experiencing flooding.

The web app also displays a flood heat map that visually shows the towns that are currently experiencing floods. The map and the heat map are essential visual components of the web application (Figs. 5, 6 and 7).

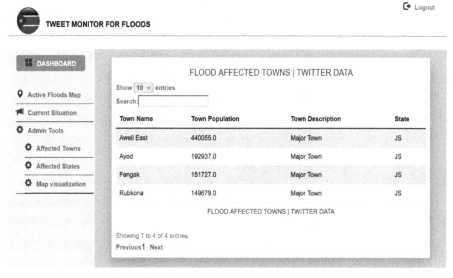

Fig. 5. Page displaying towns affected by flooding

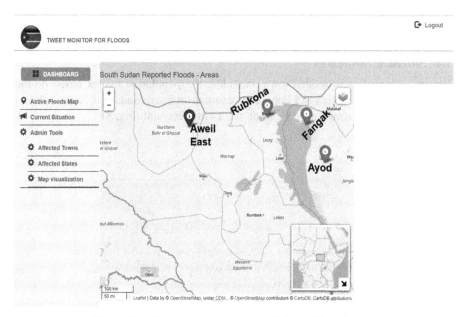

Fig. 6. Page displaying a web map with flood affected towns

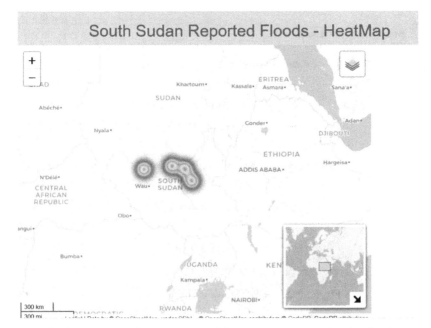

Fig. 7. Page displaying a heat map of the current towns experiencing floods

4.1.4 Situation Awareness

Information regarding a flooded town, including the population figures based on the 2008 Sudan Census and the 2017 Population estimate of South Sudan [19] are displayed on the web application and also shared on the Twitter account (Fig. 8).

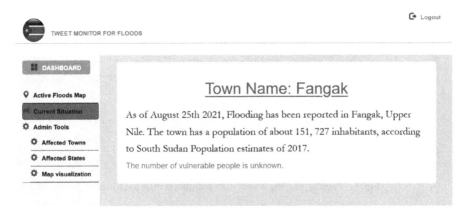

Fig. 8. Current information for situation awareness

4.2 System Backend

4.2.1 Process of Getting and Relaying Data to Twitter

The back end of the system has a connection to a Twitter account that runs on a script, called the "SSD Flood Bot". The SSD Flood Bot Twitter account is the data source for the Flood Disaster Management System for Situation Awareness and Response (Fig. 9).

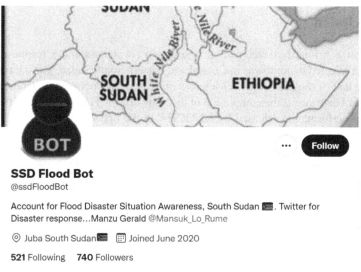

Fig. 9. Flood Bot account that streams for flood data

4.2.2 Process to Display Information on the Web Application with GIS Functions

The web application makes use of the data obtained from the Twitter account by displaying a list of the affected towns in a table, and also acts as a Geographical Information System (GIS) portal in the form of displaying the flood affected towns using markers.

An extension of the GIS functionality includes a heat map, which can provide a generation view of areas or regions that are experiencing floods.

4.3 System Operation Environment

The web system can be accessed Google Chrome version 8.0.552 or higher, Internet Explorer 8 or higher and Firefox 5 or higher. The Flood Bot separately runs as a script of its own, hosted on Heroku. It interacts with Twitter using the Twitter API and Python Library called Tweepy. Python programming language was used to implement the scripts of the flood bot.

Implemented using Python and Django as the web framework for Python, the web portal as well as the flood bot scripts were both hosted on Heroku.

4.4 Operation Target Area

With severe flooding reported in Eastern, Northern and Central South Sudan in recent years [1, 2], the study target these areas in particular. The current system has been operating since June 2021 primarily focused on collecting preliminary data during the 2021 rainy season in South Sudan. In the next rainy season, the system is planned to fully be implemented in the target areas.

5 Conclusion

The system is primarily developed as a Situation Awareness and a response aid for flooding in selected major towns in Central and Eastern South Sudan. The data collected during the half of the 2021 rainy season was only used as experimental data. Complete evaluation of data awaits the completion of the rainy season. However, part of the results agreed with information released by UNOCHA in the first week of August 2021 [9]. Hence partial evaluation based on comparative reports was successful.

Within half-way the 2021 rainy season in South Sudan, UNOCHA released a Situation Report on August 6th 2021 [5] detailing about flooding and displacement of people. In the report, two (2) counties of Ayod and Fangak were both mentioned.

At the same time, based on the data that we collected from Twitter for the month of July and August, our data indicated that flooding was reported in at least four (4) towns of Aweil East, Ayod, Fangak and Rubkona. We can therefore use correlate the situation report by UNOCHA with our current findings.

This research shows that social media, particularly twitter is vital for gathering user generated flood related data and generating information on Situation Awareness which in turn can improve awareness and disaster response by partners concerned with disasters.

We have identified and sought coordination with local and national partners such as organizations and institutions that are primary sources of information to thousands of people who do not have access to the internet, for instance local radio stations. With a partnership as such, information can be broadcasted to thousands of people.

We intend to continue collecting more data and involve organizations, institutions and individuals in our research towards the end of the 2021 rainy season in South Sudan, so that the system can be fully operational in the next rainy season in 2022.

Acknowledgment. In order to interact with data on Twitter, a Twitter developer account is needed. And to make sure that the data is used in line with the Twitter API guidelines without misusing the data and without publicly sharing vital user information, the Twitter Developer Platform has been very helpful. We would like to register our gratitude to the Twitter Developer Team, of which without the resources, getting the needed information would have been a difficult task.

References

1. UNOCHA: South Sudan Flooding Situation Report Inter-Cluster Coordination Group, as of 18 November 2020. https://www.humanitarianresponse.info/en/document/south-sudan-flooding-situation-report. Accessed 4 Dec 2020

2. Tiitmamer, N.: South Sudan's devastating floods: why there is a need for urgent resilience measures. The Sudd Institute, Juba South Sudan, 2020 November. https://suddinstitute.org/assets/Publications/5fbcef5b321bd_SouthSudansDevastatingFloodsWhyThereIs_Full.pdf. Accessed 3 Jan 2021

3. Palen, L., Liu, S.B.: Citizen communications in crisis: anticipating a future of ICT-supported public participation. In: Conference on Human Factors in Computing Systems, Chi 2007 Proceedings: Emergency Action, pp. 727–736. San Jose, May 2007

4. Truong, B., Caragea, C., Squicciarini, A., Tapia, A.H.: Identifying valuable information from twitter during natural disasters. In: Proceedings of the American Society for Information Science and Technology (2014). https://doi.org/10.1002/meet.2014.14505101162

5. Sakaki, T., Okazaki, M., Matsuo, Y.: Earthquake shakes twitter users: real-time event detection by social sensors. In: ACM International World Wide Web Conference, www, 2010, Raleigh, North Carolina, USA, pp. 851–860, April 2010

6. Imran, M., Elbassuoni, S., Castillo, C., Diaz, F.: Practical extraction of disaster-relevant information from social media. In: Proceedings of the 22nd International Conference on World Wide Web – WWW 2013 Companion, pp. 1021–1024. ACM Press, Rio de Janeiro (2013). http://dl.acm.org/citation.cfm?doid=2487788.2488109

7. Imran, M., Castillo, C.: Towards a data-driven approach to identify crisis-related topics in social media streams. In: Proceedings of the 24th International Conference on World Wide Web – WWW 2015 Companion, pp. 1205–1210. ACM Press, Florence (2015). https://doi.org/10.1145/2740908.2741729. http://dl.acm.org/citation.cfm?doid=2740908.2741729. Accessed 12 Mar 2020

8. Imran, M., Castillo, C., Lucas, J., Meier, P., Vieweg, S.: AIDR: artificial intelligence for disaster response. In: Proceedings of the 23rd International Conference on World Wide Web – WWW 2014 companion, pp. 159–162. ACM Press, Seoul (2014). https://doi.org/10.1145/2567948.2577034.http://dl.acm.org/citation.cfm?doid=2567948.2577034. Accessed 19 Aug 2020

9. UNOCHA: South Sudan: Floods – July 2021, August 2020. https://reliefweb.int/disaster/fl-2021-000108-ssd. Accessed 20 Aug 2021

10. FEMA: Review: Situation Awareness. https://emilms.fema.gov/IS2200/groups/106.html. Accessed 22 May 2020

11. Endsley, M.R.: Design and evaluation for situation awareness enhancement. In: Proceedings of the Human Factors Society 32nd Annual Meeting, vol. 1, pp. 97–101. Human Factors Society, Santa Monica (1988)

12. Endsley, M.R., Farley, T.C., Jones, W.M., Midkiff, A.H., Hansman, R.J.: Situation awareness information requirements for commercial airline pilots (ICAT). Massachusetts Institute of Technology International Center for Air Transportation, Cambridge (1998)

13. Techcrunch 2012: Twitter releases numbers related to hurricane sandy: more than 20m Tweets sent during peak. http://techcrunch.com/2012/11/02/twitter-releases-numbers-related-to-hurricane-sandy-more-than-20m-tweets-sent-between-october-27th-and-november-1st/

14. Kumar, S., Barbier, G., Abbasi, M.A., Liu, H.: TweetTracker: an analysis tool for humanitarian and disaster relief. In: Proceedings of the Fifth International Conference on Weblogs and Social Media, ICWSM, Barcelona, Spain, 17–21 July 2011

15. Funayama, T., Yamamoto, Y., Uchida, O.: Development of visualization application of tweet data for extracting information in case of disaster. In: 2017, 15th International Conference on ICT and Knowledge Engineering (ICT&KE), Bangkok, pp. 1–5 (2017). https://doi.org/10.1109/ICTKE.2017.8259620

16. Ashktorab, Z., Brown, C., Nandi, M., Culotta, A.: Tweedr: mining twitter to inform disaster response. In: ISCRAM (2014)

17. Murayama, Y., Yamamoto, K., Sasaki, J.: Recovery watcher: a disaster communication system for situation awareness and its use for barrier-free information provision. In: Murayama, Y., Velev, D., Zlateva, P. (eds.) ITDRR 2018. IAICT, vol. 550, pp. 1–11. Springer, Cham (2019). https://doi.org/10.1007/978-3-030-32169-7_1

18. Kaur, A.: Analyzing twitter feeds to facilitate crises informatics and disaster response during mass emergencies, Dissertation (2019)

19. Adams, M.J., Tenney, Y.J., Pew, R.W.: Situation awareness and the cognitive management of complex systems. Hum. Factors **37**(1), 85–104 (1995). https://doi.org/10.1518/001872095 779049462

20. The Republic of South Sudan – National Bureau of Statistics. Southern Sudan counts: Tables from the 5th Sudan Population and Housing Census, 2008. https://www.ssnbss.org/home/doc uments/census-and-survey/south-sudan-counts-2008/. Accessed 24 Jan 2021

21. Individuals using the Internet (% of Population) – South Sudan. https://data.worldbank.org/ indicator/IT.NET.USER.ZS?locations=SS

Evacuation and Rescue

Proposed Evacuation Behavior Model Using Open-Source Data: Flood Disaster Case Study

Makoto Kitsuya and Jun Sasaki[✉]

Graduate School of Software and Information Science, Iwate Prefectural University, Takizawa, Iwate, Japan
g231s008@s.iwate-pu.ac.jp, jsasaki@iwate-pu.ac.jp

Abstract. In a flood disaster, safe evacuation is essential to save lives. However, there have been problems such as low capacity or biases in evacuation centers for some flood disasters in Japan. Therefore, estimating the number of evacuees in each evacuation center during a disaster is vital for a safe evacuation. Consequently, it is necessary to develop highly accurate evacuation behavior simulation models. This paper proposes an evacuation behavior model using open-source data that are readily available from the internet. As a case study, the evacuation behavior model parameters and coefficients were obtained for a flood in Kuji City, Iwate Prefecture in Japan, where many people were affected by Typhoon Hagibis in 2019. By comparing the actual number of evacuees with the predicted number from the proposed evacuation behavior model and conducting a field survey of the actual evacuation shelters, we measured the validity of the evacuation behavior model and identified possible improvements.

Keywords: Evacuation · Behavior model · Flood disaster · Simulation

1 Introduction

Japan has experienced many natural disasters in recent years. As a disaster strikes, the meteorological agency issues weather warnings and advisories, and local governments announce evacuation-related information to encourage residents to take safety actions. However, there is a concern that information sharing, especially after a disaster occurs, may result in delays in responding to the changing disaster situation. As a result of those delays, the capacity of evacuation shelters may be exceeded. For example, 13 evacuation shelters in Iwaki City, Fukushima Prefecture, were overcrowded after Typhoon Hagibis in 2019. In another example, in 2020, 383 evacuation shelters nationwide in Japan were overcrowded after Typhoon Haishen hit Kyushu during the COVID-19 pandemic [1].

It is necessary to predict congestion in shelters to prevent such overcrowding, and an evacuation behavior model can predict the crowdedness of evacuation shelters by computer simulation. In conventional research, evacuation behavior models have been proposed, some using questionnaires and some using person trip (PT) data, but those data are difficult to obtain.

© IFIP International Federation for Information Processing 2022
Published by Springer Nature Switzerland AG 2022
J. Sasaki et al. (Eds.): ITDRR 2021, IFIP AICT 638, pp. 51–62, 2022.
https://doi.org/10.1007/978-3-031-04170-9_4

In this study, we propose an evacuation model using open-source data readily available from the internet and attempt to identify the parameters influencing shelter overcrowding. As a case study, the parameters of the evacuation behavior model in Kuji City, Iwate Prefecture in Japan during Typhoon Hagibis in 2019 are estimated, and the coefficients for each parameter are obtained. By comparing the actual number of evacuees with the number predicted by the evacuation behavior model and conducting a field survey of evacuation shelters, we measured the validity of the proposed model and identified possible improvements.

2 Related Studies

There have been many studies of disaster evacuation behavior models. Yamada et al. [2] modeled the selection of tsunami evacuation buildings (shelters), and a decision-making model for choosing an evacuation site during an earthquake and fire was developed by Nishino et al. [3]. Mancheva et al. [4] presented a multi-agent geospatial simulation of human social interactions and behavior in bush fires. These three studies used decision-making models for different disasters (tsunamis, earthquakes, and fires), but none addressed evacuation behavior modeling for a flood disaster. Flood disaster recovery of small businesses using agent-based modeling and simulation was studied by Alhabi et al. [5]. However, their simulation model was for flood disaster recovery rather than before or during the flood.

In references [2–5], behavioral model parameter estimation was based on questionnaires or PT data from a hypothetical disaster. Generally, the questionnaire does not include the characteristics of actual disasters and is therefore not true data. The PT data requires subjects to carry GPS loggers, which has the disadvantages of low data availability and high cost. In addition, these studies assume one-time decision-making for the evacuation. In the case of an actual flood disaster, multiple decisions may be made as the disaster occurs. Our study aims to build an evacuation behavior model using open-source data available from the internet that permits multiple decisions depending on the flood disaster situation.

In our previous research [6], an evacuation support system was proposed to rescue required support people, and the effect of the proposed system was reported using a multi-agent simulation. Additionally, a real-time mapping system of shelter conditions was introduced and developed to contribute to safer evacuations [7]. If the number of evacuees can be estimated before an actual flood disaster, the effectiveness of disaster response systems will increase. This potential flood disaster response improvement motivates the development of the proposed evacuation behavior model discussed in this paper.

3 Evacuation Model Concept

Figure 1 shows the concept of our evacuation model as a precondition of the proposal. In this concept, many factors were considered, including time, the population of a residential area (grid), the distance to shelters, the distance to a river, shelter capacity and facilities, and precipitation radar echo intensity. As the first step in the evacuation behavior model construction, we have identified three processes to be modeled: the decision to evacuate, the probability of an evacuation shelter being chosen, and the number of evacuees per unit time. We adopt the repeated binary logit model proposed by Fu et al. [8] for the decision-making model. The parameters for calculating the probability and the number of evacuees are determined using open-source data because it is actual data that can be easily obtained from the internet.

To use the time-series open-source data for the number of evacuees at each evacuation shelter, we assume that residents evacuate based on general decisions such as the distance to the shelter from their homes and river conditions. We set the grid to obtain the number of evacuees per unit time by population and the evacuation probability in each grid. The grid size is scaled to 250 by 250 m, which is the highest resolution available in the data.

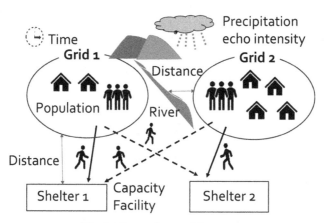

Fig. 1. Evacuation model concept

3.1 Evacuation Decision Process Model

The decision to evacuate is made using the repeated binary logit model, representing multiple decisions during the evacuation. Figure 2 shows the state transition diagram of the repeated binary logit model. It starts from the non-evacuated state, and at a time t_j, if the probability of transitions to the evacuated state is given as probability $\Pr(t_j)$, then the probability of the non-evacuated state is given as $1 - \Pr(t_j)$.

3.2 Calculation of Evacuation Shelter Choice Probability

The multinomial logit model numerically determines the utility of multiple evacuation site candidates and calculates the probability of residents choosing an evacuation site. The probability $\Pr(t, i, n)$ that subject (resident) n chooses option (evacuation shelter) i at time t, is given by Eq. (1), where $V_{t,i,n}$ is the utility function of subject n for option i at time t, and C is the total number of candidates.

$$\Pr(t, i, n) = \frac{\exp(V_{t,i,n})}{\sum_{i=0}^{C}\exp(V_{t,i,n})} \qquad (1)$$

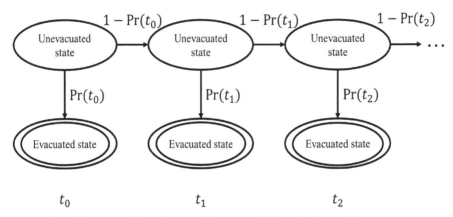

Fig. 2. State transition diagram of the repeated binary logit model to evacuate

The utility function $V_{t,i,n}$, where $x_{k,t,i,n}$ are the explanatory variables and β_k are the coefficients, is given by Eq. (2):

$$V_{t,i,n} = \sum_{k=1}^{D} x_{k,t,i,n} \beta_k \tag{2}$$

where D is the total number of explanatory variables.

3.3 Evacuee Rate Calculation

The rate of evacuees per unit time is obtained by multiplying the probability of an evacuation shelter choice, calculated in Sect. 3.2, by the number of people staying in the 250 by 250 m grid. The initial number of people staying in the grid is equal to the population of the grid at the time, t_0, and is thereafter updated to the number of people who have not yet evacuated at each time.

4 Simulation

4.1 Algorithm Overview

We estimated the evacuation behavior model parameters by comparing the proposed model's simulation results with open-source data for the actual number of evacuees. Specifically, the error between the number of evacuees predicted by the model with a unit time of 10 min and the actual number of evacuees is calculated as the root mean square error (RMSE). The parameters and coefficients are determined to minimize the RMSE using a genetic algorithm (GA).

4.2 Target Area and Data

Open-source data were used for the selected simulation site of Kuji City, Iwate Prefecture, Japan, which experienced a flood disaster from Typhoon Hagibis in 2019. During that time, the Koyahata River overflowed through a residential area, causing 455 houses to flood above ground and 561 houses to flood below ground [9]. The simulation was conducted for the period from 3:40 p.m. to 11:40 p.m. on October 12. This period was from the beginning of the evacuation by government-announced advisory and order to the end when no more evacuees were confirmed.

Figure 3 shows the distribution of the population on the 250 by 250 m grid. In total, there are 1,255 grids in the city.

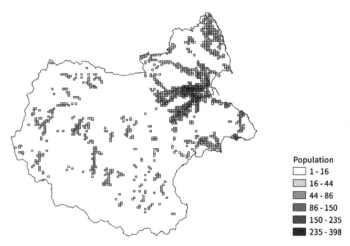

Fig. 3. Location and population of grids in Kuji City

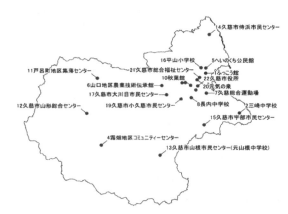

Fig. 4. Evacuation shelters in Kuji City opened during Typhoon No. 19 (Japanese characters indicate the names of shelters)

Figure 4 shows the locations of 22 evacuation centers opened in Kuji City during Typhoon Hagibis. It was confirmed that the evacuation shelters were established according to the population distribution shown in Fig. 3. The accessibility of the evacuation shelters is unclear because the topography and road conditions are not available from these maps.

4.3 Data Used in the Simulation

The data used in the simulation are shown in Table 1. All data are open-source and can be obtained from the internet.

Table 1. List of data used in the experiment

Name	Description
Iwate disaster prevention information portal (evacuation shelter information) [10]	Time-series data on the number of evacuees in each evacuation center at the time of the disaster
Designated emergency evacuation shelter data [11]	Latitude and longitude information of evacuation shelters
2015 Census, the 5th grid (250 by 250 m grid) [12]	Population per 250 by 250 m grid
2015 Census, subregions [12]	Polygon data (Shapefile) for 250 by 250 m grid
GPV precipitation echo intensity [13]	Precipitation intensity data every 10 min

4.4 Explanatory Variables

The explanatory variables used in the utility function $V_{t,i,n}$ are shown in Table 2. Different explanatory variables are used for the cases of evacuation and non-evacuation. These parameters are selected based on the criteria of objective indicators for evacuation decisions and data availability.

Table 2. List of explanatory variables

Name	When evacuated	When not evacuated
Elapsed time	✓	✓
Time of day	✓	✓
Distance between the grid and the nearest river	✓	✓
Distance between the shelter and the nearest river	✓	
Precipitation echo intensity	✓	✓

4.5 Scenarios

Three explanatory variable combinations were selected as scenarios for the simulation, as shown in Table 3. Scenario A is the simplest combination, using only elapsed time and time of day. Scenario B uses all explanatory variables except for precipitation radar echo intensity. In scenario C, all explanatory variables are used.

Table 3. Correspondence between scenarios and explanatory variables

Name	A	B	C
Elapsed time	✓	✓	✓
Time of day	✓	✓	✓
Distance between the grid and the nearest river		✓	✓
Distance between the shelter and the nearest river		✓	✓
Precipitation echo intensity			✓

4.6 Optimization Method

The R programming language was used for data preprocessing, and C++ was used for the evacuation simulation modeling. A real-valued genetic algorithm (GA) with a population of 50 and 2000 iterations is used to optimize the coefficients.

4.7 Comparison Between Actual and Predicted Number of Evacuees

Comparisons between the actual number of evacuees and the proposed evacuation behavior model results are shown in Fig. 5 for scenario A, Fig. 6 for scenario B, and Fig. 7 for scenario C. In each figure, there are 22 evacuation shelters, and for each shelter, the actual number of evacuees is shown as a red line, and the simulation prediction is shown as a blue line. The numbers in the bold typeface are the RMSE values for each shelter, and the different orange background shades correspond to the RMSE magnitudes. The evacuation center numbers are 1–5 from left to right in the top row, 6–10 in the second row, and so on, ending in numbers 21–22 in the bottom row. These shelter numbers correspond to those shown in Fig. 4. The average RMSE for each scenario is listed in Table 4.

From these comparisons, we found that scenario A had the largest error. The error was especially large for shelter numbers 20 and 21, where the number of evacuees was large. Scenario B showed an improvement in RMSE compared with scenario A. However, the number of evacuees at evacuation center number 7 is overestimated. Scenario C has the lowest RMSE, especially when the actual number of evacuees was small, although when the actual number of evacuees is large, the RMSE is large in some cases, such as in shelter number 18.

These results indicate some general directions for improving the overall accuracy of the model. Still, we could not find the cause for the RMSE change for each evacuation center, so we conducted a field survey to obtain additional information.

4.8 Field Survey

A field survey was conducted on May 26, 2021, in Kuji City, Iwate Prefecture, Japan, to understand the differences between the actual and predicted numbers of evacuees. In

Table 4. Average RMSE for each scenario

Scenario	Average RMSE
A	21.48326
B	13.33299
C	10.02989

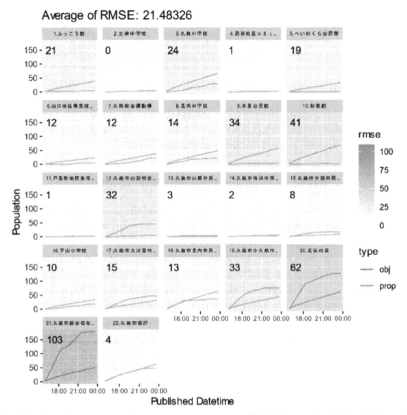

Fig. 5. Number of evacuees and root-mean square error (RMSE) at each shelter in Scenario A. The number on each graph is the RMSE for that shelter.

the field survey, we visited 14 evacuation centers located in urban areas and observed the surrounding environment. The survey was limited to the 14 urban area shelters because evacuation centers in the suburbs do not have other nearby evacuation centers, so residents do not have a choice. Figure 8 shows photographs of some of the shelters surveyed.

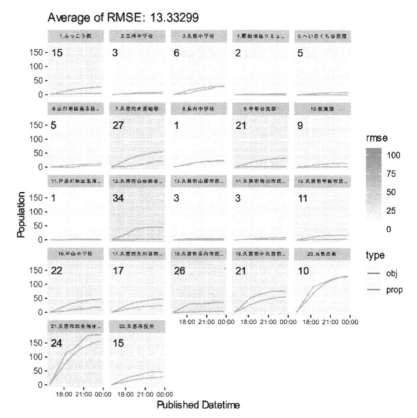

Fig. 6. Number of evacuees and root-mean square error (RMSE) at each shelter in Scenario B. The number on each graph is the RMSE for that shelter.

During Typhoon Hagibis in 2019, there were almost no evacuees in shelter numbers 5 and 10. In the case of shelter 5, there were few residents in the vicinity, and the shelter was inaccessible to evacuees on foot. Shelter 10 was easily accessible in the city center, but the building was small, and other larger evacuation centers such as the city hall and the joint government building were nearby.

For shelter numbers 17 and 19, we were able to conduct interviews with the staff. These shelters were similar because voluntary disaster prevention organizations encouraged residents to evacuate to them. They have Japanese-style rooms and other facilities and resident staff to assist the residents. We found that while some people evacuated voluntarily, many older adults were brought to the shelter by disaster prevention organization volunteers. These factors may explain why the actual numbers of evacuees are more than the model-estimated values.

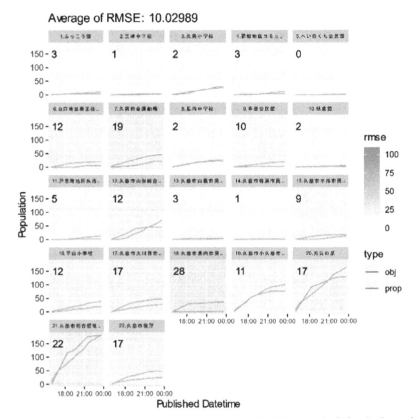

Fig. 7. Number of evacuees and root-mean square error (RMSE) at each shelter in Scenario C. The number on each graph is the RMSE for that shelter.

Shelter numbers 21 and 22 are public institutions that accepted many evacuees. In particular, shelter 21 is located on a hill with a large parking lot and has substantial resident staff, medical staff, and facilities. This sense of security is thought to have attracted many evacuees.

In general, the evacuation centers with the fewest evacuees had inconvenient access in common, such as being located in alleys or crowded areas with small parking lots. In addition, they were relatively small, unpopular, and did not appear to be used regularly. However, evacuation centers with many evacuees were superior in terms of accessibility, and it was confirmed that they were frequently used. We plan to incorporate the results of this survey into our model, including shelter accessibility, frequency of use, and the existence of voluntary disaster prevention organizations. We also intend to consider the availability of shelter facilities and staff and that some people may evacuate after a disaster has occurred.

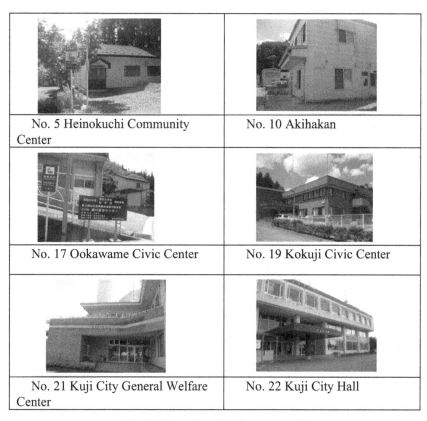

No. 5 Heinokuchi Community Center	No. 10 Akihakan
No. 17 Ookawame Civic Center	No. 19 Kokuji Civic Center
No. 21 Kuji City General Welfare Center	No. 22 Kuji City Hall

Fig. 8. Examples of shelters surveyed

5 Conclusion

This paper has described an evacuation behavior model for estimating the number of evacuees moving to shelters during floods. It proposes a method for estimating the parameters of the evacuation behavior model using open-source data. We confirmed that the model's accuracy could be improved by identifying and adding simulation parameters using actual disaster data from Kuji City, Iwate Prefecture, Japan, during Typhoon Hagibis in 2019. We also conducted a field survey to ascertain the cause of the error between the actual and predicted values for the number of evacuees and discussed possible missing elements in the model. In the future, we plan to develop a more practical evacuation behavior model and parameter estimation method based on the results of the data and field surveys.

Acknowledgments. This research is supported by the Telecommunications Advancement Foundation. We thank Robert A. Brewster, PhD, from Edanz (https://www.edanz.com/ac) for editing a draft of this manuscript.

References

1. Saga Shimbun LiVE: 383 evacuation shelters over capacity due to COVID-19 (in Japanese). https://www.saga-s.co.jp/articles/-/578443. Accessed 15 June 2021
2. Yamada, T., Kishimoto, T.: Choice behavior of refuge building selection during a tsunami in coastal areas. J. Archit. Plann. (Trans. AIJ) **80**(707), 125–133 (2015). (in Japanese)
3. Nishino, T., Himoto, K., Tanaka, T.: Modeling of destination choice for evacuation by residents in post-earthquake fire event. J. Environ. Eng. (Trans. AIJ) **76**(663), 469–477 (2011). (in Japanese)
4. Mancheva, L., Adam, C., Dugdale, J.: Multi-agent geospatial simulation of human interactions and behavior in bushfires. In: Proceedings of the 16th International Conference on Information Systems for Crisis Response and Management (ISCRAM), pp. 1–15 (2019)
5. Alhabi, M., Coates, G.: Assembling flood recovery of small business using agent-based modeling and simulation. In: Proceedings of the 16th International Conference on Information Systems for Crisis Response and Management (ISCRAM), pp. 94–104 (2019)
6. Kitsuya, M., Sasaki, J.: Proposal of evacuation support system and evaluation by multi-agent simulation in a regional disaster. In: Murayama, Y., Velev, D., Zlateva, P. (eds.) ITDRR 2019. IAICT, vol. 575, pp. 45–54. Springer, Cham (2020). https://doi.org/10.1007/978-3-030-489 39-7_5
7. Kitsuya, M., Sasaki, J.: Real-time mapping system of shelter conditions for safe evacuation. In: Sakurai, M., Shaw, R. (eds.) Emerging Technologies for Disaster Resilience. DRR, pp. 229–239. Springer, Singapore (2021). https://doi.org/10.1007/978-981-16-0360-0_12
8. Fu, H., Wilmot, C.G., Zhang, H., Baker, E.J.: Modeling the hurricane evacuation response curve. Transp. Res. Rec. **2022**(1), 94–102 (2007)
9. Fukutome, K.: Trends of evacuees regarding Typhoon Hagibis in Kuji City, Iwate Prefecture. In: The General Meeting of the AJG Spring 2020, p. 355. The Association of Japanese Geographers (2020). (in Japanese)
10. Iwate Disaster Prevention Information Portal. https://iwate.secure.force.com/
11. Evacuation Shelters of Municipalities in Iwate Prefecture. https://www.pref.iwate.jp/kurash ikankyou/anzenanshin/bosai/kokoroe/1004197.html. Accessed 15 June 2021
12. Statistics Bureau of Japan, Part 1: Matters Related to the Basic Population Census M6041, Results of the 2015 National Census. https://www.e-stat.go.jp/gis/statmap-search/data?sta tsId=T000876&code=6041&downloadType=2. Accessed 15 June 2021
13. Research Institute for Sustainable Humanosphere, Kyoto University, National Synthetic Radar GPV. http://database.rish.kyoto-u.ac.jp/index-e.html. Accessed 15 June 2021
14. MLIT Japan, National Land Data, River Data, Iwate Prefecture. https://nlftp.mlit.go.jp/ksj/ gml/datalist/KsjTmplt-W05.html. Accessed 15 June 2021

Agent-Based Tsunami Crowd Evacuation Simulation for Analysis of Evacuation Start Time and Disaster Rate in Zushi City

Yasuo Kawai[✉]

Bunkyo University, Namegaya 1100, Chigasaki, Japan
kawai@bunkyo.ac.jp

Abstract. In this study, we developed a tsunami crowd evacuation simulation system that can be operated by local governments using a game engine and open data. The purpose of this system is to visualize the evacuation behaviours of agents and obtain data for the disaster prevention planning of local governments, such as the locations of tsunami evacuation buildings and evacuation routes. The simulation results for Zushi City showed that the disaster rate increases rapidly with tsunami height and the time margin for tsunami evacuation has a significant impact on damage reduction. The locations where agents were affected revealed that there are insufficient evacuation sites, such as tsunami evacuation buildings, along inland rivers. However, Zushi City has a maximum height limit for buildings set by its landscape ordinance, so the local government and residents must work together to develop a town that balances disaster prevention and landscape.

Keywords: Tsunami evacuation · Game engine · Open data · Agent · Simulation

1 Introduction

A tsunami is a large-scale wave propagation phenomenon in the ocean caused by the rapid deformation of the topography due to an earthquake. Large tsunamis are natural disasters with very long wavelengths and large wave heights, which can penetrate deep inland from the coast and cause serious damage [1]. As a result of the 2004 Sumatra Earthquake, more than 220,000 lives were lost due to tsunamis with wave heights of up to 34 m [2, 3]. As a result of the 2011 Great East Japan Earthquake, a tsunami with wave heights of up to 40.1 m resulted in more than 18,000 deaths and serious damage to the Fukushima Daiichi Nuclear Power Plant [4, 5]. In Japan, earthquakes in Tokai, Tonankai, and Nankai are predicted to occur in the first half of the 21st century [6, 7]. Such earthquakes have caused major earthquakes and tsunami damage in the past. It has been noted that when these earthquakes occur, large tsunamis may be generated over a wide area of the Japanese archipelago.

J. Sasaki et al. (Eds.): ITDRR 2021, IFIP AICT 638, pp. 63–75, 2022.
https://doi.org/10.1007/978-3-031-04170-9_5

Previous tsunami simulations have mainly been conducted by numerical calculations [8, 9]. These numerical tsunami simulations are based on the initial tsunami waveforms estimated from the seismic waves as the earthquake occurs. This method can predict the behaviour of tsunamis from the source area to the coast of the bay. These have been used to predict tsunamis at the national level because they require large-scale calculations.

However, the hazard maps of local evacuation routes and tsunami evacuation buildings that residents of coastal areas refer to in the event of a disaster are produced by local governments based on the large-scale simulation results of inundation areas, tsunami arrival times, and tsunami heights. Because these hazard maps are developed using the data provided, they are subject to significant revision by local authorities when the original simulation results change. Since the Great East Japan Earthquake, many local governments have redesigned their hazard maps due to the large-scale risk review and data updates.

Agent-based simulations have been conducted in the past. Mas et al. proposed an evacuation model for the Great East Japan Earthquake that integrates numerical tsunami simulation and casualty estimation assessment [10]. Wang et al. studied a multimodal evacuation simulation for a short-range tsunami on the Oregon coast using Netlogo, an agent-based modelling framework [11]. Mostafizi et al. evaluated nearby vertical evacuation behaviour and evacuation sites using agent-based modelling because vertical evacuation is an alternative protective measure to horizontal evacuation in the event of a near-field tsunami [12]. There have also been studies on tsunami evacuation simulation using cellular automata [13, 14] and tsunami flow calculation using flow-based models [15, 16]. However, these approaches require specialist knowledge to operate and discuss the results. At the local government level, it is not possible to build and operate conventional tsunami simulations, which makes it difficult to conduct independent trials of detailed simulations under various conditions.

In this study, we developed a tsunami crowd evacuation simulation system that can be operated by local governments using a game engine and open data. This system focuses on the evacuation behaviour of agents, visualizes the predicted disaster areas, and obtains data for disaster prevention planning of local governments, such as the layout of tsunami evacuation buildings and evacuation routes.

2 Methods

2.1 Modelling of Target Areas

The study area was Zushi City, Kanagawa Prefecture, which is an urban area on the coast of Sagami Bay, facing the Pacific Ocean. Due to the existence of the Sagami Trough in Sagami Bay, which has a water depth of over 1000 m, this area has been repeatedly affected by tsunamis caused by earthquakes off Sagami Bay in the past. In the 1923 Taisho Kanto Earthquake Tsunami, a tsunami wave height of up to 9 m was recorded. Zushi City is located in the north-western part of the Miura peninsula, facing Sagami Bay, and is a bedroom town for Tokyo and Yokohama, with many residential buildings and a tourist resort with swimming beaches. Because of the large number of people living there and visiting, there is a need for proper disaster management planning in the area.

The geographic model of the target area was made using the Basic Map Information download service [17]. The Geospatial Information Authority of Japan (GSI) has taken the lead in the development of this system, and the basic map information is provided free of charge online. The geospatial information of the Basic Map Information is used as the basis for the development and publication of a wide range of data by local governments and private businesses, enabling them to correctly link and superimpose data from different sources. The XML data downloaded from this service can be read by the Basic Map Information Viewer [18] display software, which converts it into Shape format data and exports it (see Fig. 1).

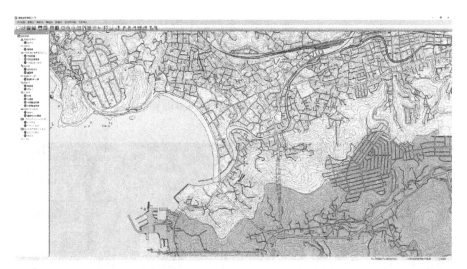

Fig. 1. Geographical information of Zushi City and its surroundings in Basic Map Information Viewer.

Next, the converted Shapefile can be loaded and displayed as a new vector layer in QGIS [19], a cross-platform open-source geographic information system (GIS) with browsing, editing, and analysis functions (see Fig. 2). In QGIS, we used TileLayerPlugin [20], a plugin for adding tilemaps to the map canvas, and Qgis2threejs [21], a three-dimensional (3D) visualization plugin using WebGL. The three.js JavaScript library was used to create 3D geographical information data with height information. The 3D data processed in QGIS was exported in STL format data as three layers: terrain, roads, and buildings.

The data in STL format was loaded into Blender, an open-source integrated 3D computer graphics software [22]. The road surface of the urban area was created by generating polygons on the surface corresponding to the road surface from the road edge data. The buildings were created from the perimeter lines of the buildings, and the assumed building heights were input from the floor–area ratios of the zoning districts on the city planning map of the target area. The 3D model data created in Blender was exported in FBX format after organizing polygons and reducing the weight of the model (see Fig. 3).

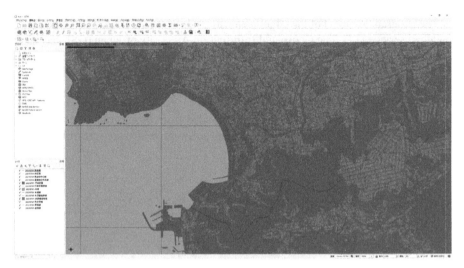

Fig. 2. Geographical information of Zushi City and its surroundings in QGIS.

Fig. 3. 3D models of terrain, buildings, and roads in Blender.

These geographic data were imported into the UNITY game engine [23], an integrated development environment, to represent the tsunami and evacuation behaviour of agents.

2.2   Tsunami Model and Evacuation Behaviour of Agents

According to the Manual on Tsunami and Storm Surge Hazard Map prepared by the Ministry of Land, Infrastructure, Transport and Tourism in Japan [24], the choice of inundation forecasting method should be accurate according to the purpose of preparation and target of evaluation. It is said that setting the numerical simulation considering the time series can obtain the high-accuracy data necessary for the preparation of a hazard map, such as data on the time course of inundation and inundation depth data of each point. However, the number of trials is limited due to the high computational cost. In contrast, a simple method is to set the tsunami run-up based on the ground height. This can be achieved with simple calculations, but it does not predict the exact flow velocity, inundation start time, and time-series effect of tsunami run-up due to topography.

This system is based on the inundation prediction method based on ground height, and the tsunami model is moved at a specified speed to partially account for the time series, such as the inundation start time. In this study, a sloping plane rotated by 0.1° was prepared as a tsunami model and inserted into the 3D terrain model to reproduce the time-series inundation according to elevation. This is a lightweight tsunami model because it does not provide for changes in flow velocities due to topography and buildings but can be represented by simple calculations (see Fig. 4).

Fig. 4. Maximum inundation area in Zushi City for a 12 m high tsunami.

In this system, we created agents to autonomously evacuate from the tsunami. Each agent acted according to a given condition, and 10,000 agents were set to evacuate at the same time. After the tsunami, the agents evacuated to the nearest high ground or tsunami evacuation building from their coordinates at a predetermined speed. Each tsunami evacuation building has a fixed capacity. Therefore, when an evacuated agent arrives at a tsunami evacuation building, if the building is over capacity, the agent cannot enter the building. After confirming that the building capacity has been exceeded, the agent searches for the nearest evacuation site from the current coordinates and starts evacuating again.

The agents prepared for this system had three age attributes: children (5–14 years old), adults (15–64 years old), and elderly (65+ years old). The moving speed of a child agent was 1.2 m/s, and the depth of the affected tsunami was 0.3 m. The moving speed of an adult agent was 1.5 m/s, and the depth of the affected tsunami was 0.6.; The moving speed of an elderly agent was 1.0 m/s, and the depth of the affected tsunami was 0.6 m. Children under 4 years of age were assumed to be evacuated alongside adult agents. Each agent was color-coded according to its type (see Fig. 5).

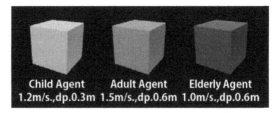

Fig. 5. Agents color-coded by age group.

The tsunami height and arrival time are registered in the configuration screen of the system. The agents with the numbers and characteristics registered in the configuration screen at the same time are randomly placed on the road surface in the target area after the simulation starts. The agents move to the nearest high ground or tsunami evacuation building, indicated in red, from their coordinates (see Fig. 6). The agents who were evacuated to high ground above the set tsunami height or to the tsunami evacuation building are represented by an orange bar to indicate where the agent evacuated to. Conversely, when the sloping plane representing the tsunami is greater than the affected tsunami height set for an agent, the agent is identified as a damaged agent. Damaged agents turn into pink bars on the spot and stay in the affected location. The areas where the pink bars are concentrated are considered to be the locations where most people are affected (see Fig. 7).

Fig. 6. Agents evacuating to nearest high ground or tsunami evacuation building.

Fig. 7. Tsunami evacuation buildings (red), number of agents evacuated (orange), and affected agents (pink). (Color figure online)

At the end of the simulation, a results screen is displayed, showing the number of affected people in each age group, and the results are exported as a CSV file. Because the agents are randomly placed on the roads, the results will vary depending on the initial conditions of the simulation. Therefore, it is possible to collect and analyse the data by repeated trials under different initial conditions.

3   Results and Discussion

Using this system, a crowd evacuation simulation was conducted for Zushi City. According to the statistics of Zushi City, there are 4787 households and 10729 inhabitants in the target area of this system, so we prepared 10000 agents for this simulation [25]. From the same statistical data, the age structure of the residents was also set in the same proportions as in the real city: 8% child agents, 60% adult agents, and 32% elderly agents. According to the Zushi City Tsunami Hazard Map, the maximum estimated tsunami height is 12.8 m, and the minimum tsunami arrival time is 9 min [26]. Therefore, in this simulation, six patterns of tsunami heights of 4–14 m (in 2 m intervals) at the time of arrival at the coast were prepared as tsunami conditions. In addition, we prepared three evacuation start times for the agents: after the tsunami reaches the coast (9 min after the earthquake), 5 min after the earthquake, and immediately after the earthquake. Because the agents were randomly placed on the road surface in the target area, we conducted 20 trials for each pattern.

First, the pattern in which agents start evacuating after the tsunami reaches the coast is examined (see Fig. 8). When the tsunami height was 4 m, the total damage rate was 0.14%, but the rate increased exponentially with height: 0.78% at 6 m, 2.56% at 8 m, and 4.85% at 10 m. When the tsunami height was 12 m, the disaster rate was 5.97%, and when it was 14 m, the rate was 9.06%, which indicates that the tsunami could cause severe damage. In the case of a tsunami height of 12 m, 4.66% of adult agents were affected, while 8.51% of child agents were affected due to their low water level to determine damage, and 7.80% of elderly agents were affected due to their low walking speed. At a tsunami height of 14 m, the disaster rate of adult agents was 7.39%, while those for child and elderly agents were 13.65% and 11.06%, respectively. Therefore, probability that children and elderly agents are affected is higher than that of adult agents.

Next, we examine the change in disaster rate according to the start time of evacuation (see Figs. 9 and 10 and Table 1). The overall disaster rate was 5.97% for the 12 m height and 9.06% for the 14 m height when the evacuation started after the tsunami arrived at the shore, whereas it was 3.32% and 5.27%, respectively, when the evacuation started 5 min after the earthquake (4 min before the tsunami arrived at the shore). In the case of evacuation immediately after the earthquake (9 min before the tsunami arrived at the coast), 2.43% of the evacuees evacuated when the tsunami height was 12 m and 2.29% when the tsunami height was 14 m. When the tsunami height was 4 m, the overall disaster rate was 0.14% when the evacuation started after the arrival of the tsunami, while the disaster rate was 0% when the evacuation started 5 min or immediately after the earthquake. Although the time between the earthquake and tsunami arrival varies greatly depending on the epicentre of the earthquake, a difference of a few minutes in the evacuation start time has a significant impact on the reduction of damage.

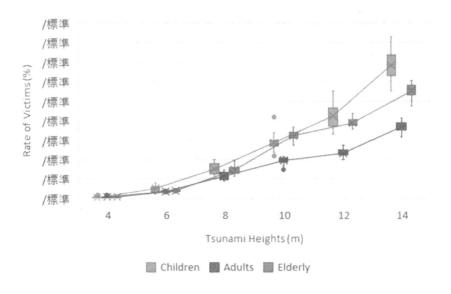

Fig. 8. Rate of damage of agents by tsunami height when evacuation begins after tsunami arrival (9 min after earthquake).

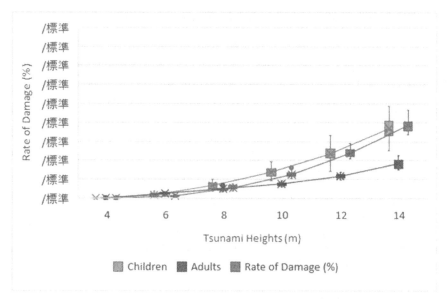

Fig. 9. Rate of damage of agents by tsunami height when evacuation begins 4 min before tsunami arrival (5 min after earthquake).

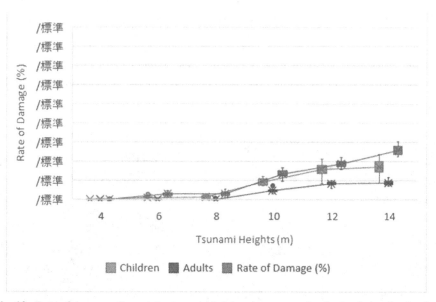

Fig. 10. Rate of damage of agents by tsunami height when evacuation begins immediately after the earthquake.

Table 1. Rate of damage by tsunami height and evacuation start time.

Tsu-nami heights (m)	Affected Rate (%)											
	Start evacuation after tsunami arrival (9 min after the earthquake)				Start evacuation 4 min before tsunami arrival (5 min after the earthquake)				Start evacuation immediately after the earthquake			
	Over-all	Chil-dren	Adults	El-derly	Over-all	Chil-dren	Adults	El-derly	Over-all	Chil-dren	Adults	El-derly
4	0.14	0.11	0.15	0.13	0.00	0.00	0.00	0.00	0.00	0.00	0.00	0.00
6	0.78	1.04	0.73	0.82	0.38	0.36	0.48	0.20	0.21	0.19	0.01	0.57
8	2.56	3.00	2.30	2.93	1.04	1.35	0.96	1.12	0.22	0.21	0.02	0.59
10	4.85	5.70	3.88	6.46	1.92	2.79	1.47	2.55	1.54	1.79	0.90	2.69
12	5.97	8.51	4.66	7.80	3.32	4.73	2.33	4.82	2.43	3.13	1.62	3.78
14	9.06	13.65	7.39	11.06	5.27	7.39	3.70	7.68	2.99	3.43	1.78	5.15

Next, see the affected areas indicated by the pink bars in Fig. 11. Along the coast, the central part was less affected, and the northern and southern parts were more affected. The agents who were near the coast when the evacuation started evacuated towards the tsunami evacuation building located in the middle of the coast or towards the high ground in the northern or southern part of the coast. Because the coast is wide, agents who evacuated parallel to the sea were affected before they reached higher ground. In addition, because the tsunami evacuation building located in the centre of the coast is a school facility (Zushi Kaisei Junior and Senior High School) and the number of evacuees who can be accommodated is limited due to the presence of students during the daytime on weekdays, the agents who could not enter the building and had to move towards other evacuation sites were also affected. In the southern part of the coast, there are only small tsunami evacuation buildings with small capacities, which caused some agents to not escape. Therefore, more tsunami evacuation buildings should be constructed along the coast.

Fig. 11. Concentrated pink bars indicate the most affected areas.

In some areas, the number of affected people was concentrated inland as well as along the coast. Zushi City has a river running through its centre, and many victims can be seen along the river. Although inland areas cannot see the sea, tsunamis traveling up rivers can cause damage to agents evacuating inland. The inland areas along the rivers are far from high ground, and there are few tsunami evacuation buildings, so many people were affected during evacuation. When local governments make disaster prevention plans, it is necessary to set up tsunami evacuation buildings not only along the coast but also in the inland areas with flat land, especially along rivers. However, the maximum height of buildings in Zushi City is limited to 10–20 m by the city's landscape ordinance. In the future, it may be necessary to relax the maximum height limit for new buildings under the condition that they are designated as tsunami evacuation buildings.

4   Conclusion

In this study, we developed a tsunami crowd evacuation simulation system using a game engine and open data, which can be used by local governments to develop disaster prevention plans. The simulation system was applied to Zushi City with different tsunami heights and evacuation start times. By using free and open-source software and game engines as the development environment and by using open geographic information data from the Geospatial Information Authority of Japan and population data from local governments as the dataset, we were able to develop a system that can be operated at the local government level.

As a result of the simulation of Zushi City, the overall disaster rate was 0.14% for evacuation after tsunami arrival at a height of 4 m. However, 5.97% and 9.06% were observed when the tsunami height was 12 m and 14 m, respectively, indicating that the damage rate increases rapidly with tsunami height. Moreover, when the evacuation started 4 min before the arrival of the tsunami, the total disaster rate was 3.32% at 12 m height and 5.27% at 14 m height, and when the evacuation started 9 min before the arrival of the tsunami, it was 2.43% at 12 m height and 2.99% at 14 m height. Although the time before the arrival of a tsunami depends on the earthquake epicentre, it was found that the time margin for tsunami evacuation has a great influence on the reduction of damage.

The locations where the agents were affected revealed that there were insufficient tsunami evacuation buildings. In particular, many inland areas along rivers were affected by the tsunami. Therefore, it is necessary to establish appropriate tsunami evacuation buildings in inland areas, which are far from high ground, in cooperation with local governments and residents. However, Zushi City has a landscape ordinance that sets a maximum height limit for buildings, so it is necessary to find a balance between disaster prevention and landscape planning.

In a real disaster, an earthquake close to the epicentre can cause damage to buildings and block roads. The speed of movement of evacuees also depends on the slope of the hill and congestion of people. In the future, we will conduct simulations to reproduce more detailed urban conditions during a disaster. Zushi City has a long stretch of beach where many marine sports are practised. Many tourists visit Zushi, mainly in summer, and 500,000 people visit the beaches annually. Therefore, it is necessary to consider simulations with agents who do not know where to evacuate, assuming that they are tourists.

In this system, small children under 4 years old are assumed to be evacuated with their parents. However, the system does not take into account the evacuation of family members, including the elderly. In the case of family evacuation, the slowest agent's speed should be applied to all members. Currently in Japan, the independent evacuation method called "Tsunami Tendenko" is recommended for each individual. However, in a real disaster, people may help their family members or acquaintances to evacuate. In the future, we will study group behaviour based on the data of family structure.

In the future, we will cooperate with local government and residents for disaster prevention planning in actual community development, such as the establishment of tsunami evacuation buildings and evacuation guidance in the agent-affected areas indicated by this system. In addition, we will refine the behavioural conditions of the agents and improve the simulation so that it is closer to an actual disaster, for example, accurately reproducing the inundation time of the tsunami and occurrence of impassable roads. Furthermore, we will apply our method not only to tsunamis but also to other natural disasters, such as floods and wildfires.

Acknowledgements. This work was supported by JSPS KAKENHI Grant No. JP 19K12665.

References

1. Nishimura, K.: Applied Geomorphology. Taimeido, Tokyo (1969)
2. Tanioka, Y., Kususose, T., Kathiroli, S., Nishimura, Y., Iwasaki, S., Satake, K.: Rupture process of the 2004 great Sumatra-Andaman earthquake estimated from tsunami waveforms. Earth, Planets Space **58**(2), 203–209 (2006)
3. Lay, T., et al.: The great Sumatra-Andaman earthquake of 26 December 2004. Science **308**(5725), 1127–1133 (2005)
4. Ranghieri, F., Ishiwatari, M. (eds.): Learning from Megadisasters: Lessons from the Great East Japan Earthquake. The World Bank (2014). https://doi.org/10.1596/978-1-4648-0153-2
5. Mimura, N., Yasuhara, K., Kawagoe, S., Yokoki, H., Kazama, S.: Damage from the Great East Japan Earthquake and Tsunami-a quick report. Mitig. Adapt. Strat. Glob. Change **16**(7), 803–818 (2011)
6. The Headquarters for Earthquake Research Promotion: Long-Term Assessment of Seismic Activity in the Nankai Trough, 2nd edn. (2013)
7. Cabinet Office: Interim report of the Nankai Trough giant earthquake model study group (2011)
8. Kanamori, H., Given, J.W.: Use of long-period seismic waves for rapid evaluation of tsunami potential of large earthquakes. Tsunamis-Their Sci. Eng. 37–49 (1983). https://doi.org/10.1007/978-94-009-7172-1_4
9. Kowalik, Z., Knight, W., Logan, T., Whitmore, P.: Numerical modeling of the global tsunami: Indonesian tsunami of 26 December 2004. Sci. Tsunami Haz. **23**(1), 40–56 (2005)
10. Mas, E., Suppasri, A., Imamura, F., Koshimura, S.: Agent-based simulation of the 2011 great east japan earthquake/tsunami evacuation: an integrated model of tsunami inundation and evacuation. J. Nat. Dis. Sci. **34**(1), 41–57 (2012)

11. Wang, H., Mostafizi, A., Cramer, L.A., Cox, D., Park, H.: An agent-based model of a multimodal near-field tsunami evacuation: decision-making and life safety. Transp. Res. Part C: Emerg. Technol. **64**, 86–100 (2016)
12. Mostafizi, A., Wang, H., Cox, D., Dong, S.: An agent-based vertical evacuation model for a near-field tsunami: choice behaviour, logical shelter locations, and life safety. Int. J. Disaster Risk Reduct. **34**, 467–479 (2019)
13. Burstedde, C., Klauck, K., Schadschneider, A., Zittartz, J.: Simulation of pedestrian dynamics using a two-dimensional cellular automaton. Phys. A **295**(3–4), 507–525 (2001)
14. Han, A.F.: TEVACS: decision support system for evacuation planning in Taiwan. J. Transp. Eng. **116**(6), 821–830 (1990)
15. Abar, S., Theodoropoulos, G.K., Lemarinier, P., O'Hare, G.M.: Agent based modelling and simulation tools: a review of the state-of-art software. Comput. Sci. Rev. **24**, 13–33 (2017)
16. Kouge, N., Sano, A.: Evacuation simulation method by approximating flow function on multi-agent model. Trans. Japan. Soc. Artific. Intell. **33**(2), 1–10 (2018)
17. Geospatial Information Authority: Basic Map Information download service. https://fgd.gsi.go.jp/download/menu.php. Accessed 31 Aug 2021
18. Geospatial Information Authority: Basic Map Information Viewer. https://fgd.gsi.go.jp/otherdata/tool/FGDV.zip. Accessed 31 Aug 2021
19. QGIS Development Team: Welcome to the QGIS project!. https://qgis.org/. Accessed 31 Aug 2021
20. Akagi, M.: TileLayer - QGIS Python Plugins Repository. https://plugins.qgis.org/plugins/TileLayerPlugin. Accessed 31 Aug 2021
21. Akagi, M.: Qgis2threejs - QGIS Python Plugins Repository. https://plugins.qgis.org/plugins/Qgis2threejs/. Accessed 31 Aug 2021
22. Blender Foundation: blender.org - Home of the Blender project - Free and Open 3D Creation Software. https://www.blender.org/. Accessed 31 Aug 2021
23. Unity Technologies: Unity Real-Time Development Platform | 3D, 2D VR & AR Engine. https://unity.com/. Accessed 31 Aug 2021
24. Ministry of Land, Infrastructure, Transport and Tourism: Tsunami and Storm Surge Hazard Map Manual (2004)
25. Zushi City: Statistics Zushi (2020)
26. Zushi City: Zushi City Tsunami Hazard Map (2015)

Rescue Strategy in Case of Large-Scale Flood Damage in the Koto Delta Region

Yoshihiro Terafuji$^{(\boxtimes)}$ and Michinori Hatayama

Kyoto University, Kyoto, Japan
terafuji.yoshihiro.22m@st.kyoto-u.ac.jp,
hatayama@dimsis.dpri.kyoto-u.ac.jp

Abstract. A wide-area evacuation plan has been formulated for the Koto Delta region because of the large population in the inundation area and the expected shortage of evacuation centers. However, carrying out wide-area evacuation as planned may be challenging due to multiple issues such as large-scale traffic congestion. Therefore, it is expected that numerous people will be isolated and their health will deteriorate due to long-term flooding. We propose an efficient rescue strategy to reduce the number of residents who are isolated for long periods of time. Therefore, we changed the conditions for rescuing isolated people by boats, such as the order of rescuing the isolated people and the evacuation rate, and estimated the changes in the number of isolated people and the time required for rescue completion under each condition. Next, we compared the estimated results under each condition to develop efficient rescue methods for isolated people.

Keywords: Rescue of isolated people · Wide area evacuation · Inundation

1 Introduction

Because the Koto Delta region is surrounded by rivers and the sea, has an area of zero-meter zone above the sea level, is located in the city center, and has a huge population, inundation is expected to continue for a long period of time over a wide area in the region, and numerous residents will be isolated during this period. Therefore, there is a risk of shortage of evacuation shelters, and it is not possible to prevent human casualties by only evacuation within the area. Therefore, Koto 5 wards have formulated an evacuation plan based on wide-area evacuation to outside the inundation area.

However, several problems associated with the feasibility of wide-area evacuation exist, such as the need to make early decisions on wide-area evacuation, the need to secure wide-area evacuation sites, and the occurrence of large-scale traffic congestion during wide-area evacuation. Therefore, there may be a large number of isolated people for whom wide evacuation will not be possible.

However, the Koto 5 Wards Large-Scale Flooding Evacuation Response Policy of 2016 [1] only states that the rescue of vertical evacuees will be studied and addressed

© IFIP International Federation for Information Processing 2022
Published by Springer Nature Switzerland AG 2022
J. Sasaki et al. (Eds.): ITDRR 2021, IFIP AICT 638, pp. 76–91, 2022.
https://doi.org/10.1007/978-3-031-04170-9_6

with the aim of efficient rescue activities and evacuation of residents from the inundation area by themselves. Information regarding specific rescue strategies is lacking.

In addition, rescue of isolated people may take a very long time. During the Kanto/Tohoku heavy rain disaster of September 2015, the Kinugawa River collapsed in Joso City, Ibaraki Prefecture, causing massive flooding. Therefore, numerous people were isolated due to inundation, and a total of 4,258 people were rescued by the fire department, police, coast guard, and Japan Self-Defense Forces [2]. Among these, the Japan Self-Defense Forces rescued 1,292 people by boat and 723 people by aircraft, for a total of 2015 people in 10 days [3]. In contrast, an estimated 444,000 residents in Koto 5 wards, including the Koto Delta region, had to be evacuated to avoid inundation [1], and depending on the number of people mobilized for rescue and the number of boats and helicopters, rescue may take an enormous amount of time. In addition, because inundation is expected to continue for a long period of time, residents whose rooms are not inundated but who are isolated will have to be rescued. Considering this, further delays in rescue can be expected.

Therefore, numerous residents are expected to be isolated in an environment where lifelines are disrupted for a long period of time. If stockpiles are depleted or lifelines are disrupted, there may be risks such as deteriorating health conditions.

Ikeuchi et al. (2011) [4] developed a simulation model to estimate the number of people isolated and rescued in the event of a large-scale flood, considering the operation of drainage facilities, improvement of evacuation rates, and rescue of isolated people, and analyzed the effects of reducing the number of isolated people and isolation time. In particular, for operation of drainage facilities, the model considers detailed conditions such as whether the operation of drainage pump stations, fuel supply, sluice gate operation, and drainage pump trucks can be performed. However, for the rescue of isolated people, detailed conditions such as the order in which the isolated people are rescued and the differences in the distribution of the isolated people, have not been considered. Therefore, there is room for consideration.

2   Research Background

2.1   Characteristics of Flooding in the Koto Delta Region

The Koto Delta region is located in the eastern part of Tokyo and comprises all of Sumida and Koto wards and part of Edogawa ward. The area is surrounded by the Sumida River on the west side, the Arakawa River on the east side, and Tokyo Bay on the south side, making it vulnerable to flooding and storm surges.

In addition, the Koto Delta region has a population of approximately 800,000, and the entire Koto 5 wards including the Koto Delta region have a population of approximately 2.6 million [1]. Thus, in the event of a large-scale flood, a huge inundation area population will be generated.

Moreover, the region is located at the sea level zero area where natural drainage is not possible. Thus, in the worst case scenario, in which the drainage facilities do not function, a large area of the region will be inundated for more than two weeks, and numerous residents will be isolated in an environment where lifelines are disrupted for a long period of time.

2.2 Issues of Wide-Area Evacuation

In the East Japan typhoon of 2019, some evacuation centers were full and people were urged to evacuate to other evacuation centers [5]. Therefore, in the event of large-scale flooding in urban areas, evacuation centers are expected to be insufficient. In Koto 5 wards, which have a population of approximately 2.6 million, most residents live in buildings inundated by more than 50 cm of water, resulting in an estimated inundated population of 2.5 million. Of these, 444,000 people are evacuees who must evacuate to a building other than the one they live in so as to avoid inundation, whereas 434,000 people are residents of apartment complexes who can evacuate to the upper floors because their houses will be inundated but the upper floors will not be inundated. In contrast, the capacity of evacuation shelters is approximately 490,000 people [1]; therefore, if many residents evacuate to evacuation shelters even if they can evacuate to the upper floors, there is a risk of a shortage of evacuation shelters. In addition, as the area is expected to be inundated for a long period of time, it is not possible to prevent human casualties only by evacuating within the region. Therefore, Koto 5 wards have formulated an evacuation plan based on wide-area evacuation outside inundation area.

In contrast, there are several problems related to the feasibility of wide-area evacuation. The first is the problem of securing shelters for wide-area evacuation. According to the Koto 5 Ward Large-Scale Flooding Evacuation Response Policy of 2016, agreements have been made with special wards and the cities of Ichikawa and Matsudo in the Chiba Prefecture for wide-area evacuation sites; however, the specific evacuation facilities are not clearly defined, and it is not clear whether there will be enough evacuation sites for the number of people to be evacuated.

Second, the problem of large-scale traffic congestion during wide-area evacuation exists. Because half of the residents who conduct a wide-area evacuation intend to use cars, a huge amount of evacuation traffic will be generated, resulting in serious traffic congestion. Furthermore, because Koto 5 Wards is surrounded by rivers and requires river crossings for evacuation, there is a concern that the bridge area will become a bottleneck and further aggravate traffic congestion.

The third problem is that making early decisions regarding wide-area evacuation is challenging. The problem of long evacuation times due to traffic congestion and long-distance travel makes it necessary to call for wide-area evacuation at an early stage. However, making decisions regarding early wide-area evacuation is difficult at this point in time because we do not have enough accurate weather information or systems in place to make such decisions [1]. In fact, in the case of the East Japan typhoon of 2019, the rainfall exceeded the standard for calling for wide-area evacuation in the Koto 5 wards; however, no call was made because it was expected to cause confusion among residents due to the impending planned suspension of railroad services [6].

3 Previous Studies and Purpose of this Study

Several previous studies have dealt with the evacuation of residents and rescue of isolated people in the event of a large-scale flood in the Koto five wards, including the Koto Delta region.

Katada et al. (2013) [7] conducted a scenario analysis of a hypothetical collapse of the Arakawa River for Edogawa Ward using a simulator that specifically and comprehensively represents the situation during a flood. Through this analysis, the direction of response measures specific to large cities, such as reducing the evacuation demand and dispersing evacuees, was clarified, in addition to improving residents' awareness, thoroughly communicating information, and supporting those in need of disaster relief.

Kato and Miyagawa (2011) [8] conducted a simulation in which all residents conducted a wide-area evacuation by rail, along the Sobu Line in Katsushika Ward, and analyzed the feasibility of such a scenario. They found that the transportation capacity of the railroad would be a bottleneck.

However, these studies focused on the wide-area evacuation of residents before a large-scale flood occurs and did not address the rescue of isolated people after a large-scale flood occurs.

Ikeuchi et al. (2011) [4], as the secretariat of the Central Disaster Management Council of the Cabinet Office's "Expert Committee on Large-Scale Flood Countermeasures," conducted estimated the number of isolated people and the duration of isolation in the event of a large-scale flood caused by the collapse of the Arakawa River, etc. and analyzed the effects of mitigation measures. Their inundation analysis model incorporated the operational status of drainage facilities in the basin because they considered it important to understand the duration of inundation and drainage status. In addition, a model for rescuing isolated people during flooding was developed based on interviews with the Fire and Disaster Management Agency, the National Police Agency, and the Ministry of Defense. Using these models, they showed that the number of isolated persons can be reduced to zero three days after leveed collapse by conducting damage mitigation measures such as increasing the evacuation rate, operating drainage facilities, and rescuing isolated people by boat in several types of flooding such as the Koto Delta storage type flooding.

However, in their study, the average distance between the starting and rescue points of the boat where the isolated person was rescued was used as the distance traveled by the boat to estimate the rescue time of the isolated people. Therefore, unlike the actual population distribution, the time required for rescue was estimated based on the assumption that all isolated persons exist at one point, which may affect the estimation results. In addition, they assumed that all boats will be placed at practically one point in their study, although in reality, boats may be placed at multiple starting points to rescue isolated people, and there is no indication of how it is appropriate to place boats and how to distribute the number of boats. Moreover, as a case in which the effect of reducing the number of isolated people and the rescue time of isolated people can be observed, the case where drainage facilities are in operation or the evacuation rate is improved is shown. However, for cases in which drainage facilities are not in operation or the evacuation rate is low, the method of reducing the number of isolated people and the rescue time is not sufficiently considered.

For research on rescuing isolated people during flooding, Ozkan et al. (2019) [9] and Chandra et al. (2016) [10] collected data on the affected area by UAVs and other means to speed up rescue operations and analyzed the shortest route for rescue boats based on their data. However, with regard to speeding up the rescue of isolated people, the order in which isolated people are rescued has not been focused on, and there is room for consideration.

The purpose of this study was to propose a strategy for efficiently rescuing isolated people considering the points that have not been considered in previous studies. Specifically, considering the population distribution of isolated people, we will set up the boat starting point and estimate the distance traveled by boats for each rescue point. We will also estimate the changes in the number of isolated people when rescue activities are conducted. It also shows how the pace of rescue differs when the order of rescuing isolated people is considered, starting with isolated people closest to the rescuer, compared to when it is not.

The results will be used to study strategies for efficiently rescuing isolated people. Residents on lower floors are more likely to suffer from direct physical damage from flooding and need to be rescued as soon as possible, and their evacuation rate is expected to be relatively high. In contrast, residents on upper floors are less likely to suffer direct damage from flooding, and the evacuation rate is expected to be relatively low. However, if they are isolated for a long period of time, their health may deteriorate due to the disconnection of lifelines, and they need to be rescued. Thus, we will examine strategies for efficiently rescuing isolated people by focusing on the possible differences in damage and evacuation rates depending on the floor on which the residents live.

4   Estimation of Changes in the Number of Isolated People in the Koto Delta Region When Rescue Operations are Conducted

In the Koto Delta region, which consists of Sumida, Koto, and part of Edogawa wards in Tokyo and is surrounded by the Sumida River and the Arakawa River, we estimated the number of isolated people immediately after the Arakawa River flooded and the changes in the number of people isolated when rescue operations were conducted by boat.

4.1   Data and Estimation Methods

To estimate the number of isolated people, we used the population data in 250 m mesh units and small area units (From now on, these are collectively referred to as the population aggregation unit area) from the 2015 National Census from e-Stat [11] as population data, and data from the Tokyo Metropolitan Government prepared in 2012 from the Geospatial Information Authority of Japan [12] as flood inundation area map data. For population aggregation unit area, estimations were conducted using one of the two patterns shown in Table 1.

As for isolated people, the depth of water at which evacuation becomes difficult is set at 50 cm, based on the study conducted by Ikeuchi et al. [4], and the people among the residents in the area where the water depth is 50 cm or more who do not evacuate are considered as isolated people. Furthermore, we estimated the number of isolated people.

To estimate the number of isolated people, we first estimated the number of people in the population aggregation unit area whose depth of inundation was 50 cm or more. This was performed using one of the two patterns shown in Table 1. Then, we multiplied the

Table 1. Data and estimation methods

Data and estimation methods	Pattern	Content of pattern
Population data	A1	Use population data in 250 m mesh units
	A2	Use population data in small area units
How to estimate the population in the inundation area with a depth of 50 cm or more	B1	Assume that the number of isolated people is the same as the number of people in the population aggregation unit area and estimate the number of isolated people without dividing the area proportionally
	B2	Estimate the number of isolated people by dividing the area proportionally according to the area of inundation depth of 50 cm or more in the population aggregation unit area
Set evacuation rates	C1	40% of all residents are evacuated
	C2	Residents living on the third floor or higher of apartment buildings do not evacuate; 40% of other residents evacuate
	C3	The evacuation rate is not set at the beginning, but the evacuation rate required to complete rescue in 7 days is calculated based on conditions such as the daily rescue time
Set the boat starting point	D1	Set at the center of gravity of the 250m mesh of the non-inundated area which does not include the inundated area
	D2	Set at the center of gravity of the small area of the non-inundated area which does not include the inundated area
	D3	Set a bridge leading to the Koto Delta region, which could be a bottleneck for rescue from outside the Koto Delta region
Set rescue point	E1	Set at the center of gravity of the 250 m mesh that includes inundation areas with a depth of 50 cm or more
	E2	Set at the center of gravity of the small area that includes inundation areas with a depth of 50 cm or more
How to estimate the boat travel distance	F1	For each rescue point, use the straight-line distance to the nearest boat starting point
	F2	Use the number of isolated people at the rescue point as the weight and take the weighted average of the straight-line distance between each rescue point and the nearest boat starting point

(continued)

Table 1. (*continued*)

Data and estimation methods	Pattern	Content of pattern
The daily rescue time	G1	12 h a day rescue
	G2	24 h a day rescue
The order of rescuing isolated people	H1	Estimate the number of rescued people assuming that isolated people of all rescue points are in one rescue point using the average value for the boat travel distance (pattern G3)
	H2	Estimate the number of rescued people, assuming that all boats are allocated in order of rescue point with the shortest boat travel distance
	H3	Allocate all boats to each boat starting point, considering the boat travel distance to the rescue point and the number of isolated people at the rescue point. Estimate the number of rescued people, assuming that rescuing isolated people at multiple rescue points from multiple boat starting points is performed in the order of the shortest boat travel distance

population of the area with a depth of 50 cm or more by 1 - the evacuation rate (%)/100 to estimate the number of isolated people in the area.

The evacuation rate was estimated based on the study by Ikeuchi et al. [4], using pattern C1 as the basic case, and considering the residential floors, using one of the three patterns shown in Table 1.

For the capacity and number of boats used for rescue, we used data of the boats of the National Police Agency, the Fire and Disaster Management Agency, and the Ministry of Defense shown in Table 2, which were used in the study by Ikeuchi et al. [4].

Table 2. Capability and number of boats

		Ministry of defense	National police agency	Fire and disaster management agency
Number of rescued people by 1 boat (person/1 boat)		11	2	3
Ship speed (km/h)	Outward way	2.6	2.0	2.0
	Return path	2.0	1.2	1.2
Number of boats		Approximately 300	Approximately 600	Approximately 1000

For the time required for the rescue cycle, we used the following values used in the study by Ikeuchi et al.:

- Release mooring at boat starting point: 2 min
- Onward travel time: travel distance/onward travel speed
- Mooring at the rescue point: 3 min
- Boarding of rescued people at rescue point: 1 min per person
- Unmooring at the rescue point: 2 min
- Return travel time: travel distance/return travel speed
- Mooring at the boat starting point: 3 min
- Boarding of rescued people at the boat starting point: 1 min per person

The capability of the boat was averaged by the number of three types of boats, and the capacity of the boat was set at 3.4 people. We averaged the transfer capability by dividing it into the time required for a round trip transfer and the time required for non-transfer activities such as mooring, un-mooring, and disembarkation. The time required for round-trip travel was not calculated from the average value of the boat travel speed itself because the boat travel speed differed between outbound and inbound trips; the average value of the time required for round-trip travel of 1 km each way was used. Accordingly, we assumed that the averaged boat had the ability to take 75.7 min to travel 1 km one way and back, and 16.8 min for non-travel tasks.

As for the boat starting point, estimation was conducted using one of the three patterns shown in Table 1. Figure 1 shows the boat starting point in each pattern.

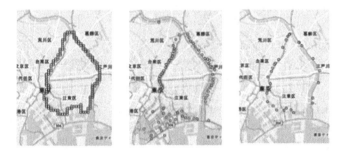

Fig. 1. Boat starting point (Left: pattern D1, Center: pattern D2, Right: pattern D3)

For the rescue point, estimations were conducted using one of the two patterns shown in Table 1. Figure 2 shows the rescue point in each pattern.

For the boat travel distance, estimations were conducted using one of the three patterns shown in Table 1. In pattern F2, the boat travel distance D was estimated as follows:

$$D = \frac{\sum_{r=1}^{N} d_r p_r}{\sum_{r=1}^{N} p_r} \tag{1}$$

d_r : straight-line distance between the rescue point and the nearest boat starting point (For each rescue point).

Fig. 2. Rescue point (Left: pattern E1, Right: pattern E2)

p_r : number of isolated people in each rescue point.

N : total number of boat starting points.

For the daily rescue time, estimations were conducted using one of the two patterns shown in Table 1.

For the order of rescuing isolated people, estimations were conducted using one of the three patterns shown in Table 1. For the order of rescuing isolated people, estimations were conducted using one of the three patterns shown in Table 1. The travel time between the rescue points should essentially be considered, but this time is not included in the time required for rescue in pattern H2. In pattern H3, the distribution of boats to each boat starting point of all boats was calculated using the following formula:

$$r_s = \frac{\sum_{r=1}^{N_{sr}} d_{sr} p_{sr}}{\sum_{s=1}^{N_s} \sum_{r=1}^{N_{sr}} d_{sr} p_{sr}}, N_{sb} = r_s N_b \qquad (2)$$

N_s : total number of boat starting points.

N_{sr} : number of all rescue points to be covered by each boat starting point.

d_{sr} : straight-line distance between rescue point and the nearest boat starting point (for each rescue point).

p_{sr} : number of isolated people in each rescue point.

r_s : percentage of boats allocated to each boat starting point.

N_{sb} : number of boats to be allocated to each boat starting point.

N_b : total number of boats.

4.2 Comparison of the Difference in the Size of Population Aggregation Unit Area

The results obtained by estimating the changes in the number of isolated people in the case of rescue by boat may differ depending on the size of the unit of population data used for estimation. This is because boat travel distances to the rescue point of the isolated people may change based on different assumed distributions of the isolated people. Therefore, it is thought to be ideal to use detailed population data that are closer to the actual distribution of the population to estimate the changes in the number of isolated persons in the case of rescue activities.

To investigate the differences in the results obtained by estimating the changes in the number of isolated people in the case of rescue activities depending on the differences in the size of the population aggregation unit area, we changed only the conditions of the population aggregation unit area and compared the estimation of the changes in the number of isolated people in the case of rescue activities between Pattern A1 (250 m mesh unit) and Pattern A2 (small area unit).

Comparing their sizes, the area with an inundation depth of 50 cm or more in the Koto Delta region covered 575 units in the 250 m mesh unit of Pattern A1 and 243 units in the district unit of Pattern A2, with the 250 m mesh unit representing an area that is more than twice as small on average as the small area unit.

The other common conditions were set as pattern B1 for the presence or absence of proportional distribution of area, pattern C1 for the evacuation rate, pattern D1 for the boat starting point, pattern E1 for the rescue point, pattern F1 for boat travel distance, pattern G1 for the daily rescue time, and pattern H2 for the order of rescue.

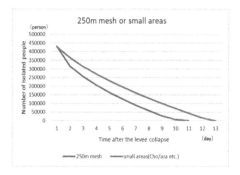

Fig. 3. Comparison of the 250 m mesh and small areas

Figure 3 shows that there is no significant difference in the number of isolated people one day after collapse of the levee before rescue begins because the difference in the size of the population aggregation unit area; however, the number of days required for rescue in Pattern A2 is two days more than that in Pattern A1.

According to these results, it may be necessary to use detailed population data that are closer to the actual population distribution because differences in the size of the population aggregation unit area may significantly affect the estimation of the required number of days to rescue isolated people in the event of rescue operations.

4.3 Comparison of the Difference in the Order of Rescuing Isolated People

When rescuing isolated people by boat, it is thought that the easily rescued isolated people near the border with the non-inundated area will be rescued first, rather than isolated people deep in the inundation area. However, the Cabinet Office's estimation of the changes in the number of isolated people in the case of rescue activities uses the average of the distances traveled from the boat starting point to each rescue point; thus, the order of rescue is not considered according to the proximity of the rescuer to the isolated people.

Thus, considering the order of rescuing isolated people, we compared results of the estimated changes in the number of isolated people among the following two cases: rescuing in the order from isolated people who are at a rescue point close to the boat starting point or rescuing isolated people regardless of the distance from the boat starting point to the rescue point.

For the specific conditions for estimation, only the conditions for the order of rescuing isolated people and boat travel distance were changed, and when the condition for the order of rescue was Pattern H3, the condition for boat travel distance was Pattern F1. When the condition for the order of rescue was Pattern H1, the condition for boat travel distance was Pattern F2. Furthermore, we compared the estimation for the case in which the rescuer rescued isolated people in the order from them closest to the boat starting point (pattern H3) and the case in which the rescuer rescued them regardless of the distance to the boat starting point (pattern H1).

The other common conditions were set as pattern A1 for the population aggregation unit area, pattern B2 for the presence or absence of the proportional distribution of area, pattern C1 for the evacuation rate, pattern D1 for the boat starting point, pattern E1 for the rescue point, and pattern G1 for the daily rescue time.

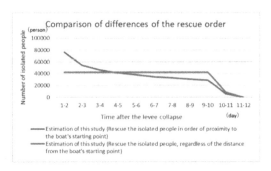

Fig.4. Comparison of differences of the rescue order

Figure 4 shows that the number of rescues per day remained constant at approximately 40,000 from the second day to the tenth day when rescuing isolated people regardless of their distance from the boat starting point (Pattern H1 and Pattern F2). In contrast, when rescuing isolated people in order from them closest to the boat starting point (Pattern H3 and Pattern F1), the number of rescued people per day on the second day was approximately 80,000. However, as days passed, the number of rescued people per day gradually decreased, and on the tenth day, the number of rescued people per day was approximately 30,000, which is less than the number of rescued people per day when it is assumed that isolated people are rescued regardless of the distance from the boat starting point.

This result shows that the pace of rescue is faster and more isolated people can be rescued during the first few days of rescue when it is assumed that isolated people are rescued in order from them closest to the boat starting point, compared to when it is assumed that isolated people are rescued regardless of their distance from the boat starting point. Therefore, by focusing on wide-area evacuation of residents who live in the inundation area far from the non-inundation area and who are expected to be isolated away from boat starting point, it may be possible to reduce the number of residents who are isolated for a long time and rescue them in a shorter period of time.

4.4 Comparison of the Difference in the Evacuation Rate of the Residents on Upper Floors

The Koto Delta region is an area that is expected to be inundated for long periods of time of more than two weeks. Therefore, not only the residents on the lower floors who may be directly affected by the flooding but also the residents on the upper floors need to be rescued because their health may deteriorate due to disconnection of lifelines if they are isolated. However, the Koto Delta region has relatively more residents living in upper floors in the country. The population of Koto 5 wards, including the Koto Delta region, is approximately 2.6 million. In contrast, an estimated 1.6 million people live in inundation areas with a depth of 50 cm or more but have rooms that are not inundated due to living on upper floors and are able to stay in their homes [1]. This indicates that numerous residents live on upper floors. In addition, the evacuation rate of residents living on upper floors may be lower than that of residents living on lower floors because they are less likely to suffer from direct damage from flooding. Therefore, it is conceivable that a large number of residents on upper floors may be isolated.

Accordingly, we investigate how much the number of isolated people before rescue begins differs between cases in which residents on upper floors evacuate and cases in which they do not evacuate, and therefore, how much the number of days required to complete the rescue of isolated people differs. Specifically, we changed only the conditions for the evacuation rate and compared the estimated changes in the number of isolated people when rescue activities were carried out under two patterns: Pattern C1 (evacuation rate of all residents is 40%) and Pattern C2 (evacuation rate of residents on the third floor or higher of apartment buildings is 0%, and the evacuation rate of other residents is 40%).

The other common conditions were set as pattern A1 for the population aggregation unit area, pattern B2 for the presence or absence of proportional distribution of areas, pattern D2 for the boat starting point, pattern E2 for the rescue point, pattern F1 for boat travel distance, pattern G1 for the daily rescue time, and pattern H3 for the order of rescue.

Figure 5 shows that the number of isolated people one day after the collapse of the levee before rescue began was approximately 380,000 when 40% residents on the upper floors evacuated (Pattern C1), whereas it was approximately 530,000 when the residents on the upper floors did not evacuate (Pattern C2), which indicates an increase of approximately 150,000. The results show that the number of isolated people greatly varies depending on whether residents on upper floors evacuate in the same way as residents on lower floors. In addition, when we consider the number of days required to complete rescue, we found that in the case of Pattern C1, rescue was completed after 12 days, whereas in the case of Pattern C2, rescue was completed after 16 days, which is 4 days later. This result shows that if residents on upper floors do not evacuate in the

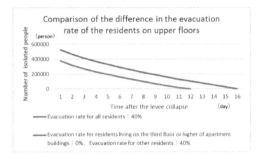

Fig. 5. Comparison of the difference in the evacuation rate of the residents on upper floors

same way as those on lower floors, there may be a significant delay in the completion of rescue.

This indicates that the impact of isolation without evacuation of residents on the upper floors, who are less likely to suffer direct damage from inundation, on the rescue of isolated people is significant, and that the evacuation rate for residents on upper floors should be as high as that for residents on lower floors.

4.5 Estimation of the Evacuation Rate Required to Complete Rescue in 7 days

In the aftermath of a major flood, lifelines such as electricity, water, and gas are expected to be out of service for long periods of time. Thus, drinking water and food must be stockpiled. To prepare for such a disruption of lifelines after a disaster, the Cabinet Office [13] and Koto Ward [14] and Edogawa Ward [15] in the Koto Delta region have called for the stockpiling of drinking water and foodstuffs for about one week if possible. Therefore, it is expected that a certain percentage of residents in the Koto Delta region will have a one-week stock-pile. Consequently, if the period of isolation exceeds one week, the number of isolated people whose health condition deteriorates due to lack of drinking water and food will probably increase.

Therefore, we estimated the required evacuation rate of residents on the third floor or higher of a high-rise apartment building and that of other residents to complete the rescue of isolated people in seven days, in the case of 12-h rescue operations per day and 24-h rescue operations per day.

The specific conditions for the estimation were set as pattern A2 for the population aggregation unit area, pattern B2 for the presence or absence of proportional distribution of area, pattern C3 for evacuation rate, pattern D2 for the boat starting point, pattern E2 for the rescue point, pattern F1 for boat travel distance, and pattern H3 for the order of rescue.

Figure 6 shows that when rescue is conducted for 12 h a day, if the evacuation rate for all residents is the same regardless of the floor they live on, the required evacuation rate for all residents is 67%, at which rate, rescue of isolated people will be completed in 7 days. In addition, if the evacuation rate is divided into residents on the third and higher floors of the apartment building, who are residents of the upper floors, and other residents, the result is that the required evacuation rate of residents on the third and higher

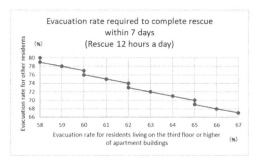

Fig. 6. Evacuation rate required to complete rescue within 7 days (Rescue 12 h a day)

floors of the apartment building is 58%, even if the evacuation rate of other residents is 80%, for completing the rescue of isolated persons after seven days. Thus, when rescue is conducted for 12 h a day, the residents must evacuate at a very high rate to complete the rescue of isolated people by 7 days later, and the possibility of completing the rescue is quite low.

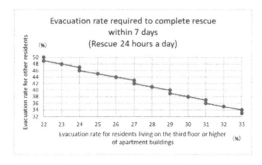

Fig. 7. Evacuation rate required to complete rescue within 7 days (Rescue 24 h a day)

Figure 7 shows that when rescue is conducted for 24 h a day, if the evacuation rate of all residents is the same regardless of the floor they live on, the required evacuation rate for all residents is 33%, at which rate, rescue of the isolated people is completed after 7 days. When the evacuation rate was divided into residents on the third floor or higher of the apartment building, who are residents of the upper floors and other residents on the lower floors, the result is that the required evacuation rate of the residents on the third floor or higher of the apartment building is 22%, if the evacuation rate of other residents is 50% for completing the rescue of the isolated persons after seven days. Thus, in the case of 24-h rescue per day, if the evacuation rate of residents on lower floors is approximately 40% and the evacuation rate of residents on upper floors is approximately 25%, that is if the evacuation rate is relatively realistic, there is a possibility of completing rescue of isolated people by 7 days later.

5 Summary and Future Work

From the results of the previous chapters, it is considered that the Koto Delta region has a high percentage of households living on upper floors, which may lead to a large number of isolated people on upper floors and a significant delay in completing the rescue of isolated people.

In fact, if rescue operations were conducted for 12 h/d, a high evacuation rate of 60% or more would be required to complete the rescue of isolated people by 7 days after the collapse of the levee, indicating that numerous residents on the upper floors who did not evacuate could be isolated for more than a week. Furthermore, in the case of a 24 h rescue operation per day, if the evacuation rate is 30–40%, the rescue of isolated people can be completed by 7 days after the collapse of the levee. However, the estimated number of days required to complete the rescue of isolated people differs depending on the size of the used population aggregation unit area; thus, if population data with a detailed population distribution closer to the actual situation are used, the results show that the rescue will not be completed by 7 days after the collapse of the levee.

Therefore, the number of isolated residents must be reduced by having residents on upper floors conduct wide-area evacuations as well. In contrast, if numerous residents evacuate in a wide area, traffic congestion may occur; thus, it is necessary for residents to conduct a wide-area evacuation in a way that will shorten the number of days required to complete the rescue of isolated people. In the previous Section, we showed that when the order of rescuing isolated people was considered and the isolated people were rescued in order of closest to the boat starting point, more isolated people could be rescued during the first few days than when the order of rescuing isolated people was not considered. This result may suggest that by especially strongly encouraging wide-area evacuation on residents on upper floors far from non-inundated areas and reducing the number of isolated people located far from rescuers, the number of isolated people who take time to be rescued will be reduced and the number of days required to complete rescue of isolated people will be efficiently shortened. In other words, to have the same number of residents conduct a wide-area evacuation and effectively reduce the time required to rescue isolated people, it is considered effective to have residents on upper floors far from the non-inundated area conduct a wide-area evacuation.

At present, residents who do not evacuate within the inundation area with a depth of 50 cm or more are defined as isolated people and changes in the area with a depth of 50 cm or more are not considered. However, in reality, it is unlikely that drainage facilities will operate at all and no drainage will take place. Therefore, it is possible that the drainage will gradually narrow the area above the 50 cm depth of inundation, and residents whose isolation has been resolved will occur. Therefore, in future research, we will consider efficient rescue strategies based on the fact that the inundation area will change with operation of drainage facilities.

References

1. The Koto 5 Wards Large-Scale Flooding Evacuation Response Policy. https://www.city.ada chi.tokyo.jp/documents/33490/koto5ku_evacuation_guidelines.pdf. Accessed 6 Aug 2021

2. Ito, H., Yamamoto, M., Yuasa, N.: Interim report on the flood damage survey in Joso City. Civil Eng. Mater. **58**(6), 42–45 (2016)
3. Disaster Relief for Flooding in Ibaraki Prefecture - Ministry of Defense. https://www.mod. go.jp/js/Activity/Disaster_relief/2709kinugawa.htm. Accessed 30 Nov 2021
4. Ikeuchi, K., Ochi, S., Yasuda, G., Okamura, J., Aono, M.: Estimates of the number of stranded persons and the rescue waiting time in case of large floods with effectiveness analysis of the mitigatory operations. In: Proceedings B1 of JSCE, vol. 67, No. 3, pp.145–154 (2011)
5. Typhoon No. 19: A series of "miscalculations" at evacuation centers: flooded, packed, and cold. https://www.nikkei.com/article/DGXMZO51042310W9A011C1CC1000/. Accessed 6 Aug 2021
6. Typhoon No. 19: Wide-area Evacuation Questioned (Jiron Koron) | Jiron Koron | Commentary Archives - NHK Commentary Committee Room. https://www.nhk.or.jp/kaisetsu-blog/100/414424.html. Accessed 6 Aug 2021
7. Katada, T., Kuwasawa, N., Shida, S., Kojima, M.: Scenario analysis on evacuation strategies for residents in big cities during large scale flood. In: Proceedings B1 of JSCE, vol. 69, No. 1, pp.71–82 (2013)
8. Kato, T., Miyagawa, Y.: Analysis on possibility of long distant evacuation by railways in below-sea-level area in Tokyo. J. Inst. Indust. Sci. Univ. Tokyo **63**(4), 495–499 (2011)
9. Ozkan, M.F., Carrillo, L.R.G., King, S.A.: Rescue boat path planning in flooded urban environments. In: 2019 IEEE International Symposium on Measurement and Control in Robotics (ISMCR), pp. B2-2-1-B2-2-9 (2019)
10. Chandra, M., Niyogi, R.: Web services based path guidance to rescue team alert system during flood. In: 2016 Ninth International Conference on Contemporary Computing (IC3), pp. 1–6 (2016)
11. Statistics on a Map (Statistical GIS) Government Statistics Portal. https://www.e-stat.go.jp/gis. Accessed 6 Aug 2021
12. National Land Data Download Service. https://nlftp.mlit.go.jp/ksj/. Accessed 6 Aug 2021
13. Let's start with what we can do! Disaster Prevention Measures Part 3 - Cabinet Office Disaster Prevention Information Page: Disaster Prevention Information Page. http://www.bousai.go.jp/kohou/kouhoubousai/h25/73/bousaitaisaku.html. Accessed 6 Aug 2021
14. Koto Ward Homepage. https://www.city.koto.lg.jp/260353/fukushi/hoken/eyo/bichiku-pan fuletto.html. Accessed 6 Aug 2021
15. Are your household stockpiles sufficient? Edogawa Ward Homepage. https://www.city.edogawa.tokyo.jp/e008/bosaianzen/bosai/jijo/bichiku.html. Accessed 6 Aug 2021

COVID-19 Issues

Trial of Building a Resilient Face-To-Face Classroom Based on CO_2-Based Risk Awareness

Tomohiro Kokogawa[✉]

International Professional University of Technology in Tokyo, Tokyo, Japan
t.koko@ieee.org

Abstract. The COVID-19 pandemic forced many schools to switch to online classes. Although there has been a movement to return to face-to-face classes since then, many schools are still struggling to ensure safety during classes and subsequent examinations in a face-to-face environment. In this study, we attempted to visualize the relationship between class usage and building air conditioning management by installing CO_2 sensors at fixed points in classrooms and also applied them to environmental monitoring during examinations to grasp the risks in real time and provide a response.

Keywords: COVID-19 · CO_2 · Risk awareness · Situation awareness

1 Introduction

The novel coronavirus disease (COVID-19), which was first reported in Wuhan, China, at the end of 2019, caused a worldwide pandemic, and it is still difficult to determine when the pandemic will be over.

In Japan, the government issued a request for the temporary closure of elementary, junior high, and high schools in late February 2020 when the infection began to spread in the country. Although universities were not subject to the request, many of them responded by canceling graduation and entrance ceremonies and postponing the start of classes for the new semester. The pandemic continued to spread, leading to the declaration of a national state of emergency, and many universities were forced to close their campuses and shift to online classes.

Since late May 2020, when the state of emergency was lifted nationwide, there has been a gradual return to face-to-face classes, but with the outbreak of the second wave of infection soon after, full recovery has not been possible. Many universities tried face-to-face classes with staggered attendance or introduced hybrid (online and face-to-face) teaching.

The shift to online classes, which could be said to have been forced, brought about various adverse effects; however, the National Institute of Informatics promoted a cyber-symposium to share best practices and know-how about education online and at various universities promoted as "digital transformation (DX) for educational institutions" [1]. However, in classes that can only be conducted face-to-face, especially those that involve

J. Sasaki et al. (Eds.): ITDRR 2021, IFIP AICT 638, pp. 95–106, 2022.
https://doi.org/10.1007/978-3-031-04170-9_7

practical training and skills, face-to-face classes must be continued while dealing with the fear of infection risk, causing great stress not only for students but also for school personnel.

The biggest problem is that the risk of infection is difficult to measure. Thanks to the efforts of the government's expert panel and others, the factors that increase the risk of COVID-19 infection were identified at an early stage and provided in the easy-to-understand phrase "Three Cs" (Closed spaces, Crowded places, and Close-contact settings) [2]. However, the level of environment we should be prepared to consider safe remains a matter of trial and error.

Initially, droplet and contact infections were considered the main routes of COVID-19 infection, but later, the possibility of infection by microdroplets (aerosols) with a diameter of 5 μm or less was pointed out [3]. Even if social distance is maintained, the risk of infection occurs when microdroplets drift around the room for a long time, so ventilation is more important. However, ventilation is difficult for people to sense physically, and it is difficult to know how much ventilation is being provided especially in high-rise buildings where windows cannot be opened for structural reasons.

In this paper, we report on an attempt to visualize the degree of ventilation in a university campus located in a high-rise building by measuring CO_2 concentrations and evaluating the extent of situation awareness [4] about the infection spread risk in face-to-face classes and examinations and to direct our responses against these infection risks.

2   Case Study and Issues

2.1   Case Study

The target university, the International Professional University of Technology in Tokyo (IPUT), to which the author belongs, has just been established in April 2020 as a new professional and vocational university in Japan. The major differences from conventional universities are the high percentage of full-time practitioner teachers (more than 40%), the high percentage of practical training classes in the curriculum (more than 33%), and the number of students per class is limited to 40 or fewer [5]. The campus is located in a high-rise building (50 floors above ground) in Shinjuku, Tokyo.

Due to the effects of the onset of the COVID-19 pandemic just before the establishment of IPUT, we had to take various emergency measures to maintain business as usual, although none of the previously planned on-campus events or classes was held. Table 1 is a summary of the typical response to addressing educational continuity taken since establishing IPUT.

To initiate classes to our first students as soon as possible, we established a communication tool *Slack* (http://slack.com/) to connect all students and the faculty and built an online classroom environment as soon as was practicable. By the end of the consecutive holidays in May, we were able to start online classes for all subjects based on the original timetable.

However, practical training and skills classes, which are characteristic of a "professional and vocational university," would be hindered by running online classes only, so we also considered an immediate return to face-to-face classes in anticipation of the lifting of the emergency declaration. In addition, there was concern from an early stage that students' stress would increase due to the continuation of online classes and the fact that they would not be able to see their friends due to the continued self-restraint [6].

Table 1. Timetable of educational continuity response at International Professional University of Technology

Timeline	Events
Early March 2020	End of general entrance examinations (as originally scheduled)
Mid-March 2020	Decision to cancel the entrance ceremony (to be held online) and postpone the start of classes for 2 weeks
Early April 2020	The university started. The entrance ceremony and student orientations were conducted online
Mid-April 2020	Online classes began for parts of subjects with a special timetable
Mid-May 2020	Online classes began for all subjects with the original timetable
Mid-June 2020	Students attended the campus for the first time. Distributed attendance (2 days a week for each student), shifted to mixed online/face-to-face (hybrid) classes
Early October 2020	The second semester started, with one more face-to-face class day per week
Early January 2021	In response to the second emergency declaration, face-to-face class days were reduced by 1 day per week
Early April 2021	Second school year started. Five levels of hybrid classes were provided. Starting with level 1 (three face-to-face class days per week), it changed in response to the pandemic situation in Tokyo
Late August 2021	In response to the situation of a worsening infection spread (fifth wave) and the fourth emergency declaration, the level at the end of August 2020 was reduced to level 4 (full online classes each day)

To resume face-to-face classes, the following measures were implemented to reduce the infection spread risk:

- Reducing the number of students on campus by staggering attendance
- Halving the capacity of classrooms
- Measuring body temperature at the entrance of the school building
- Setting up disinfectant (ethanol) on each floor
- Establishing rules for daily life, such as prohibiting lunch with more than three people gathered
- Reminding students frequently about safety measures at the beginning of classes and through administrative communications such as *Slack*

As a result of the above measures, fortunately, both faculty and students were able to get through the first year without causing any infection clusters.

In addition, there were many issues in ensuring the fairness and impartiality of the online entrance examinations and routine examinations, as well as the preparation and operation of the online examinations, so we abandoned online examinations and conducted all examinations face to face. For the entrance examinations in particular, unlike routine examinations, which are always conducted with the same members (current students), an unspecified number of examinees from all over the country visit the campus for the first time, so it was necessary to take stricter measures against infection in preparation for the possible introduction of viruses. On the other hand, the students who took the examinations were also anxious about going to Shinjuku, Tokyo (an area where many infections occur), and required an environment where they could take the examinations with peace of mind.

2.2   Ventilation Issues

However, the fact that the entire campus is located in a high-rise building makes it difficult to take countermeasures. Due to the structure of the building, it is not possible to open the windows, and there is no spontaneous ventilation. Even if the doors of classrooms are opened, the ventilating effect cannot be expected because the entire floor is a kind of sealed space. Air conditioning is managed centrally throughout the building, and since several other schools (vocational schools and universities) are housed in the same building, it is difficult to control the air conditioning according to the circumstances of a specific school or room. In addition, ventilation is more difficult for people to sense physically than heating and cooling, and it is difficult to grasp the operational status of the ventilation system.

The measurement of carbon dioxide (CO_2) concentration has been attracting attention as a means of visualizing ventilation. When people are in a room, CO_2 is rapidly generated by their breathing, and if the ventilation is inadequate, the CO_2 concentration in the room will increase. By measuring this, it is expected to determine how well ventilation is working.

High CO_2 concentrations are known to have adverse effects on the human body, such as headaches, dizziness, and nausea, and have also been linked to poor concentration and even falling asleep in class [7]. The Ministry of Education, Culture, Sports, Science and Technology recommends that the concentration of CO_2 in classrooms should be 1,500 ppm or less [8], and the Ministry of Health, Labor and Welfare stipulates that the concentration should be 1,000 ppm or less [9]. Therefore, in buildings of a certain size, CO_2 concentration is monitored, and ventilation control is considered to be based on it. However, this criterion is not based on the presence or absence of ventilation, but on the extent of the CO_2 concentration, and is intended to prevent health hazards caused by high CO_2 concentrations. On the other hand, when focusing on ventilation, the increase or decrease in CO_2 concentration is more important than the increase or decrease in concentration, and ventilation control has not been implemented from this perspective. In addition, the increase or decrease of CO_2 depends on the movement of people in and out of the room, and ventilation is affected by temperature and humidity, making uniform control difficult.

Therefore, in this study, we decided to start by placing CO_2 measurement devices in classrooms to capture the daily increase and decrease patterns. Then, we identified the problems and risks of the current ventilation system to realize more effective ventilation in the face-to-face environment. In addition, we conducted short-term monitoring of events and studied how we could apply this information to individual responses.

Figure 1 shows schematically the relationship between ventilation and CO_2 concentration. When there are people in the room, the amount of CO_2 emitted by breathing increases with time, but it reaches equilibrium at a certain concentration when ventilation is provided to some extent. As the number of people in the room increases, the amount of CO_2 emitted increases and the concentration also rises, but if sufficient ventilation is provided, the concentration soon reaches equilibrium or decreases as in the upper row. On the other hand, if the number of people in the room is small but ventilation is inadequate, the CO_2 emitted by people is not discharged outside the room, and the concentration continues to increase. The right case is the most problematic because microdroplets contained in exhaled air remain in the room for a long time even if the number of people is small, and the risk of infection is considered to be high if there are infected people present. However, with conventional building air conditioning control, the problem will not be noticed until it reaches the environmental hygiene management standard (1,000 ppm), and there is a strong possibility that ventilation will not occur. On the other hand, it is not practical to forcibly ventilate all rooms. A large amount of outside air will affect the temperature and humidity in the room, and the power consumption of the air conditioning system, including heating, cooling, and humidification, may significantly increase.

As described above, an air conditioning control that balances infection control (ventilation), maintenance of the building environment (temperature and humidity), and economic efficiency (reduction of electricity consumption) is not an easy task, and the solution will require observation of actual room usage and air conditioning circumstance to establish a pattern.

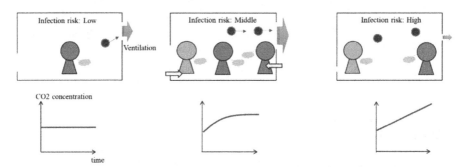

Fig. 1. Relationship between CO_2 and ventilation

3   Measurement System

The non-dispersive infrared (NDIR) method is a typical method of CO_2 detection, but the measuring instruments are relatively expensive. Some inexpensive measuring instruments estimate and calculate the equivalent CO_2 from the concentration of volatile organic compounds (VOCs) (especially ethanol concentration), which poses a problem with accuracy [10]. In addition, most of the measuring instruments on the market do not have a log function and only display the measured value at the time, making it difficult to capture the trend of increase or decrease. Therefore, we decided to build a prototype measuring instrument using an NDIR CO_2 sensor device. We obtained sensor devices, *SCD30* (https://www.sensirion.com/jp/environmental-sensors/carbon-dioxide-sensors/carbon-dioxide-sensors-scd30/), which is also able to measure temperature and humidity simultaneously.

We used the *M5StickC Plus* (https://docs.m5stack.com/en/core/m5stickc_plus) microcontroller for the sensor gateway. *M5StickC Plus* is an IoT development board using *ESP32* as the microcontroller chip and has a small LCD screen and Wi-Fi communication functions. We also use *Ambient* (https://ambidata.io/) as an IoT cloud network service to gather and visualize sensor data.

The system configuration is shown in Fig. 2. *SCD30* sensor data is measured by *M5StickC Plus* via I2C interfaces, periodically sent to *Ambient* via Wi-Fi, and displayed as a graph on a web browser.

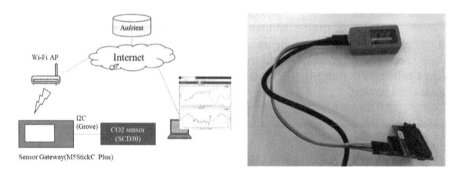

Fig. 2.   System configuration and overview

4   Experiments

4.1   Measurement at an Event

Since it is necessary to find the best solution for air conditioning control of classrooms in regular use while considering the economic efficiency of the entire building, it is not easy to respond to individual cases. Therefore, we conducted a trial of CO_2 monitoring and response during events targeting the entrance examinations (for candidate students) and routine examinations (for current students), which are major events at universities.

Figure 3 shows the overall examination implementation system for entrance examination: three prototype measuring instruments were installed at the examination sites (paper test room, interview test room, and anteroom), and the measurement results were monitored and displayed centrally in the examination office. In the case of the routine examinations, two paper test rooms were used simultaneously although there were no interview tests.

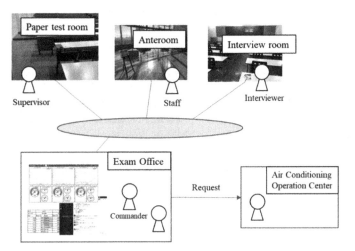

Fig. 3. Response structure for exams

The examination office and the staff at the examination site (supervisors, interviewers, guidance staff, etc.) used *Slack* to communicate, and a system was created in which the examination office and staff could share the progress of the test and changes in CO_2 concentration. If there was a problem, the commander could identify it immediately and take appropriate action (such as contacting the air conditioning operation center). An example of comments in *Slack* is shown in Fig. 4.

The instruments were installed on the morning of the examination day to stabilize the measurement values. The measurement interval was set to 30 s. The measurement results of three instruments were shown in a single browser window using graphs and meters. An example of the measurement view is shown in Fig. 5.

The total view design in the examination office is constructed by referring to the emergency management concept of "Plan/Do/See," which was implemented to the emergency management support system "*KADAN*." [11] The *Slack* acts as the "Do" screen, and the CO_2 view acts as the "See" screen. The "Plan" screen is also implemented, but on a simple Excel sheet as a program progress list.

The experiment was conducted on the entrance examinations (one comprehensive selection, four general selection) and the routine examinations held from January to March, 2021. Table 2 shows the number of comments on *Slack* during the examinations and the number of comments on the topic of CO_2 concentration. The number of comments divided into threads is counted for each comment. The number of responses indicates the number of requests for increasing ventilation to the air conditioning control center of the building.

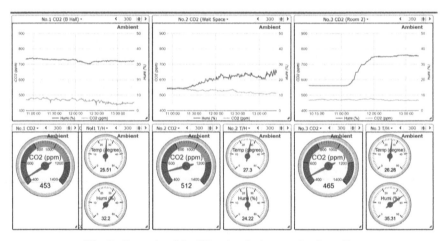

[Room B] 14:01 It seems over 1000 ppm in Room A.
[Exam Office] 14:03 Is Room B having a problem? I will call the Air Conditioning Operation Center now.
[Room B] 14:04 About 700 ppm in Room B. Is there a difference in the number of people in the room? If it exceeds 1000 ppm, concentration loss and drowsiness become more of a problem than infection control, especially during the exam.
[Exam Office] 14:06 It looks like the air conditioning was turned off. (why?) I'll have it turned on.
[Room A] 14:08 I am experiencing stagnation in the air!
[Teacher] 14:08 I LOL'd.
[Room A] 14:16 Air quality is improving in Room A, because a student who was sleeping suddenly woke up!
[Exam Office] 14:18 Finally it is below 900 ppm in Room A.
[Teacher] 14:49 I just looked around both classrooms and the air quality is clearly different. I think it depends on the number of people, but in extreme cases it may be unequal.

Fig. 4. Example of comments in *Slack* (English translations are shown on the right)

Fig. 5. Example of the CO_2 view in the examination office

For the entrance examinations, *Slack* was divided into two channels: one for the overall management and the other for the interview rooms, but only the data from the overall management channel is counted because the latter was specialized for managing the progress of the interviews. For the routine exam, we also had two separate channels, one for general management and the other for the exam room, but since this was only a written exam, the exam room channel was also used for general management, so only the data from the exam room channel is counted. For the entrance exam, CO_2-related comments accounted for 27.6% and 21.8%, respectively, of the data for the routine exam, suggesting that CO_2-related comments made a significant contribution to the management of the exam.

Table 2. Number of comments in *Slack*

Exam type	Total comments	CO_2-related comments	Number of responses for ventilations
Comprehensive	39	13	3
General 1	31	8	1
General 2	49	13	1
General 3	24	4	0
General 4	20	7	1
Routine 1	113	27	1
Routine 2	74	13	1
Routine 3	5	2	0

During the entrance examination on January 30, the CO_2 concentration in the paper test room was slightly high before the examination began, so we asked the air conditioning control center to increase ventilation. As a result, the CO_2 concentration improved, but the classroom suddenly began to dry out, and the humidity dropped below 10% during the test. The air conditioning control center was urgently requested to operate the humidifier. This was a valuable lesson that monitoring ventilation alone is not enough. In subsequent examinations, the balance with humidity was maintained, and the need for monitoring each individually in the written examination room was almost eliminated.

However, another problem arose in the interview room. There were two interviewers in a classroom with a capacity of about 40 people, and the number of examinees was few (one examinee for the comprehensive selection and five for the general selection). However, when the interviewer entered the test room, the CO_2 concentration began to rise and continued to rise throughout the interview test, which means a higher-risk situation, as shown in Fig. 1. As a result, the increase in CO_2 concentration was noticed during the first set of interviews and enhanced ventilation was requested, and the CO_2 concentration finally leveled off or started to decrease after the second set of interviews (Fig. 6, left). It is highly possible that the students were so relieved by the sufficiently low concentration that they did not increase ventilation, and it is necessary to review the operation of the room by consciously starting ventilation just before the start of the examination.

For the routine exam, since it was a routine event for current students only, the exam office did not take any special measures at first; however, the increase in CO_2 concentration was more pronounced than for the entrance exam, and the commander had to request the air conditioning control center to take action urgently (Fig. 6, right). In addition to the report of the increase in concentration, there were mentions of the stagnant air and the degree of concentration of the students.

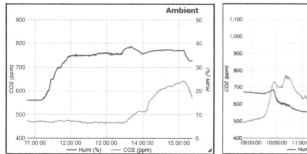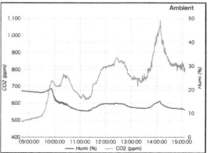

Fig. 6. Example of CO_2 measurement during exams

4.2 Measurement of the Whole Campus

Under normal circumstances, classes are held in many classrooms at the same time, and it is difficult to request ventilation measures for each classroom as described above. Therefore, we aimed to familiarize ourselves with the overall situation of ventilation in the building by observing changes in CO_2 concentration in multiple classrooms at the same time, to enable us to get risk awareness and to take appropriate measures.

As an experiment, CO_2 measurement instruments were installed in six classrooms (two classrooms on each of three floors), and an example of how the situation can be monitored is shown in Fig. 7. Measurements were taken at 2-min intervals, and bar graphs were displayed to make it easier to notice any sharp increase in CO_2 concentration (which means increased infection risk). This graph can be viewed online at any time by faculty members, and when ventilation is insufficient, they can see the overall situation, including the situation in surrounding rooms, and take measures such as switching the priority of ventilation between classrooms or temporarily evacuating to another classroom.

We have started to evaluate the operation of the system; however, due to the spread of cases of infection in Tokyo, the number of hybrid classes has been down, which means the frequency of face-to-face classes has been reduced. Therefore, we have not yet had a chance to take specific actions.

As another means of getting risk awareness, we have begun to experiment with the use of electronic bulletin board displays (LED matrix arrays), which are expected to enable faculty and students to notice risks by viewing them in classrooms and corridors without having to open their PCs or smartphones, especially since web-based viewing takes up a large area of the PC screen and interferes with classes. The figure shows an example of the display, with arrows indicating the increase or decrease in addition to the CO_2 concentration in the room (Fig. 8).

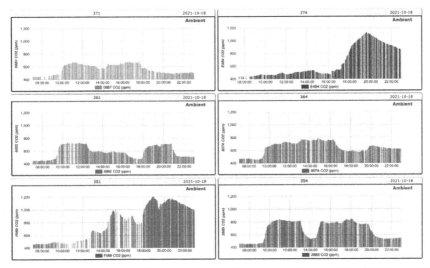

Fig. 7. Risk visualization on multiple classrooms. The capacity of rooms 371, 374, 361, and 351 is about 100 seats, while 364 and 354 are laboratory-style rooms with about 40 seats

Fig. 8. Risk visualization using an LED matrix array

5   Conclusion

By measuring CO_2 concentrations during classes and examinations on a university campus in a high-rise building, we attempted to understand the risk of COVID-19 infection from the viewpoint of ventilation and to actively utilize the results for responses. Through the measurement, it became clear that the pattern of increase and decrease in CO_2 concentration is not so simple to evaluate, and visualization showed that it can be used for risk situation awareness and proactive response to ventilation control.

In the future, by installing sensors in a wider area, we will construct an environment in which we can grasp the risk situation from both an aspectual and temporal perspective and study the possibility of realizing an environment in which students can take face-to-face classes and examinations safely.

References

1. National Institute of Informatics: DX symposium for educational institutions. https://www.nii.ac.jp/event/other/decs/. Accessed 30 Aug 2021. (in Japanese)
2. Ministry of Health and Labor Welfare Japan: Information on health and medical consultation. https://www.mhlw.go.jp/stf/covid-19/kenkou-iryousoudan_00006.html. Accessed 30 Aug 2021
3. Center for Disease Control and Prevention: Scientific Brief: SARS-CoV-2 Transmission. https://www.cdc.gov/coronavirus/2019-ncov/science/science-briefs/sars-cov-2-transmission.html. Accessed 30 Aug 2021
4. Endsley, M.R.: Toward a theory of situation awareness in dynamic systems. Hum. Factors **37**(1), 32–64 (1995). https://doi.org/10.1518/001872095779049543
5. Ministry of Education, Culture, Sports Science and Technology Japan: Characteristics of Professional and Vocational Universities (PVU) and Professional and Vocational Junior Colleges (PVJC). https://www.mext.go.jp/en/policy/education/highered/title02/detail02/1373918.html. Accessed 30 Aug 2021
6. Nippon Foundation: Awareness Survey of 18-Year-Olds–Coronavirus and Stress. https://www.nippon-foundation.or.jp/en/news/articles/2021/20210325-55959.html. Accessed 30 Aug 2021
7. Fujiwara, T., Nagao, K.: Research on evaluation of classroom environment and class concentration using IoT devices. FIT2019 **4**, 331–332 (2019). (in Japanese)
8. Ministry of Education, Culture, Sports Science and Technology Japan: Standards of environmental sanitation at schools, 2020. https://www.mext.go.jp/a_menu/kenko/hoken/1353625.htm. Accessed 31 Aug 2021. (in Japanese)
9. Ministry of Health and Labor Welfare Japan: About the management standard of environmental sanitation for buildings. https://www.mhlw.go.jp/bunya/kenkou/seikatsu-eisei10/. Accessed 31 Aug 2021 (in Japanese)
10. Ishigaki, Y., et al.: Accuracy verification of low-cost CO_2 concentration measuring devices for general use as a countermeasure against COVID-19, medRxiv preprint (2021). https://doi.org/10.1101/2021.07.30.21261265
11. Kosaka, N., et al.: Applicability assessment of an emergency management support system "KADAN". In: Proceedings of 2019 IEEE International Conference on Big Data and Smart Computing, pp. 532–538 (2019). https://doi.org/10.1109/BIGCOMP.2019.8679466

Analysis of Quote Retweets for COVID-19 State of Emergency Related Tweets Posted from Prefectural Governors' Accounts in Japan

Keisuke Utsu[1]([envelope]), Natsumi Yagi[1], Airi Fukushima[1], Yuma Takemori[1], Atsushi Okazaki[1], and Osamu Uchida[2]

[1] Department of Communication and Network Engineering, School of Information and Telecommunication Engineering, Tokai University, Minato, Tokyo, Japan
utsu@utsuken.net
[2] Department of Human and Information Science, School of Information Science and Technology, Tokai University, Hiratsuka, Kanagawa, Japan
o-uchida@tokai.ac.jp

Abstract. The novel coronavirus disease (COVID-19) pandemic has seriously affected countries all over the world. In Japan, a state of emergency has been declared several times in some prefectures. Information related to the spread of infection is provided to the public via central or local government websites and social media accounts. In particular, some prefectural governors have used Twitter accounts to provide information related to the pandemic, and this use of social media has been attracting attention. One of the advantages of Twitter is its ability to disseminate information instantly. In order to prevent the spread of infection, it is desirable to respond to changes in the situation and provide information in a timely manner. In this study, we focused on three Twitter accounts used by prefectural governors in Japan and aimed to clarify users' reactions to posts (tweets) related to the state of emergency posted from those accounts. We collected quote retweets for the top quote-retweeted tweets posted between January 1, 2020, and July 31, 2021, and classified them as either positive or negative.

Keywords: COVID-19 · Social media · Twitter

1 Introduction

The novel coronavirus disease (COVID-19) pandemic has seriously affected countries all over the world. In Japan, the number of infected people first began to increase in January 2020. States of emergency in this country are declared by the Prime Minister on a prefectural basis. On April 7, 2020, a state of emergency was declared for the first time in Japan. Since then, such declarations have been issued several times in some prefectures. The principal measures taken during these declared states of emergency have been requests to refrain from going out without good reason, encouragement of teleworking, shortening of business hours, and the closure of schools. The specific restrictions and

J. Sasaki et al. (Eds.): ITDRR 2021, IFIP AICT 638, pp. 107–120, 2022.
https://doi.org/10.1007/978-3-031-04170-9_8

requests implemented under each state of emergency varied depending on the time period and the prefecture. In Japan, strict regulations such as lockdowns and curfews are not legally enforced.

In recent years, public institutions have begun to use Twitter to provide information proactively on daily matters and at times of disaster, and this use of social media has been attracting attention as a means of information sharing [1, 2]. There is an increasing number of local governments opening official social media accounts to provide information to citizens. In response to the COVID-19 pandemic, it has been important to react immediately to changes in the situation and to provide information and requests to citizens in a timely manner. Twitter posts (tweets) related to the infection have been analyzed [3–7], and tweets related to the vaccination have been discussed [8, 9]. Regarding the infection, statements made by world leaders and state governors at press conferences have been a particular focus of public attention. Tweets posted by world leaders and state governors have been discussed outside Japan [10–13]. In Japan, some prefectures have been disseminating information through their governors' Twitter accounts, and those tweets have attracted Twitter users' attention. However, there has been no major study that focuses on the analysis of tweets posted from the accounts of prefectural governors in Japan and the reactions of users to those tweets. Providing information from a governor's social media account is considered to make that information seem more highly credible because the governor's words can reach residents in an immediate and direct manner. It is necessary to discuss the effectiveness of this type of information dissemination.

The authors have already studied the Twitter accounts of prefectural governors who have made posts about the COVID-19 infection, and analyzed the top retweeted tweets [14]. In this study, we focus on the Twitter accounts of three governors: Mr. Hirofumi Yoshimura, the governor of Osaka prefecture, Ms. Yuriko Koike, the governor of the Tokyo metropolitan area, and Mr. Naomichi Suzuki, the governor of Hokkaido prefecture. This study aims to clarify the reactions of users to tweets related to the state of emergency in each region that were posted from those accounts. We collect quote retweets for the top quote-retweeted tweets posted between January 1, 2020, and July 31, 2021, and classify them as either positive or negative.

The rest of this paper is organized as follows: Sect. 2 introduces related studies. Section 3 shows the collection of tweets posted from the governor's account and presents an analysis of the quote retweets for the governor's top quote-retweeted tweets related to the state of emergency declared in his or her region. Section 4 summarizes this study.

2 Related Studies

There have been many studies to analyze tweets related to the COVID-19 infection. Banda et al. [3] presented a large-scale curated dataset of tweets related to the infection. Xue et al. [4] examined COVID-19-related discussions, concerns, and sentiments using tweets. They concluded that "Real-time monitoring and assessment of Twitter discussions and concerns could provide useful data for public health emergency responses and planning."

In Japan, Yoshida [5] reviewed the state of social media during an early period of the pandemic, and introduced public datasets of social media data including those from outside Japan. Toriumi et al. [6] collected Japanese tweets containing words related to the infection and analyzed the use of emotive words in the tweets to analyze how people feel about the virus. The analysis results show that "The occurrence of a particular social event can change the emotions expressed on social media." Yomoda [7] collected Japanese tweets containing words related to the infection during an early period of the pandemic and analyzed them using a quantitative text analysis technique. The analysis results show that "Concerns and stress related to coronavirus varied over a wide range of aspects, including fear of infection, stress due to restriction of daily behavior and recreational activities, concerns over government epidemiological measures and economic damage, and concerns arising from media information."

COVID-19 vaccine-related tweets have also been discussed. Yousefinaghani et al. [8] identified public sentiments and opinions vis-à-vis the COVID-19 vaccines based on tweets. They concluded that "Understanding sentiments and opinions about vaccination using Twitter may help public health agencies to increase positive messaging and eliminate opposing messages in order to enhance vaccine uptake." Lyu et al. [9] present a topic modeling, sentiment and emotion analysis of COVID-19 vaccine-related discussion on Twitter. They concluded that "Public COVID-19 vaccine-related discussion on Twitter was largely driven by major events about COVID-19 vaccines and mirrored active news topics in mainstream media."

Tweets from world leaders and state governors have been a focus of attention, and have also been discussed outside Japan. Haman [10] examined how many leaders have used Twitter during the COVID-19 pandemic, in what way, and the impact they had on the public by using it. Haman stated that "The research implies that citizens are interested in being informed about emergencies through social networks and government officials should use them." Rufai and Bunce [11] explored the role of Twitter as used by Group of Seven (G7) world leaders in response to COVID-19. They performed a context analysis to categorize tweets into appropriate themes and analyzed associated Twitter data. They conclude that "Twitter may represent a powerful tool for world leaders to rapidly communicate public health information to citizens, with a preference for tweets containing official government-based information sources." Dwianto et al. [12] examined the responses of Joko Widodo's and Donald Trump's tweets regarding COVID-19 policies. According to the article, analysis results of responses to both presidents' tweets reveal higher negative sentiments than positive ones. Qodir et al. [13] examined the official Twitter account for the governor of Jakarta, Indonesia, using a social network analysis method to examine communication patterns between the government and the public. This article concludes that the official account of the governor on social media is effective in a pandemic to assuage public panic and extend public trust in the government.

3 Analysis of Tweets

In this study, we focus on tweets posted from three accounts belonging to prefectural governors in Japan and analyze reactions of users to the tweets.

3.1 Governors' Accounts to Be Analyzed

We focus on the following three accounts belonging to prefectural governors:

- Hirofumi Yoshimura, the governor of Osaka Prefecture, @hiroyoshimura, https://twitter.com/hiroyoshimura
- Yuriko Koike, the governor of the Tokyo metropolitan area, @ecoyuri, https://twitter.com/ecoyuri
- Naomichi Suzuki, the governor of Hokkaido Prefecture, @suzukinaomichi, https://twitter.com/suzukinaomichi

These governors' accounts posted relatively more tweets related to the infection than other governors' accounts. As of August 1, 2021, the Tokyo, Osaka and Hokkaido regions ranked first, second, and seventh, respectively, among the 47 prefectures in Japan, for the cumulative number of cases of COVID-19 infection [15]. For reference, Fig. 1 shows when states of emergency and intensive anti-virus measures (introduced in February 2021) were declared in the three relevant regions. In April 2020, a state of emergency was declared throughout Japan. In 2021, states of emergency had been declared three times by August 31, including in the Tokyo and Osaka regions.

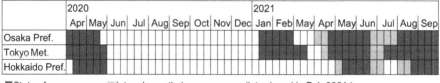

■State of emergency   ■Intensive anti-virus measures (introduced in Feb 2021-)

Fig. 1. Details of the states of emergency issued in the Osaka, Tokyo, and Hokkaido regions

3.2 Tweets Collection

We collected tweets posted from the accounts of the three governors during the period from January 1, 2020, to July 31, 2021, using the Twitter API v2 [16]. The collection was conducted on August 1, 2021. For the account of Governor Koike, there were no tweets from June 21 to July 20, 2021. Tweets posted from this account during this period may have been deleted prior to our collection of them. Figures 2, 3 and 4 show the number of tweets posted from each governor's account in the following categories (i) to (iii).

(i)   Total tweets
(ii)   The original tweets including COVID-19 related words, which are Corona (コロナ), virus (ウイルス), infection (感染), vaccine (ワクチン), vaccination (接種), test (検査), positive (i.e. of a test result) (陽性), sickbed (病床), severe illness (重症), mild illness (軽症), patient (患者), self-restraint (自粛), recuperation (療養), contact (接触), and emergency (緊急事態). These words were selected from among the words occurring most frequently in tweets posted from the governors' accounts that the authors considered to be related to COVID-19.

(iii)   The original tweets that included the word "emergency." The reason we focus on the word "emergency" here is that this study intends to analyze tweets specifically related to declared "states of emergency (緊急事態宣言)."

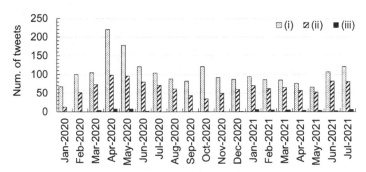

Fig. 2. The number of tweets posted per month from the account of Governor Yoshimura

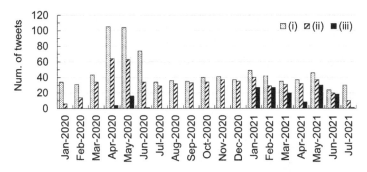

Fig. 3. The number of tweets posted per month from the account of Governor Koike

The content of the tweets in category (ii) included, for example, statements about the spread of infection (such as the number of infected people and PCR tests), statements about the declaration of a state of emergency, measures and responses to the spread of infection, statements about campaigns, requests for self-restraint, opinions and comments. Regarding the number of tweets in category (ii), the three governors commonly posted the largest number of tweets in April 2020. This may be due to the fact that a state of emergency was declared in their regions for the first time in that month, and as a result, they posted many tweets related to the infection. The tweets corresponding to category (iii) were found mainly during the periods when a state of emergency had been declared.

3.3 Analysis of Quote Retweets of Governors' Tweets

In order to analyze users' reactions to tweets posted from the governors' accounts relating to the states of emergency, we collected quote retweets for the top five quote-retweeted

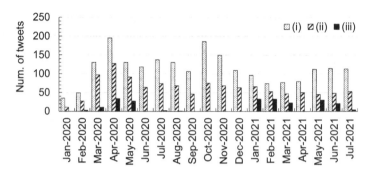

Fig. 4. The number of tweets posted per month from the account of Governor Suzuki

tweets in category (iii) in each year of 2020 (January 1–December 31) and 2021 (January 1–July 31) for each governor's account. Then we classified the quote retweets as either positive or negative. Although there is an alternative method of focusing on replies to examine a user's reaction, we focus on quote retweets because they are more likely to aid the spread of information. Figures 5, 6 and 7 show the number of quote retweets for the tweets in category (iii) for each governor's account. In the figures, the top five quote-retweeted tweets in each year of 2020 and 2021 are indicated by balloons as T01 to T30. Tables 1, 2 and 3 show the contents of the original tweet, its ID, the date and time of posting, and the number of retweets (RTs) and quote retweets (QRTs) it received.

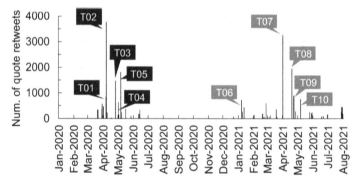

Fig. 5. The number of quote retweets for each tweet posted from the account of Governor Yoshimura

We collected the quote retweets for each tweet of T01–T30 using the Twitter API v2 [16], and selected the tweets to be analyzed using the following procedure:

1. For Governor Yoshimura, we focused on the quote retweets that were posted within 24 h of the governor's original tweet being posted. As for Governors Koike and Suzuki, we focused on the quote retweets that were posted within 120 h of the governors' original tweets being posted, because the number of quote retweets for

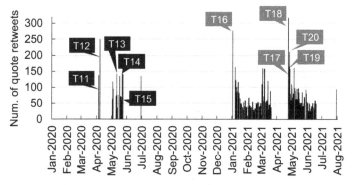

Fig. 6. The number of quote retweets for each tweet posted from the account of Governor Koike

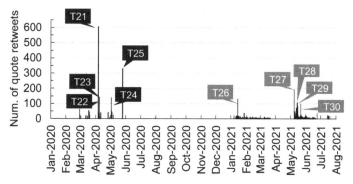

Fig. 7. The number of quote retweets for each tweet posted from the account of Governor Suzuki

Governor Koike's and Governor Suzuki's tweets is smaller than that for Governor Yoshimura's tweets.

2. If there were multiple quote retweets by one account, we focused only on the first quote retweet.
3. If there were more than 100 quote retweets satisfying (1) and (2), 100 of them were selected randomly; if there were less than 100, all of them were selected.

The quote retweets selected by the above procedure were classified by three of the authors involved in this paper into one of the following categories:

- (P) Positive content (such as an approving or encouraging message)
- (N) Negative content (such as an opposing or critical message)
- (E) Neither (P) nor (N): Not a comment on the governor's tweet, or unknown.

Table 1. Top quote-retweeted tweets for Governor Yoshimura: T01–T10

	Contents
	Tweet ID, Date/Time, Retweets (RTs), Quote retweets (QRTs)
T01	• Messages for people including a request to refrain from panic-buying foods and goods ID: 1247022999993077760, Date/Time: 13:47, Apr 6, 2020, RTs: 19.2k, QRTs: 836
T02	• Video message from the governor related to a state of emergency ID: 1247517477468114951, Date/Time: 22:31, Apr 7, 2020, RTs: 43.7k, QRTs: 3,771
T03	• Opinions including a request for pachinko parlors to restrict admission ID: 1253963991337955329, Date/Time: 17:28, Apr 25, 2020, RTs: 10.1k, QRTs: 1,477
T04	• Opinions related to measures for preventing a medical collapse ID: 1256204571770142722, Date/Time: 21:51, May 1, 2020, RTs: 4.8k, QRTs: 628
T05	• Message for the Minister in charge of Economic Revitalization in Japan ID: 1258026380601655297, Date/Time: 22:30, May 6, 2020, RTs: 8.1k, QRTs: 1,809
T06	• Reporting the number of new cases • Information that the governor was considering requesting the declaration of a state of emergency ID: 1347118393388724225, Date/Time: 18:50, Jan 7, 2021, RTs: 2.4k, QRTs: 724
T07	• Comment for TV news ID: 1377631360051863554, Date/Time: 23:38, Apr 1, 2021, RTs: 1.6k, QRTs: 3,277
T08	• Information that the governor requested that the central government declare a state of emergency ID: 1384006532048723978, Date/Time: 13:50, Apr 19, 2021, RTs: 4.9k, QRTs: 1,959
T09	• Video message from the governor related to a state of emergency ID: 1385560154079334404, Date/Time: 20:44, Apr 23, 2021, RTs: 3.1k, QRTs: 894
T10	• A video message from the governor related to the extension of a state of emergency ID: 1390648829410648065, Date/Time: 21:44, May 7, 2021, RTs: 2.4k, QRTs: 767

Then, classifications made by two or more of the authors were taken as the discriminated result for the quote retweet. If the classifications made by all three authors differed among (P), (N), or (E), the result was taken to be (E).

Figures 8, 9 and 10 show the classification results for each of the quote retweets of T01–10, T11–T20, and T21–30, respectively. In the figures, the numbers of classified quote retweets are shown in brackets. The proportion of (E) classifications is larger than that of (P) and (N) for many tweets, however the details of the tweets classified as (E) will be discussed in a future paper. In the following, we discuss the quote retweets classified as (P) and (N).

The discussion of the quote retweets for the tweets posted from Governor Yoshimura's account is as follows. Comparing tweets in 2020 (T01–T05) with those in 2021 (T06–T10), those in 2020 showed a large proportion of positive content, while those in 2021 showed a large proportion of negative content. It seems that, in Osaka Prefecture, with a state of emergency declared for the second and third times in 2021, there were more quote retweets indicating dissatisfaction with the governor's pandemic response posted in 2021 than in 2020. The tweet with the largest percentage of positive content was T02 (P: 62%), and the tweet with the largest percentage of negative content was T09 (N: 53%). Both of those tweets are about a video message from the governor related to a state of emergency. Table 4 shows the original texts and English translations of T02 and T09.

The discussion of the quote retweets for the tweets posted from Governor Koike's account is as follows. Comparing tweets in 2020 (T11–T15) with those in 2021 (T16–T20), those in 2020 showed a large proportion of positive content, while those in 2021

Table 2. Top quote-retweeted tweets for Governor Koike: T11–T20

	Contents
	Tweet ID, Date/Time, Retweets (RTs), Quote retweets (QRTs)
T11	● Information that the governor requested that the central government declare a state of emergency.
	ID: 1246787821282582528, Date/Time: 22:12, Apr 5, 2020, RTs: 1.8k, QRTs: 137
T12	● Request for people to refrain from going out due to the declaration of a state of emergency
	ID: 1247523431546884096, Date/Time: 22:55, Apr 7, 2020, RTs: 3.4k, QRTs: 250
T13	● The number of new cases
	● Information about an extension of a state of emergency
	ID: 1259826644228820992, Date/Time: 21:44, May 11, 2020, RTs: 1.1k, QRTs: 141
T14	● Information about easing the business suspension request
	ID: 1263823455436210176, Date/Time: 22:26, May 22, 2020, RTs: 0.7k, QRTs: 142
T15	● Information that the central government will discuss lifting a state of emergency
	ID: 1264540976279810049, Date/Time: 21:57, May 24, 2020, RTs: 1.4k, QRTs: 140
T16	● The number of severe cases, deaths, and new cases
	● Information that the governor requested that the Minister in charge of Economic Revitalization declare a state of emergency
	ID: 1345335212645912576, Date/Time: 20:44, Jan 2, 2021, RTs: 0.7k, QRTs: 278
T17	● The number of severe cases, deaths, and new cases
	● Video message to appeal for a reduction in the flow of people during vacation
	ID: 1385614660435537924, Date/Time: 0:20, Apr 24, 2021, RTs: 0.3k, QRTs: 168
T18	● The number of severe cases, deaths, and new cases
	ID: 1385950210627563524, Date/Time: 22:34, Apr 24, 2021, RTs: 0.4k, QRTs: 318
T19	● Encouragement of the use of paid vacation
	● The number of severe cases, deaths, and new cases
	ID: 1386301142125072384, Date/Time: 21:48, Apr 25, 2021, RTs: 0.2k, QRTs: 164
T20	● The number of severe cases, deaths, and new cases
	● Request for people to refrain from trips crossing prefectural borders
	ID: 1386668587847327748, Date/Time: 22:08, May 26, 2021, RTs: 0.2k, QRTs: 211

showed a large proportion of negative content. This trend is similar to that for Governor Yoshimura's tweets. It seems that, in the Tokyo metropolitan area, with a state of emergency declared for the second and third times in 2021, there were more quote tweets indicating dissatisfaction with the governor's pandemic response posted in 2021 than in 2020. The tweet with the largest positive content was T12 (P: 28%), which requested people to refrain from going out due to the declaration of a state of emergency. The tweet with the largest negative content was T17 (N: 58%), which contained information on the number of severe cases, deaths, and new cases. The tweet quoted a tweet with a video message requesting a reduction in the flow of people during vacation. Table 5 shows the original texts and English summaries of T12 and T17.

The discussion of the quote retweets for the tweets posted from Governor Suzuki's account is as follows. Comparing the tweets in 2020 (T21–T25) with those in 2021 (T26–T30), the differences in the time trends were not as great as those for the accounts of Governors Yoshimura and Koike. Unlike the Osaka and Tokyo regions, a state of emergency had not been declared again in Hokkaido Prefecture in the period up to July 31, 2021, and thus it seems that the percentage of negative quote retweets of tweets from Governor Suzuki's account did not increase as it did in the case of tweets from the other two governors' accounts. The tweet with the largest percentage of positive content was T26 (P: 39%), which featured criticism of the national government strategy. Although

Table 3. Top quote-retweeted tweets for Governor Suzuki: T21–T30

	Content
	Tweet ID, Date/Time, Retweets (RTs), Quote retweets (QRTs)
T21	● Opinion for a news item regarding a declaration of a state of emergency in Hokkaido
	ID: 1246962933952688128, Date/Time: 9:48, Apr 6, 2020, RTs: 3.2k, QRTs: 308
T22	● Opinion for a news item regarding a declaration of a state of emergency in Hokkaido Prefecture
	ID: 1247045561158488065, Date/Time: 15:16, Apr 6, 2020, RTs: 1.5k, QRTs: 153
T23	● Request for people to cooperate to prevent the spread of infection
	ID: 1247694817343098881, Date/Time: 10:16, Apr 8, 2020, RTs: 2.6k, QRTs: 138
T24	● Information about sending notification by e-mail when the central government extends the period of a state of emergency
	ID: 1256469795148451845, Date/Time: 15:25, May 2, 2020, RTs: 1.7k, QRTs: 139
T25	● Information about lifting a state of emergency ● Request for people to refrain from going out and making trips to Sapporo, and a request for business suspension
	ID: 1264784711122972673, Date/Time: 14:05, May 25, 2020, RTs: 4.4k, QRTs: 333
T26	● Criticism of the national government strategy
	ID: 1349711663730069506, Date/Time: 22:35, Jan 14, 2021, RTs: 1.0k, QRTs: 132
T27	● Denial of misinformation in the news
	ID: 1390995004802232323, Date/Time: 20:40, May 8, 2021, RTs: 1.1k, QRTs: 193
T28	● Message related to a declaration of a state of emergency
	ID: 1393202065136963585, Date/Time: 22:50, May 14, 2021, RTs: 0.7k, QRTs: 107
T29	● Message related to a declaration of a state of emergency
	ID: 1393558413582479360, Date/Time: 22:26, May 15, 2021, RTs: 0.4k, QRTs: 85
T30	● Request to refrain from contact with other people and going out
	ID: 1395704237573562376, Date/Time: 20:33, May 21, 2021, RTs: 0.3k, QRTs: 97

there were two tweets with almost the same percentage of negative content, which were T29 and T30 (N: 29%), of those two tweets the one which had the smallest percentage of positive content was T30. The tweet was about refraining from contact with other people and called for people to refrain from going out. Table 6 shows the original texts and English summaries of T26 and T30.

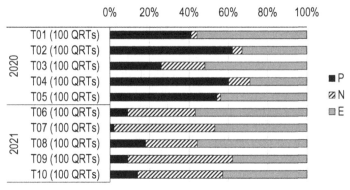

Fig. 8. Classification result of quote retweets for T01–T10 posted from the account of Governor Yoshimura

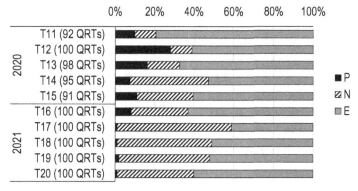

Fig. 9. Classification result of quote retweets for T11–T20 posted from the account of Governor Koike

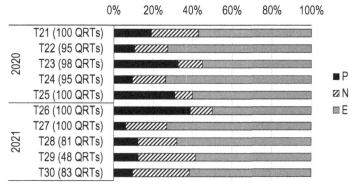

Fig. 10. Classification result of quote retweets for T21–T30 posted from the account of Governor Suzuki

Table 4. Original texts and their English translations for T02 and T09 posted from the account of Governor Yoshimura

	Original Japanese text	English translation
T02	本日、緊急事態宣言が出されました。僕から皆様への メッセージです。https://*** *(A video of the governor's message was embedded.)*	Today, a state of emergency has been declared. This is a message for you.
T09	本日、緊急事態宣言が決定されたことに関し、僕から のメッセージです。なんとかこの危機を乗り越える為、ご協 力をお願い申し上げます。 https://*** *(A video of the governor's message was embedded.)*	This is a message for you regarding the decision to declare a state of emergency today. I would like to ask for your cooperation in overcoming this crisis.

Table 5. Original texts and their English summary for T12 and T17 posted from the account of Governor Koike

	Original Japanese text	English summary
T12	本日の緊急事態宣言発令を受け、都は緊急事態措置として、都民の皆様へ『徹底的な外出自粛』を要請します。大目的は、【都民の皆様の命を守る】こと。人との接触を避けることが最大の対応策です。自分を、大切な人を守るため、皆様の行動変容がカギです。　一丸となって、この難局を乗り越えましょう https://*** *(Two images regarding requests made of citizens were embedded.)*	In response to today's declaration of a state of emergency, the metropolitan government requests all residents of Tokyo to refrain from going out. The objective is to protect the lives of the people. The best way to deal with this threat is to avoid contact with people. *The tweet also includes a message of encouragement for citizens to overcome the crisis.*
T17	≪緊急事態宣言発出決定≫　新型コロナウイルスの23日の重症者52人。検査件数3日間移動平均10091件。お亡くなりになられた5名の方のご冥福を心よりお祈り致します。新規感染者759人。7日間平均対前週比128.7%　都民、事業者の皆様にはご協力を頂いてきました。人流を抑えるため力を結集しましょう。　https://*** *(A video of a message from the governor was embedded.)*	[Decision taken to declare a state of emergency] 52 people were severely ill with COVID-19 on the 23rd. The three-day moving average for the number of tests administered was 10091. We sincerely pray for the souls of the five people who passed away. The number of newly-infected people was 759. The seven-day average of new cases was 128.7% compared to the previous week. *The tweet also includes a request to reduce the flow of people.*

Table 6. Original texts and their English summary for T26 and T30 posted from the account of Governor Suzuki

	Original Japanese text	English summary
T26	緊急事態宣言の対象地域になる、ならないで、国からお金がもらえる、もらえないと違いが出てくるのはおかしい。感染拡大の影響は全国幅広く及んでいる。感染を抑えるために全国が一丸となり、取り組んでいるなか、分断を生むような対策については、再考いただきたい。https://*** *(A news article was embedded.)*	It is not appropriate that there would be a difference in whether or not the prefecture can receive financial support from the government based on whether the prefecture is under a declared state of emergency or not.
T30	【緊急事態宣言メッセージ】市中での感染が広がり、感染経路の不明な事例も多いなど、誰もが、どこでも感染する可能性があります。人と人との接触を徹底的に抑えてください。特に週末は、外出を控えてください。道民の皆様のご協力をお願いします。https://*** *(A video of a message from the governor was embedded.)*	[Message regarding the state of emergency] The infection is spreading throughout the city. There are many cases where the route of infection is unknown. Anyone can be infected. Please reduce your contact with other people and avoid going out, especially on weekends.

4 Conclusions

This study aimed to clarify the reactions of users to tweets relating to COVID-19 states of emergency posted by three governors in Japan: Hirofumi Yoshimura, the governor of Osaka prefecture, Yuriko Koike, the governor of the Tokyo metropolitan area, and Naomichi Suzuki, the governor of Hokkaido prefecture.

We collected quote retweets for the top quote-retweeted tweets posted from each of these accounts between January 1, 2020, and July 31, 2021, and classified the quote retweets as either positive or negative. In particular, Governor Yoshimura's tweet posted during a state of emergency in Osaka prefecture in 2020 received a large proportion of positive quote retweets. However, for both Governors Yoshimura and Koike, the percentage of negative quote retweets for his or her 2021 tweets was larger than that for his or her 2020 tweets. This suggests that negative content may account for a large percentage of quote retweets when a state of emergency is declared again in the future. For Governor Suzuki, the variation in the classification of quote retweets of tweets posted in 2020 and of those posted in 2021 was not as large as for Governors Yoshimura and Koike.

Some limitations exist in this study. Firstly, for many tweets, the proportion of those classified as neither positive nor negative was larger than that of those classified as clearly positive or negative, and thus the details of the tweets classified as neither positive nor negative will be discussed in a future paper. Secondly, the number of quote retweets examined was limited. We plan to analyze a larger number of tweets using a sentiment analysis service based on natural language processing in a forthcoming paper.

It is expected that cases of COVID-19 infection will continue and that the governors' accounts will continue to post COVID-19-related information. Therefore, we will continue to collect and analyze the governors' tweets and user responses to them.

Acknowledgments. This research was supported by JSPS KAKENHI Grant Number 18K11553.

References

1. Imran, M., Castillo, C., Diaz, F., Vieweg, S.: Processing social media messages in mass emergency: a survey. ACM Comput. Surv. **47**(4), 67 (2015). https://doi.org/10.1145/2771588
2. Uchida, O., Utsu, K.: Utilization of social media at the time of disaster. IEICE Fundam. Rev. **13**, 4 (2020). https://doi.org/10.1587/essfr.13.4_301. (in Japanese)
3. Banda, J.M., et al.: A Large-Scale COVID-19 Twitter chatter dataset for open scientific research—an international collaboration. Epidemiologia 2021 **2**(3), 315–324 (2021). https://doi.org/10.3390/epidemiologia2030024
4. Xue, J., et al T.: Twitter discussions and emotions about the COVID-19 pandemic: machine learning approach. J. Med. Internet Res. **22**(11), e20550 (2020). https://doi.org/10.2196/20550
5. Yoshida, M.: The state of social media during the COVID-19 pandemic –Japan's situation, research trends and public datasets–. Trans. Jpn. Soc. Artif. Intell. **35**, 5 (2020). https://doi.org/10.11517/jjsai.35.5_644. (in Japanese)
6. Toriumi, F., Sakaki, T., Yoshida, M.: Social emotions under the spread of COVID-19 using social media. Trans. Jpn. Soc. Artif. Intell. **35**, 4 (2020). https://doi.org/10.1527/tjsai.F-K45. (in Japanese)

7. Yomoda, Y.: Concerns and stress caused by the novel coronavirus disease (COVID-19) pandemic: a quantitative text analysis of Twitter data. Jpn. J. Phys. Educ. Health Sport Sci. **65**, 757–774 (2020). https://doi.org/10.5432/jjpehss.20048. (in Japanese)
8. Yousefinaghani, S., Dara, S., Mubareka, S., Papadopoulos, A., Sharif, A.: An analysis of COVID-19 vaccine sentiments and opinions on Twitter. J. Infect. Dis **108**, 256–262 (2021). https://doi.org/10.1016/j.ijid.2021.05.059
9. Lyu, J.C., Han, E.L., Luli, G.K.: COVID-19 vaccine-related discussion on Twitter: topic modeling and sentiment analysis. J. Med. Internet Res. **23**, 6 (2021). https://doi.org/10.2196/24435
10. Haman, M.: The use of Twitter by state leaders and its impact on the public during the COVID-19 pandemic. Heliyon **6**, e05540 (2020). https://doi.org/10.1016/j.heliyon.2020
11. Rufai, S.R., Bunce, C.: World leaders' usage of Twitter in response to the COVID-19 pandemic: a content analysis. J. Public Health. **42**(3), 510–516 (2020). https://doi.org/10.1093/pubmed/fdaa049
12. Dwianto, R.A., Nurmandi, A., Salahudin, S.: The sentiments analysis of donald trump and Jokowi's Twitters on Covid-19 policy dissemination. Webology. **8**(1), 389–405 (2021). https://doi.org/10.14704/WEB/V18I1/WEB18096
13. Qodir, Z., Zahra, A.A., Nurmandi, A., Jubba, H., Hidayati, M.: The role of the leader in a pandemic: government communication to induce a positive perspective among the public concerning the COVID-19 outbreak. J. Critic. Rev. **7**(15), 27–35 (2020). https://doi.org/10.31838/jcr.07.15.05
14. Okazaki, A., Uchida, O., Utsu, K.: Analysis of Tweets related to COVID-19 posted by accounts of prefectural governors in Japan. IEICE Techn. Rep. **120**(324), LOIS2020-26, 21–26 (2021). (in Japanese)
15. NHK. https://www3.nhk.or.jp/news/special/coronavirus/
16. Twitter API v2. https://developer.twitter.com/en/docs/twitter-api/early-access

Insights from the COVID-19 Pandemic
for Systemic Risk Assessment and Management

Jose J. Gonzalez[1,3](✉) and Colin Eden[2,3]

[1] Centre for Integrated Emergency, Management (CIEM), University of Agder, Kristiansand, Norway
josejg@uia.no
[2] Strathclyde Business School, Glasgow, UK
colin.eden@strath.ac.uk
[3] Stepchange AS, Kristiansand, Norway

Abstract. The COVID-19 pandemic has activated hundreds of interdependent long-lasting risks across all sectors of society. Zoonotic diseases are on the rise, fuelled by climatic change, by encroachment and destruction of habitats, and by unsustainable practices. Risk assessment and management must be greatly improved to prevent even worse consequences than COVID-19 if the next pandemic is caused by an agent with higher infectiousness and lethality. Insights from a project on systemic pandemic risk management reveal that the interdependency of risks creates cascading effects mediated by millions of vicious cycles which must be addressed to gain control over a pandemic. We propose a method for systemic, cross-sectoral risk assessment that detects the myriad of causal influences resulting from the risks, allowing to identify and mitigate the most potent risks, i.e., those participating in the highest numbers of vicious loops.

Keywords: Systemic risk · Cascading effects · Vicious cycles · Risk system analysis · Risk mitigation

1 Introduction

1.1 Have We Learnt Enough from COVID-19 to Manage New Pandemic Waves Better?

At the time of writing this work, the COVID-19 pandemic continues to be a global problem nearly two years after the World Health Organization (WHO) activated its Incident Management Support Team to ensure coordination of activities and response across the three levels of WHO (Headquarters, Regional, Country) for public health emergencies [1]. The COVID-19 pandemic has affected many countries in a roller-coaster pattern, often with increasing heights for the 2nd, 3rd, 4th or even the 5th pandemic wave.

Norway and Denmark were among the best performers in the world, with low numbers of COVID-19 cases per million and low lethality (ratio deaths/cases). But then, the

© IFIP International Federation for Information Processing 2022
Published by Springer Nature Switzerland AG 2022
J. Sasaki et al. (Eds.): ITDRR 2021, IFIP AICT 638, pp. 121–138, 2022.
https://doi.org/10.1007/978-3-031-04170-9_9

14th December 2021, Denmark had 1193 COVID cases per million and Norway had 888, although the share of people that have been fully vaccinated in both countries is higher than 70% and the percentage of people vaccinated at least once is about 80% [2]. The graphs for both countries (Fig. 1) show that their last COVID-19 wave even surpasses the highest peaks in the UK (872 cases per million) and in the USA (756 cases per million), which both happened in January 2021.

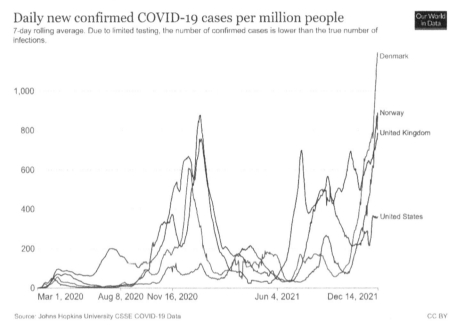

Fig. 1. COVID-19 statistics of daily cases per million people for selected countries. (c) Our World In Data https://ourworldindata.org

The fact that COVID-19 is still a major problem nearly two years after it became a global problem should cause concern. The United Nations Environment Programme alerts that diseases transmitted from animals to humans (zoonoses) are on the rise [3, p7]. Never have so many opportunities existed for pathogens to pass from wild and domestic animals to people. More than 20 new human zoonotic pathogens have been detected since 1990 and over 60% of all known infectious diseases in humans are zoonotic [4, p38].

The share of people that have been fully vaccinated in many countries in the Third World is below 10% by mid December 2021 [2]. In many cases the share is below 2%. Unsatisfactory hygienic conditions combined with high population densities in poor countries favour the evolution of aggressive virus variants that in our globalized world can cross continents in a few days. We may experience new pandemic waves with virus variants that are more contagious, that have higher mortality and that existing vaccines do not provide adequate protection against.

Risk assessment and management is crucial for disaster preparedness and response [5]. We contend that the nearly universal failure to control COVID-19 may be due to the inadequate current practices of risk assessment and management of pandemics.

The Global Assessment Report on Disaster Risk Reduction 2019 from the United Nations Office for Disaster Risk Reduction (UNDRR) is a powerful message that systemic risk assessment and management is indispensable to achieve the goals of the Sendai Framework [6]. The awareness of systemic risk is the recognition that the interactions between risks create a network, or system, of associated risks and outcomes, where the outcomes of risks are risks themselves, and where the resulting consequences can be complex. Risks are a system where a single risk can cause a plethora of other risks, and, very importantly, cause vicious cycles of risks. Vicious cycle is a short name for a chain of events that reinforce themselves through a feedback loop.

Applied to risks, vicious cycles are the mechanisms that allow small risks to grow into major problems, as in this quote from the Global Assessment Report on Disaster Risk Reduction 2019: "Systemic risks might be easy to mitigate early on. However, failure or even intentional ignorance to capture the role of underlying drivers of systemic risk will allow small risks to grow into major problems, increasing the opportunity costs of failed interventions and missed opportunities." [6, p71]. Since disasters do not follow scripts, it is unavoidable that underlying drivers of systemic risk will emerge during the response to disasters. In other words, systemic risk management is indispensable during disaster response.

The Global Assessment Report on Disaster Risk Reduction 2019 advocates stochastic risk management models. In Sect. 4.1 "The risk systemicity approach" we delineate a different approach that has been successfully applied to systemic risk assessment of large engineering projects since the 1990s. We have adopted and extended this method to pandemics.

Pandemics, and other major disasters have disruptive cross-sectorial effects. A recent call in the risk management literature, in 2016, recognises the immaturity of risk assessment with respect to complexity: *"...substantial research and development to obtain adequate modelling and analysis methods – beyond the 'traditional' ones – to 'handle' different types of systems... which are complex systems and often inter-dependent"* [7, p10].

In the context of COVID-19, Amaratunga et al. [8] contend that *"current policies that are designed to address conventional risks are unable to capture and deal with the complexity and interconnectedness of systemic risks. Hence, a policy mechanism that facilitates 'systemic risk governance' is much called for."* Solarz and Waliszewski [9] argue for understanding the holistic nature of the COVID-19 pandemic, and they suggest that *"in the long run, it will be possible to monitor the pandemic via an integrated, holistic system of systemic risk management."* However, neither Amaratunga et al. nor Solarz et al. have developed methods or policies for systemic (holistic) risk assessment and governance.

A recent article applies systemic risk and response management in the Republic of Korea. The study explored the official database of the Korea Centers for Disease Control and Prevention and then identified the disaster risks and countermeasures from the government press briefings and news media in the same period. The study proved three lessons-learned to enhance pandemic response management: 1) Respond rapidly, even when lacking information and knowledge about the new type of risk. 2) Establish a multi-sectoral response. 3) The government should prioritise transparency [10].

To the best of our knowledge, so far only one country, Norway, has performed a full evaluation of all relevant aspects of the national management of the COVID-19 pandemic. The Norwegian government appointed the 24th April 2020 an interdisciplinary committee of experts that delivered 14th April 2021 a report to this effect. The Corona Committee Report lists seventeen main findings [11]. Main finding no. 1 concludes that overall, the authorities have handled the pandemic well. (When the report was delivered, Norway had among the European countries the lowest mortality from the pandemic and was among the least affected economically). Not quite consistent with the first main finding, the second main finding criticizes the government for insufficient preparedness, even though the Norwegian Directorate for Civil Protection had evaluated a major pandemic as the most probable and most serious national crisis.

The third main finding further weakens the message of the first finding: "*In its emergency preparedness efforts, the Government has paid little attention to how risk in one sector is affected by risks in other sectors. A crisis preparedness system in which each sector evaluates its own risks and vulnerabilities, will fail if no one takes responsibility for evaluating the sum of the consequences for society at large. There is a need for a cross-sectoral system that can accommodate the interaction of risks across all sectors. This is a lesson applicable to preparedness in general.*"

Surprisingly, the Norwegian Corona Committee does not refer to the Global Assessment Report on Disaster Risk Reduction 2019 [6]. This omission makes the Corona Committee Report's less compelling and may explain why the message of the third finding has not yet triggered much interest so far among the Norwegian authorities. Also, the Norwegian Corona Committee does not recognize that systemic risk management requires more than considering the systemic aspects for preparedness. Systemic risk management is indispensable for mitigating the high number of vicious cycles that escalate the pandemic risks (cf. §4.1).

The wording "evaluating the sum of the consequences" in the third main finding of the Norwegian Corona Committee could be perceived as adding up consequences identified in one sector 1 with those identified in other sectors. But joint consideration of all relevant sectors together increases the system size, and the number of consequences does not often increase linearly as a sum, but exponentially. And so is the case for major pandemics, (cf. §4.1).

During the same period as the Norwegian Corona Committee conducted its evaluation, a Norwegian funded project on systemic pandemic risk management with international participation had started in parallel with the committee's evaluation. The project has developed a cross-sectoral system for systemic risk assessment and management that captures how the risks in the various sectors interact with each other with respect to health care. The project's methods can be adapted to disaster preparedness and response in general when complex interactions between risks are apparent, i.e., beyond pandemics [12].

A pandemic is a complex dynamic system. The risks act through vicious cycles. Vicious cycles are mostly interconnected, which drive complex, compounded effects

[12]. This is the domain of "dynamic complexity" that is resistant against interventions [14, p96–97].

To the best of our knowledge no country has designed its COVID-19 response based on systemic risk assessment and systemic risk response. Hence, the question posed as this section's heading, "Have we learnt enough from COVID-19 to manage new pandemic waves better?", must be probably answered with a 'no' with respect to potential new COVID-19 waves, and 'not yet' with respect to future major pandemics.

1.2 The Aim of This Paper and How It Is Organized

In this paper, we discuss the key characteristics that a systemic risk assessment and management method must satisfy to conduct risk and vulnerability assessments with full consideration of the systemic inter-dependencies of a major pandemic, and to develop strategies for preparedness and responses to a major pandemic like COVID-19. COVID-19 has reminded us that a major pandemic can have long duration and that it can have several waves. Further, that one must be prepared for the unexpected during response. The Global Assessment Report on Disaster Risk Reduction 2019 emphasizes that systemic risks are emergent, and not necessarily obvious … until the disaster occurs, and that unanticipated risks emerge [6, p38]. Our approach is in accord with this request: "The Sendai Framework impels a move away from an obsession with prediction and control towards an ability to embrace multiplicity, ambiguity and uncertainty." [6, p, 43].

We organise this paper as follows. In Sect. 2 "Characteristics of a major pandemic in the globalization era", we summarise key aspects that are relevant for a systemic approach. In Sect. 3 "Risks in the light of systemic interdependencies", we review how risk must be approached and defined to allow for a systemic risk assessment. In Sect. 4 "Order of magnitude of pandemic cascading effects", we first summarise our method. Thereafter we discuss the meaning of cascading effects in the context of a major pandemic and the order of magnitude of cascading effects occurring in a major pandemic such as COVID-19. In Sect. 5 "Discussion" we point to future research and developments, and we summarise our findings in the light of the Global Assessment Report on Disaster Risk Reduction 2019.

2 Characteristics of a Major Pandemic in the Globalization Era

COVID-19 is in terms of number of cases, deaths, and global impact the largest pandemic disaster since the Spanish Flu 1918–1920.

A recent publication [15] presents strong evidence that the challenges of the COVID-19 pandemic are unique, owing to the characteristics of the cascading effects, the long duration of the pandemic and the need to prioritize risk mitigation in a hierarchical manner, which altogether make the character of the COVID-19 pandemic very different from other disasters. Indeed, hierarchical prioritization must follow from attention to the relative significance of risk within the context of the whole system of risks. The authors of reference [15] also point out that is no clear distinction between the impact and response phases in the COVID-19 pandemic. Casualties continued to mount even as response activities were implemented. Indeed, the roller-coaster pattern implies that impact, response, and recovery attempts overlap. We add that these phases often do not occur simultaneously, even in neighbouring countries.

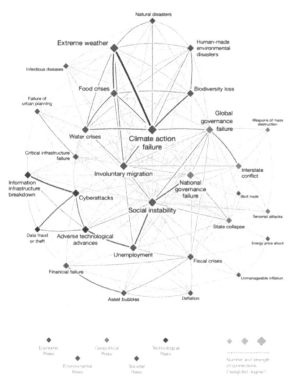

Fig. 2. The Global Risks Interconnections map. The Global Risks Report 2020 (c) World Economic Forum

Infectious diseases are the origin of pandemics, and the occurrence and propagation of pandemics find numerous direct and indirect channels for exponential propagation.

Figure 2 illustrates one view of the global interconnections, which bundle numerous cause-effect influences coupling environmental, societal, geopolitical, technological, and economic risks. These influences are the origin of the increase in zoonoses, and with that the risk of major pandemics. The drivers of zoonoses are unsustainable patterns of consumption and production causing climate change, habitat loss and fragmentation, loss of biodiversity, pollution, and poor waste management [4, p38]. But then the characteristics of COVID-19, and arguably of major pandemics to come, are consequences of the interconnections and interdependencies in the era of globalization. The large number of cascading effects, particularly of vicious cycles that drive exponentiation; the long duration of the pandemic; the emergence of new and more aggressive virus variants in part responsible for new waves with even higher case incidence: they all relate to the flood of interdependent risks enabled by the interconnections.

Numerous factors outside of the health system impacted on the management of the COVID-19 pandemic, e.g., infodemics, mass gatherings, travels, logistics and even criminal behaviour, …, and vice versa: the pandemic itself impacted on numerous outside factors which had causative effects on the pandemic.

Vicious cycles must be detected, understood, and responded to with measures that are anchored in proper understanding of the systemic interdependencies and the resulting dynamic complexity [14]. Quoting Senge [16], dynamic complexity is characterised by *"…cause and effect are subtle…the effects over time of interventions are not obvious. Conventional forecasting, planning and analysis methods are not equipped to deal with dynamic complexity."*

The next section discusses the concept of risk in the context of systemic interdependencies.

3   Risks in the Light of Systemic Interdependencies

3.1   Adequate Risk Definition in the Presence of Dynamic Complexity

Risk is typically understood as an adverse circumstance and the chance (probability) of its occurrence. The Oxford English Dictionary defines risk as *"(Exposure) to the possibility of loss, injury, or other adverse or unwelcome circumstance; a chance of something bad happening."* [17] The Oxford Dictionary of Economics defines risk as *"A form of uncertainty where, while the actual outcome of an action is not known, probabilities can be assigned to each of the possible outcomes."* [18] The Dictionary of the Social Sciences defines risk as *"Generally, the chances of malign events or uncertainty of outcome. Risk may or may not be quantifiable in terms of specific likelihoods of outcomes, but its most common use implies that the underlying probabilities of various outcomes are known. These probabilities may either be objectively specified, as in the case of a lottery, or may reflect an individual's private subjective beliefs."* [19].

In practice, risk occurs in systems, and systems can be complex. There is general awareness that complexity makes it difficult to model a system and predict its behaviour, i.e., to compute probabilities for risk assessment [20–25]. There is less awareness that there are different kinds of complexity, and that the complexity type has crucial importance for risk assessment and management.

A recent work [25] examines complexity and discusses its relation to risk. The authors consider as the key issue how risk can be assessed based on the knowledge of the system elements and the assumptions about these elements. Their approach is still anchored in the classical triplet definition of risk in terms of events/scenarios (s), probabilities (p) and consequences (c), i.e. (s, p, c) [26]. The perspective of the authors of reference [25] on complexity is of the knowledge at the system level being poor, even if one has strong knowledge at the sub-system level. In other words, it is not possible to model the system behaviour in this way of thinking about risk. They argue accordingly that the risk assessment has strong limitations, hampering risk management.

The perspective in reference [25] is from complex engineering systems. But most engineering *systems* do not have dynamic complexity that is resistant to interventions. Exceptions are large engineering *projects*, which do exhibit dynamic complexity characterized by numerous interdependencies and dynamics across sectors and disciplines. As consequence, disruptions of large engineering projects (considerable delays and cost overruns) are ubiquitous [27–29].

The complexity of the engineering systems as analysed in reference [25] is *numerosity*, i.e., large number of components and activities. In other words, they exhibit "detail complexity" rather than "dynamic complexity". Pandemics (and many other disaster types), but also large engineering projects, have more than just a high number of parts. They are characterised by a high number of interdependencies that are dynamic, i.e., change over time, and that to a large degree cannot be described by known relations (by laws of Nature or using correlations). Interdependencies in both large engineering projects and pandemics are often non-linear and act with significant time delays [13, 14].

3.2 Quantitative Analysis of Qualitative Models of Systemic Risk

The dynamic complexity of major pandemics implies that assessing most present risks in terms of probabilities is a futile task. A major pandemic triggers many time-dependent risks (adverse circumstances) within and across societal sectors. The risks are interdependent, i.e., the dynamics of any risk influences the dynamics of other risks. In our Systemic Pandemic Risk Management project experts identified in round numbers 220 hundred risks across society. The interdependencies between risks count in round numbers 600 or more. Most of such influences defy quantitative description, owing to insufficient knowledge.

Consider ascertaining the probability of new virus variant to occur, its infectiousness and its lethality (which likely would be time dependent as well). The behaviour over time of direct and indirect pandemic risks is strongly influenced by the agent's infectiousness and its consequences in terms of case incidence and death case rate.

Consider the quantitative risk assessment of infodemic and the impact of different messages in social media; the invention of conspiracy theories that would influence citizens' behaviours (trust in the authorities; disruptive activities; propensity of vaccination, etc.).

Even if it was possible to obtain the required insights, it would not happen in near real time. Near real time insight would be indispensable to achieve an agile response to the pandemic, based on fast update and analysis of the risk model.

A reasonably complete model of a pandemic for mitigation would be impossible to design and simulate in near real time, because of its sheer size and complexity, with its difficulties compounded by the need to act agile against a problem with new and emergent features.

In contrast, qualitative descriptions, based on experience and general observation, are possible. Models can be constructed that reflect the experience and wisdom of those who have sought to manage at least parts of the system. Bringing together these views begins to develop a holistic view.

The behaviour over time of direct and indirect pandemic risks is strongly influenced by the agent's infectiousness and its consequences in terms of case incidence and death case rate. Infectious agents evolve over time. We do know that in many cases it is beneficial for an infectious agent to become less virulent. It can then spread without causing too much damage to the host, thus increasing the probability of being transmitted. But it has happened before, the most famous case shaping the second wave of the Spanish Flu 1918–1920, that the infectious agent evolved to much higher infectiousness and lethality [30]. This evolution of the Spanish Flu virus has been explained by practices in the Western front of World War I, where individuals immobilized by illness were transported repeatedly from one cluster of susceptible hosts to another, in trenches, tents, hospitals, and trains. Such practices aided more virulent variants to infect and kill people without paying the price of reduced transmission [31].

For COVID-19 it has been argued that different social practices in Sweden and Norway may explain the significant difference of case mortality between these otherwise similar neighbour countries. When reference [32] was published 19th November 2020, Sweden, which had not enacted strict containment measures, had more than three times as many deaths per 100 cases as Norway. At the time of writing this article, Sweden, which in the meantime had enacted stricter containment rules, has a case fatality ratio of 1,22%, still more than three times as many deaths per 100 cases as Norway, whose case fatality ratio is 0,36% (source: Johns Hopkins Coronavirus Center https://coronavirus. jhu.edu/map.html, retrieved 14th December 2021).

Traditional risks assessment methods cannot cope with interdependent risks and the dynamic complexity of a pandemic. Most pandemic risks cannot be computed. Instead, risk must be considered as "a phenomenon that has the potential to deliver substantial harm, whether or not the probability of this harm eventuating is estimable" [33, p10], or whether the behaviour over time of this harm can be computed or estimated from its causes (which are mostly other risks).

Because of the different meanings that may be given to the nature of causation – intensity, strength, probability etc. – the judgments about the causal relations will always be disputed. However, an overriding consideration is the practical constraints on providing sensible quantification of so many risks and their relationships.

The method discussed in the next section has quantitative flavour added to qualitatively representing risks in maps that include vast numbers of causal loops. By identifying, through an analysis of the structure of the risk system, the most potent risks and the most potent causal relations, and ranging them hierarchically according to degree of potency, portfolios of strategies can be designed to mitigate those potent risks and causal influences.

Ultimately risk mitigation depends on the judgments of policymakers, and the role of modelling is to assist the policymakers about the validity of the risk system and analysis of it, thus enabling them to improve their decision making.

4   Order of Magnitude of Pandemic Cascading Effects

4.1   The Risk Systemicity Approach

The fundament and point of departure of our project on systemic pandemic risk management are methods developed through decades of research on strategic management and systemic risk assessment and mitigation for engineering projects. Among the numerous references we mention [12, 34, 35]. Recently, the risk systemicity approach was extended to societal resilience [36]. The research on strategic management and systemic risk assessment and mitigation employed tools known as Group Explorer and Decision Explorer [37] that have recently inspired the internet-based tool *strategyfinder*™.

A recent paper [12] has extensively described the risk systemicity approach for pandemics and the results obtained using *strategyfinder* in risk workshops with carefully selected experts on health care risks and in the various sectors that interact with each other with respect to health care.

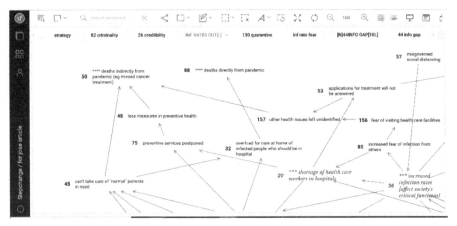

Fig. 3. An enlarged screenshot of the canvas of *strategyfinder*™ depicting a view of the pandemic model developed for the Systemic Pandemic Risk Management project. See the main text for details

Therefore, in this paper it should suffice to summarize the key features of the risk systemicity approach.

The risk systemicity approach uses a special collaborative software to elicit and collect wisdom, experience, and knowledge from a carefully selected interdisciplinary expert team in a structured way. This software – *strategyfinder*™ – allows the experts to 'meet' via the internet and work on a causal map of the interconnected risks. A facilitator works with the group to help ensure that the different individual perspectives are structured to reveal significant causal chains of argument that allow for further reflection, extension, and debate amongst group members.

Each participant (expert) is able to add material to the map in a manner that means as changes and additions are made to the map all participants can see these changes. The participants add links representing causal influences, which often lead to discovering feedback loops (vicious and virtuous cycles, and balancing/controlling feedback loops).

Figure 3 shows part of a view of the pandemic risk model. Views are created by a facilitator who also has the rights to export the risks from the complete map of interconnected risks (which, of course, are found in a view itself) to the selected view. Views showing model sections depict selected scenarios of the complete model. The view shown on focuses on risks influencing risk #88 "deaths directly from pandemic" and risk #50 "deaths indirectly from pandemic (e.g. missed cancer treatment)". Risks are numbered automatically by *strategyfinder* as they appear on the canvas. The numbers are otherwise unimportant (i.e., unrelated to the relevance of the risk). Arrows express cause-effects.

E.g., risk #45 "can't take care of 'normal' patients in need" affects (increases) the risk #50 "deaths indirectly from pandemic (e.g. missed cancer treatment)".

The view shown on Fig. 3 was developed by the facilitator after the workshop with experts. The facilitator added information (such as asterisks and colours) that is relevant for workshops to occur later (such as quality assurance of the model, development of mitigating strategies).

The system of risks presented in a causal map format then allows participants to i) explore and validate a map of the system of risks, and ii) develop impactful strategies that are also practical. The *strategyfinder* software has powerful tools for analysing the risk map, to detect feedback loops, in particular the most potent feedback loops and find the most central parts of the risk system, to rate strategies and explore the different views of group members about impact and practicality, and so guide the participants during this strategy development process towards realistic actions and goals.

The extension and adaptation of the risk systemicity approach to pandemics meets new challenges related to the large number of risks and the richness of interdependencies among the risks. Our pandemic risk model obtained in the workshops with experts has, in round numbers, 220 risks factors, with interconnections in the order of 600, yielding in round numbers 5 million of interconnected vicious cycles, most of them highly interconnected with other vicious cycles. So many vicious cycles in the model can be seen as characterizing the nature of a pandemic and the difficulties in managing one. It follows that the management of such a complex challenge cannot be met with conventional strategies addressing isolated risks, even if the strategy targets ten, twenty or even thirty identified risks. Using the *strategyfinder* analysis tools it is possible to find those risks that if mitigated would be likely to have the biggest impact in terms of reducing the long-term impact of infections and both indirect and direct deaths. It is these risks that become the focus of strategy development. To ensure best strategy coverage, portfolios of effective and practical strategies targeting multiple risk factors in highly compounded vicious risks networks are developed.

4.2 Cascading Effects as Vicious Cycles

The previous considerations have implications for the concept of cascading effects in major pandemics (and probably in other major disasters). The term "cascading effects" (sometimes expressed as "cascade effects") appears frequently in the disaster literature, but it is also often used in other domains (ecology, finances, forensics, history, medicine, and some others). Curiously, the term "cascading effects" is rarely precisely defined. It is taken for granted in much of the literature. Even in reference works such as Oxford Dictionary of Ecology (*Cascade effect: A sequence of events in which each produces the circumstances necessary for the initiation of the next*) [38] or the Handbook of Transitions to Energy and Climate Security (*"cascading disasters" or "cascading consequences" where multiple disasters happen either simultaneously or in close proximity to one other*) [39] the definitions lack a metric for cascading effects.

Taking the concept of cascading effect for granted, the literature tends to (sometimes) illustrate the concept with sentences like e.g., *"cascading effects, which tend to create extreme events: the overload of one component of the system challenges other components, which therefore causes a propagation of problems through the system. ...*

They tend to occur when the interdependencies in the system exceed a critical strength" [40], and then proceed to model and compute the impacts of the tacitly defined cascading effects in terms of proxies such as the level of criticality of crowd density [40], the spread of impacts [41], or the fraction of the functional entities [42].

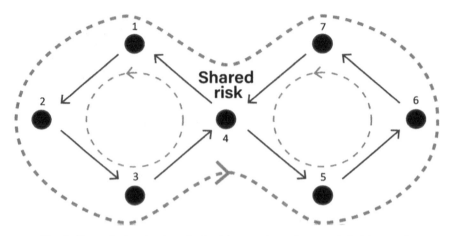

Fig. 4. Example showing two single vicious cycles and one nested vicious cycle

Consider the example shown on Fig. 4. It shows seven risks labelled 1...7, forming two single vicious loops and one nested vicious loop where risk 4 is passed through twice. Each causal link (arrow) can cause a cascading effect if activated. For example, if risk 1, say "insufficient PPE to protect health staff attending infectious patients", is active then it influences risk 2 (say, "increase of health staff infected in hospitals"). The vicious cycle on the l.h.s. of the figure could have these two additional risks "3: "diminishing the availability of health care staff" and "4: higher number of infected people in the general populations", which – owing to the increased need of health care for a higher number of infected persons – would exacerbate risk 1. Each risk increases the next risk in the vicious cycle and the negative consequences get reinforced. In this example all the cascading effects occur within the same sector (the health care sector). One has inner-sector cascading effects. But if one risk or more risks would relate to a difference sector one would have inter-sector cascading effects. Indeed, in many instances the l.h.s. may be a vicious cycle in one sector and the r.h.s. in another, and through risk 4 they interact to create the nested inter-sector vicious cycle.

The usual definitions of cascading effects tend to only mention the influence from one effect (risk) to another effect (*"the overload of one component of the system challenges other components"* [40]). But the real issue is the chain of effects going round and round in the vicious cycle. It is the reinforcing of the negative consequences that creates systemic disruption and exponentiation.

Now consider again Fig. 4. Does the nested vicious cycle $1 \to 2 \to 3 \to 4 \to 5 \to 6 \to 7 \to 4 \to 1$ have additional impact beyond the impacts caused by the single vicious cycles $4 \to 1 \to 2 \to 3 \to 4$ and $4 \to 5 \to 6 \to 7 \to 4$?

Indeed it does, and nested vicious cycles must therefore be counted in addition to the single vicious cycles to fully estimate the impacts of cascading effects and to find the most potent risks and potent causality.

Think of risk 3 as flood of misleading information (risk occurring in the information and telecommunication sector), risk 4 as diminishing trust in politicians (risk occurring in the government sector), risk 5 as decreasing citizen willingness to be vaccinated, and risk 7 as increasing infections in the population, ultimately increasing risk 4 (diminishing trust to politicians), etc. This shows that compounded inter-sector cascading effects between the three mentioned sectors requires adding up the individual cascading effects traversing the nested vicious loop $1 \rightarrow 2 \rightarrow 3 \rightarrow 4 \rightarrow 5 \rightarrow 6 \rightarrow 7 \rightarrow 4 \rightarrow 1$.

As mentioned in §4.1 the systemic pandemic risk model obtained in the workshops with experts has, in round numbers, 220 risks factors, yielding over 5 million of vicious cycles, most of them highly nested. The *strategyfinder* software counts the vicious cycles using the algorithm of reference [43]. Since the huge number of vicious cycles is likely to challenge the reader's intuition, we provide a mathematical expression to count the number of vicious cycles, single and nested in a "n-leaves-clover". (Fig. 4 displays a 2-leaves-clover of vicious cycles.) We choose the "n-leaves-clover" example because the number of vicious cycles in it can be easily found using the binomial theorem. The total number of vicious cycles in a n-leaves-clover model is $\binom{n}{0} + \binom{n}{1} + \binom{n}{2} + \ldots \binom{n}{n-1} + \binom{n}{n} - 1 = 2^n - 1$, of which n are single and $2^n - n - 1$ are nested.

Thus, one gets an exponential increase in vicious cycles depending on the number of leaves (single vicious cycles). If there are, say, 20, vicious cycles sharing one common element both the total number of vicious cycles and the total number of nested vicious cycles surpasses one million.

In our pandemic risk systemicity model there are many vicious cycles sharing one common risk, and also quite many vicious cycles sharing two or even more common risks. Thus, while possibly surprising and counterintuitive, we can trust the algorithms that count more than 5 million vicious cycles, most of them highly nested, in our risk systemicity model.

With such huge number of vicious cycles driving the dynamics of the pandemics one suspects it is the joint contribution of many vicious cycles that account for the complex dynamics of a pandemic.

Here is it where the quantitative analysis of the risk system as a directed graph enters. A risk having many incoming causal arrows is exposed to potential cascading effects from many different risks (each incoming causal arrow having the potential to cause a cascading effect in the receiving risk). Many outgoing causal arrows may imply that the risk in question has many paths to effectuate cascading effects (each outgoing causal arrow being a potential source to pass a cascading affect).

The most potent risks are those that if mitigated will have the most significant impact on the risk system. Satisfactory mitigation implies the risk can be deleted from the risk system and so the structure of the risk system changes. When the risk system contains nested vicious cycles then the most potent risk will be that which if mitigated (deleted) minimizes the number of remaining vicious cycles. Thus, the most potent risk is that which creates a significant cascading effect (where a cascade implies escalating risks through vicious cycles).

Shortage of Health Care Workers in Hospitals

Agreed Strategies, their Purpose, and Implementation Teams

Establish high-level infection protection (PPE) for healthcare and emergency workers
In order to:
Directly avoid shortage of Health Care Workers in Hospitals, and
Control local outbreaks in hospitals, and so avoid having exhausted health care workers and so reduce possibility of low productivity of working health care staff because o shortage of staff
Implementation Team: Chief physician at short-term nursing home, Hospital contingency planner

Priority of vaccination for health care workers
In order to:
Directly avoid shortage of Health Care Workers in Hospitals, and
Avoid local outbreaks of virus in nursing homes, and in hospitals
Avoid delays in ordinary medical education
Implementation Team: Crisis manager Kristiansand Municipality, Physician specialist in public health

Limit visits and staff exchange
In order to:
Avoid local outbreaks of virus in nursing homes, and in hospitals
Implementation Team: Chief physician at short-term nursing home, Crisis manager Kristiansand Municipality

Not allow student health care workers to be in different locations
In order to:
Avoid local outbreaks of virus in nursing homes, and so
Avoid care home residents being hospitalized and shortage of care home staff
Implementation Team: University of Agder, Faculty for health and sport sciences

Effective communication and cooperation between hospital and municipality
In order to:
Avoid local outbreaks of virus in nursing homes, and so
Avoid care home residents being hospitalized and shortage of care home staff
Implementation Team: Physician specialist in public health

Avoid transportation by bus for health care workers
In order to:
Avoid local outbreaks of virus in nursing homes, and so
Avoid care home residents being hospitalized and shortage of care home staff
Implementation Team: Crisis manager Kristiansand Municipality

Arrange core hospital staff in cohorts

Fig. 5. Portfolios of strategies address each key risk scenario to provide enough points of attack in case that some of the strategies fail to achieve desired effect. The picture shows such portfolios for the key risk "shortage of health care workers in hospital".

Such quantitative analysis of a qualitative risk system can be used to devise portfolios of strategies to mitigate the pandemics. As described in [12] the analysis for the strategy development workshops involves three steps:

i.   find all the vicious cycles,
ii. find the risks that appear in the most vicious cycles, and
iii. find which causal links, if deleted, would reduce the maximum number of vicious cycles.

Finding the most potent risks and most potent causal links between risks then means that strategies are developed i) to mitigate the most potent risk, and ii) to break the most potent link. This requires a portfolio of strategies, on the basis that some will fail. When either or both mitigation strategies have been developed then these risks or causal links are 'deleted' from the risks system and the next most potent risks and causal links found, and the strategy development process continued.

To this effect, the facilitator/analyst uses the sequence of maps developed by the group to compose a document on the agreed portfolio of strategies (Fig. 5 shows the first page of the document). For each portfolio, the rationale of the strategy is explained in terms of its causal implications.

5 Discussion

"The pandemic has reminded us, in the starkest way possible, of the price we pay for weaknesses in health systems, social protection and public services." [4, p38].

Whereas the risk systemicity approach has been successfully been applied in practice within industrial settings, the project on systemic pandemic risks management is at the stage of proof of concept. The challenge is its adoption in hospitals, major organisations, and government agencies for civil protection and disaster assistance. The adoption depends on the perception that risk systemicity is needed, but also in tight collaboration between scientists and practitioners. The approach must be used on a multi-organisational basis to ensure multi-disciplinary/trans-disciplinary expertise and policy-makers.

For pandemics and major disasters, the risk systemicity approach is still at the stage of an invention. The distance from invention to innovation (wide adoption in practice) can be large, and achieving the innovation stage often takes much time [44].

To facilitate the adoption of the risk systemicity approach our project on systemic pandemic risk management is developing support for automated risk scenario identification, automated analysis of impacts for prioritizing and generation of policy options writing scenarios.

The use of computer software is critical. As shown, risk systems related to pandemics and disasters are likely to have millions of vicious cycles, and these need to be identified. Although *strategyfinder* has appropriate algorithms for their identification, and for many other useful analyses of complex networks, the computational effort means that it is not currently possible to undertake these analyses quickly (within a few seconds) when used through internet browsers. A facilitator needs to be able to undertake analyses in real-time when working with a group of policy makers. The analysis for potency needs be possible as the group work on possible strategies – 'what happens if' analyses need to be reported to the group 'instantly'. Analyses such as 'closeness', 'betweenness' and 'connectedness' are also important contributors to the process of understanding the nature of a risk system. These analyses are available in current versions of *strategyfinder* but need to be embedded in appropriate facilitation processes of the sort that are being developed and tested.

The UN Secretary-General stated April 2, 2020 *"We simply cannot return to where we were before COVID-19 struck, with societies unnecessarily vulnerable to crisis. We need to build a better world."* [45].

The UNDRR's Global Assessment Report on Disaster Risk Reduction 2019 [6] recognizes that systemic risk assessment and management of disasters is a *sine qua non*. However, the report advocates stochastic risk management models, ignoring other approaches. The sheer number of the emergent risks that must be addressed in near real time for proper response to a major pandemic do exclude stochastic models of pandemic risks from practical consideration for pandemic response, at least for the time being. In contrast, our risk systemicity approach can be used in near real time by capturing the wisdom of appropriately selected interdisciplinary teams. Such teams can be reconfigured to accommodate for expertise to capture emerging risks. Risks are phenomena that have the potential to deliver substantial harm, whether or not the probability of this harm eventuating is estimable. Since the risks participate in vicious cycles, the risks will be reinforced and ultimately cause harm. Hence, our approach targets the most potent risks and the most potent causal links – those that if mitigated will have the most significant impact on the risk system.

Systemic risks are ubiquitous in humankind's Grand Challenges. Quoting again UNDRR's "Global Assessment Report on Disaster Risk Reduction 2019": *"the systemic risks … are embedded in the complex networks of an increasingly interconnected world. The behaviour of these networks defines quality of life and will shape the dynamic interactions among the Sendai Framework, the 2030 Agenda, the Paris Agreement, New Urban Agenda and the Agenda for Humanity. Ultimately, the behaviour of these networks determines exposure and vulnerability at all scales."*

For the need to improve approaches toward systemic risks and dynamic (systemic) complexity watch the TEDx talk "Can technology help against technology?" [46].

Acknowledgements. We thank the Research Council of Norway for funding the innovation project "Systemic Pandemic Risk Management", grant #315444.

References

1. Listings of WHO's response to COVID-19. https://www.who.int/news/item/29-06-2020-cov idtimeline. Accessed 15 Dec 2021
2. Coronavirus (Covid-19) Vaccination. https://ourworldindata.org/covid-vaccinations. Accessed 15 Dec 2021
3. United Nations Environment Programme, Preventing the Next Pandemic: Zoonotic diseases and how to break the chain of transmission. Nairobi, Kenya (2020)
4. United Nations, A UN framework for the immediate socio-economic response to COVID-19 (2020)
5. Etkin, D.: Disaster Theory: An Interdisciplinary Approach to Concepts and Causes. Elsevier Science Publishers, Amsterdam (2016)
6. United Nations Office for Disaster Risk Reduction (UNDRR), Global assessment report on disaster risk reduction 2019. https://www.undrr.org/publication/global-assessment-report-dis aster-risk-reduction-2019#:~:text=The%202019%20Global%20Assessment%20Report% 20on%20Disaster%20Risk,the%20state%20of%20the%20global%20disaster%20risk%20l andscape. Accessed 21 Sept 2021
7. Aven, T.: Risk assessment and risk management: review of recent advances on their foundation. Eur. J. Oper. Res. **253**, 1–13 (2016)
8. Amaratunga, D., et al.: Disaster risk governance and systemic risks: policy challenges associated with the COVID19 Pandemic Governance. In: Senaratne, R., Amaratunga, D. (eds.) National Conference on Covid-19: Impact, Mitigation, Strategies and Building Resilience (BMICH), Colombo, Sri Lanka (2021)

9. Solarz, J.K., Waliszewski, K.: Holistic framework for COVID-19 pandemic as systemic risk. Eur. Res. Stud. J. **XXIII**(Special Issue 2), 340–351 (2020)
10. Kim, Y., Poncelet, J., Min, G., Lee, J., Yang, Y.: COVID-19: systemic risk and response management in the Republic of Korea. Prog. Disaster Sci. **12**, 100200 (2021)
11. The Corona Commision Report, The authorities' handling of the COVID-19 pandemic (2020). https://www.regjeringen.no/contentassets/5d388acc92064389b2a4e1a449c5865e/no/sved/01kap02engelsk.pdf
12. Gonzalez, J.J., et al.: Elicitation, analysis and mitigation of systemic pandemic risks. In: Adrot, A., Grace, R., Moore, K., Zobel, C. (eds.) Proceedings of the 18th ISCRAM Conference – Blacksburg, VA, USA, May 2021
13. Ackermann, F., Eden, C., Williams, T., Howick, S.: Systemic risk assessment: a case study. J. Oper. Res. Soc. **58**(1), 39–51 (2007)
14. Grösser, S.N.: Complexity management and system dynamics thinking. In: Grösser, S.N., Reyes-Lecuona, A., Granholm, G. (eds.) Dynamics of long-life assets, pp. 69–92. Springer, Cham (2017). https://doi.org/10.1007/978-3-319-45438-2_5
15. Peleg, K., Bodas, M., Hertelendy, A.J., Kirsch, T.D.: The COVID-19 pandemic challenge to the all-hazards approach for disaster planning. Int. J. Disaster Risk Reduct. **55**, 102103 (2021)
16. Senge, P.: The Fifth Discipline: The Art and Practice of the Learning Organization. Century Business, London (1992)
17. The Oxford English Dictionary Britannica Academic. Accessed 15th June 2021
18. Dictionary of Economics, 4th edn. Reference Rev. 27(3), 14–15 (2013)
19. Calhoun, C. (ed.): Dictionary of the Social Sciences. Oxford University Press, Oxford (2002)
20. Bar-Yam, Y.: Dynamics of Complex Systems. Addison-Wesley, Boston (1997)
21. Mitchell, M.: Complexity: A Guided Tour. Oxford University Press, Oxford (2009)
22. Vatn, J.: Can we understand complex systems in terms of risk analysis? Proc. Inst. Mech. Eng. Part O: J. Risk Reliab. **226**, 346–58 (2012)
23. Johansen, I.L., Rausand, M.: Defining complexity for risk assessment of sociotechnical systems: a conceptual framework. Proc. Inst. Mech. Eng. Part O: J. Risk Reliab. **228**, 272–290 (2014)
24. Bjerga, T., Aven, T., Zio, E.: Uncertainty treatment in risk analysis of complex systems: the case of STAMP and FRAM. Reliab. Eng. Syst. Saf. **156**, 203–209 (2016)
25. Jensen, A., Aven, T.: A new definition of complexity in a risk analysis setting. Reliab. Eng. Syst. Saf. **171**, 169–173 (2018)
26. Kaplan, S., Garrick, B.J.: On the quantitative definition of risk. Risk Anal. **1**, 11–27 (1981)
27. Eden, C., Ackermann, F., Williams, T.: The amoebic growth of project costs. Proj. Manag. J. **36**(1), 15–27 (2005)
28. Lyneis, J.M., Ford, D.N.: System dynamics applied to project management: a survey, assessment, and directions for future research. Syst. Dyn. Rev. **23**, 157–189 (2007)
29. Howick, S., Ackermann, F., Eden, C., Williams, T.: Delay and disruption in complex projects. In: Dangerfield, B. (ed.) System Dynamics. ECSSS, pp. 315–339. Springer, New York (2020). https://doi.org/10.1007/978-1-4939-8790-0_118
30. Spinney, L.: Pale Rider: The Spanish Flu of 1918 and how it Changed the World. Jonathan Cape, London (2017)
31. Ewald, P.W.: Evolution of virulence, environmental change, and the threat posed by emerging and chronic diseases. Ecol. Res. **26**(6), 1017–1026 (2011). https://doi.org/10.1007/s11284-011-0874-8
32. Spinney, L.: Coronavirus is evolving. Whether it gets deadlier or not may depend on us, in The Guardian. London, UK (2020). https://www.theguardian.com/commentisfree/2020/nov/19/coronavirus-evolving-deadlier-evidence-social-distancing-covid-19. Accessed 14 June 2021
33. Lupton, D.: Risk, 2nd edn. Routledge, London (2013)

34. Williams, T.M., Ackermann, F., Eden, C.: Project risk: systemicity, cause mapping and scenario approach. In: Kahkonen, K., Artto, K.A. (eds.) Managing Risks in Projects, pp. 343–352. E&FN Spon, London (1997)

35. Ackermann, F., Howick, S., Quigley, J., Walls, L., Houghton, T.: Systemic risk elicitation: using causal maps to engage stakeholders and build a comprehensive view of risks. Eur. J. Oper. Res. **238**(1), 290–299 (2014)

36. Pyrko, I., Eden, C., Howick, S.: Knowledge acquisition using group support systems. Group Decis. Negot. **28**(2), 233–253 (2019). https://doi.org/10.1007/s10726-019-09614-9

37. Eden, C., Ackermann, F.: Making Strategy: The Journey of Strategic Management. Sage Publications Ltd, London (1998)

38. Allaby, M.: Oxford Reference - A Dictionary of Ecology, 5th edn. Oxford University Press, Oxford (2015)

39. Femia, F., Werrell, C.: The climate and security imperative. In: Looney, R.E. (ed.) Handbook of Transitions to Energy and Climate Security, pp. 41–57. Routledge, London (2016)

40. Helbing, D., Mukerji, P.: Crowd disasters as systemic failures: analysis of the Love Parade disaster. EPJ Data Sci. **1**(1), 1–40 (2012). https://doi.org/10.1140/epjds7

41. Rehak, D., Senovsky, P., Hromada, M., Lovecek, T., Novotny, P.: Cascading impact assessment in a critical infrastructure system. Int. J. Crit. Infrastruct. Prot. **22**, 125–138 (2018)

42. Wang, W., et al.: An approach for cascading effects within critical infrastructure systems. Physica A **510**, 164–177 (2018)

43. Johnson, D.B.: Finding all the elementary circuits of a directed graph. SIAM J. Comput. **4**, 77–84 (1975)

44. Ridley, M.: How innovation works. London: 4th Estate, London, UK (2020)

45. Guterres, A.: Recovery from the coronavirus crisis must lead to a better world (2020). https://www.un.org/sg/en/content/sg/articles/2020-04-02/recovery-the-coronavirus-crisis-must-lead-better-world. Accessed 14 Dec 2021

46. Gonzalez, J.J.: Can technology help against technology? TEDx Talk, 5th November 2021. https://youtu.be/aIqqj5VcCXM

IT Use for Risk and Disaster Management

Leveraging Geospatial Technology in Disaster Management

Manoj Rajan[✉] and S. Emily Prabha

Karnataka State Natural Disaster Monitoring Centre (KSNDMC), Government of Karnataka, Bengaluru, Karnataka 560064, India
manoarya@gmail.com

Abstract. The increased frequency of disasters has become a peril to human habitation across the globe, and leveraging Geospatial technology for effective disaster risk reduction and management for all phases of disaster management is the way forward. Geospatial technologies have to be leveraged to facilitate disaster management by producing models for visualisation of the effect of the disaster, efficient methods to mitigate and effectively deploy teams to undertake rescue, reconstruction and rehabilitation. Karnataka State has been actively involved in Disaster Risk Reduction (DRR) through the inclusive cooperation of all stakeholders. The paper describes Leveraging Geospatial Technology Innovations in Disaster Management, the conceptual geospatial database design envisaged, and the decision support tools developed for emergency management. The State has developed Karnataka State Disaster Management Information System (KSDMIS), a Geospatial Web Application for Collecting Data on Disaster Events. KSDMIS is a state-of-the-art technological disaster management technology with real-time infrastructure to collect & store data, analyse, communicate and auto-generate event-based Reports or Memorandum. The State has also developed the "Geospatial Enabled District Disaster Management Plan (GEDDMP)" System. GEDDMP system is a technology-driven solution designed and developed to create a Geospatial foundation by structuring information and generating plans for disaster management.

Keywords: Disaster management · Geospatial technology · KSDMIS · GEDDMP · Disaster risk reduction

1 Introduction

1.1 Disaster Scenario

Karnataka has been experiencing various natural disasters, both hydro-meteorological and geological, every year. The devastating weather phenomena have led to successive Drought, Flood, Hailstorms, Lightning, Strong surface winds and intense vertical wind shear, causing massive loss of life and property in the State. 80% of the Geographical area in the State has been frequently affected by Drought, and nearly 22% of the Geographical

J. Sasaki et al. (Eds.): ITDRR 2021, IFIP AICT 638, pp. 141–159, 2022.
https://doi.org/10.1007/978-3-031-04170-9_10

area is prone to moderate earthquakes. The State has 24% of its Geographical area prone to cyclones and heavy winds; landslides affect the areas with more than 30% slopes. The coastline of 359 km in the State is prone to sea-erosion and Tsunami; Hailstorms almost every year cause damage to crops, human lives and livestock.

Natural disasters have been causing massive loss of life and property in various parts of the country in recent decades. Having a vast geographical area and hosting a vast population, effective management of disasters is a humongous task. Lack of coordination and speedy address of rescue operations, mostly manually driven, is one of the major causes of human lives lost. Though we cannot prevent natural disasters, they could be managed effectively through proper planning.

1.2 Geospatial Technology

Geospatial technology has the exceptional ability to collect, store, analyse, and distribute information. All phases of Disaster management depend on data from a variety of sources. Relevant data has to be collected seamlessly, organised and displayed logically to determine the size and scope of Disaster management programs. During an actual disaster, it is imperative to have the correct data, at the right time, accessible and displayed logically to respond and take appropriate action. Disasters can impact all or several sectors of the Government departments. Emergency workers find it challenging to access interdepartmental staff and resources without this capability, resulting in disaster responders guessing, estimating, or making decisions without adequate information. Geospatial technology provides a mechanism to centralise and visually display critical information during disasters. By utilising geospatial technology, all departments can share information through databases on computer-generated maps in one location. Most of the data requirements for emergency management are spatial and can be located on a map. This paper will illustrate how Geospatial technology can fulfil data requirement needs for planning and emergency operations and how Geospatial technology can become the backbone of disaster management. Disaster management activities are focused on three primary objectives. These objectives are protecting life, property, and the environment.

Geospatial technology can be adopted to save lives and reduce damages in all aspects of emergency management. Responders who know where impacts are most significant, where critical assets are stored, or where infrastructure is likely to be damaged can act more quickly, especially during the "crucial golden hour".

1.3 Geospatial Technology Innovations in Disaster Management

Geospatial Technology plays a huge role in disaster management because the features impacted by disasters are geographically located and have geographic addresses. Karnataka State is prone to numerous natural disasters. Frequent disasters have resulted in the loss of lives and livelihoods, caused immense damage to infrastructure and disrupted critical services. The socio-economic losses undo years of growth and development, primarily affecting the most vulnerable and marginalised populations. Hitherto, data on disaster loss, damage and expenditure are taken through physical/paper mode and in different formats like Excel, MS Word, PDF, images. The districts collating the data sets have been a cumbersome and time-consuming process. The collection of factual data on disaster events is necessary to assist with quick relief, rehabilitation, recovery & rebuilding, assessing the loss due to disaster, preparing the reports, event-based memorandum, and updating the Disaster Management plans. Further, the non-availability of centralised data hampers decision-making during emergencies, and it is difficult to monitor compliance on expenditure from SDRMF and NDRMF. Karnataka State Disaster Management Authority (KSDMA) and Karnataka State Natural Disaster Monitoring Authority (KSNDMC) have developed an integrated disaster database called Karnataka State Disaster Management Information System (KSDMIS) - An Geospatial web application for collecting data on disaster events for bringing uniformity in disaster classifications, criteria and parameters of loss and injuries to humans, livestock, loss of livelihood, and other capital losses including losses to private property and business.

Technology Automation and Artificial intelligence have advanced over the past few years. They have been solving real-world problems with close to human-like logical & analytic thinking with decision making. Being a technology hub of the world, India needs to adopt the technology-driven solution to effectively and efficiently contain and manage disasters and save precious lives and property. As the scale, complexity, & challenges in coordination and managing, disasters are enormous and often beyond human capabilities. It is logical to use such advanced technologies to mitigate the impact. Software technologies will also be able to process information and make logical decisions & judgements without getting affected by ad-hoc and unstructured impulses. The Geospatial-DDMP is a technology-driven solution designed and developed to create a Geospatial foundation by structuring information and generating plans for disaster management. A digital geo-information database and generation of State and District Disaster Management Plan through auto mode is a prime output of the Geospatial-DDMP platform. It enables to touch all aspects of disaster management and facilitates automatic response systems, decision making, tracking, documentation and 'lessons learnt' to mitigate risks in future.

2 Karnataka State Disaster Management Information System (KSDMIS) - A Geospatial Web Application for Collecting Data on Disaster Events

KSDMIS is a state-of-the-art disaster management technology with real-time infrastructure to Collect & Store data, Analyse, Communicate and auto-generate event-based Reports or Memorandums. The authentic information geo-stamped with GPS location & time is collected using the Web and mobile interfaces. The KSDMIS intends to dispense with the manual collection process and ensure collecting last-mile disaster-related data using appropriate technology that ensures transparency, data integrity, real-time data availability, and data collation. The KSDMIS enables the data collection from ground level to district level and State level in predefined standardised templates for data collection, updation and validation to ensure accuracy and quality. The data from KSDMIS will form the basis of hazard and vulnerability analysis and prepare the Annual report as mandated under Sub Section 2 of Section 70 of the Disaster Management Act, 2005. KSDMIS is crucial for assessing and tracking risks and progress towards resilience, without which the State cannot mainstream disaster risk reduction into developmental activities. It will also be a step towards implementing the Prime Minister's 10-point agenda plan to address disaster risks and Sendai Framework Disaster Risk Reduction. KSDMIS auto-generates the memorandum of Losses and damages by collating the geo-stamped data submitted from various field locations across the State, including statistics, maps, photos, and other documents related to the extreme event. KSDMIS uses a GPS enabled handheld Mobile to capture geo-stamped location and time details of a site with photo/audio/signature. KSDMIS has data collection templates to capture all details of losses, including human and animal loss, crop loss, infrastructure damages, industries, national highways, private properties, relief camp details, search and rescue operation, crop loss subsidy and housing assistance, monitoring drinking water supply & repair works using the SDRF/NDRF fund. The database created will provide help identifying the mitigation.

2.1 About Karnataka

Karnataka is India's eighth largest State in a geographical area covering 1.92 lakh km^2 and accounting for 6.3% of the country's geographical area. The State is delineated into 31 districts and 227 taluks spread over 27,481 villages. Bengaluru is the capital of Karnataka and the city known as the Silicon Valley of Asia due to its flourishing Information Technology industry. The location of Karnataka state is provided in Fig. 1.

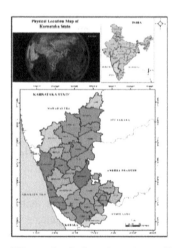

Fig. 1. Location map of Karnataka, India, where the application shall be adopted.

2.2 Objectives of KSDMIS Application Software

Data collection in real-time/near real-time in predefined templates from the disaster-affected area. Geospatial view of damaged areas and helping to plan appropriate mitigation measures. Geospatial authenticated Memorandum generation for Government of India Submission. Calculation of losses under various categories and fund requirements.

Data authenticity by Geo stamping. The database will provide help in the identification of mitigation projects.

2.3 Benefits of KSDMIS Application Software

KSDMIS provides authenticated Geo-stamped information from the field. All information collected from the field is Geo stamped from the KSDMIS app, along with the survey and loss/damage details.

- **Real-time system:** The final report of losses and damages and memorandum can be generated in real-time as the Geo stamped photos get synchronised to the servers directly from the field.
- **Ground-up (Village level data):** The data is collected from each location and tagged to the village level. The software reporting engine provides granular information and is statistically summarised at Panchayat, Taluk, District, and State levels.
- **Database driven:** Data management is structured with information tagged with location masters and standard jurisdiction IDS (District, Taluk, Panchayat and Village). Digital database provides a framework to generate MIS reports and identify gaps in procedures automatically.
- **Repeatable:** Database can be dynamically updated from the App and web portal where respective districts can add or modify information. Continuous update to information ensures repeatability and up-to-date information.
- **Traceable and avoids duplication:** Since the data collection and reporting are encompassed in a single software system and authenticated GPS and photographic information, it helps traceability and avoids duplication.
- **Last-mile data collection from Mobile Phones:** Native mobile App helps collect data from the field. The App is resilient to no-network zones and is designed to work in the field. The data is stored on the phone and synchronised in no-network whenever network/wifi becomes available.
- **Standardised surveys:** The survey engine of the system can automatically generate mobile and web surveys from a template. The surveys get synchronised to the mobile App. This ensures that the data collection is standardised.
- **Tamper Proof:** Photographs with GPS ensure that the data cannot be tampered with as there is a reference to validate the same.
- **Reduce human errors:** Since the reporting engine is software-driven and automatically generates reports depending on the user profiles, it reduces human errors and calculation mistakes.
- **Accessible:** Web-driven system makes the information accessible to various user groups depending on the privilege over the Internet.
- **Accountability:** Since the data is submitted from the place of the event by a user who has unique access & login credentials, it makes the submitters accountable for the accuracy of the data.
- **Low cost:** Memorandum & report generation is at the click of a button with minimal manual intervention, avoids paper trails, saves time and is cost-effective. The App runs well on low-cost devices and has low RAM and CPU requirements.

2.4 KSDMIS Application Software Structure

The KSDMIS has been designed with distinct features for accurate and authentic data collection with ease from the field by the designated officers, periodically updating data and generating event-based reports or memorandum.

KSDMIS system has three technology components. They are,

1. Handheld GPS mobile which can capture field information such as Forms/questionnaires, Photo/video/audio and Signatures on touch screen and automatically transfer the same to a Geo-information database wirelessly through 3G/GPRS
2. Geo-information Database which can store field data classified under jurisdictions and surveys
3. Backend system interprets data from geo-information database and Auto-classifies survey data, auto-computes statistics needed for submitting a memorandum, and generates memorandum, MIS reports, and maps.

The field staff performs all data collection, survey, monitoring, authentication, feedback, and disaster response activities using the login protected handheld mobile. The data is finally presented as a webpage through the backend interface or periodically auto-generated documents (Memorandum). For the user, there are two interfaces to submit the data: the Mobile interface (Android) and the Web interface. Both interfaces have the same secure logins for each district. Field data is submitted using a mobile interface (level 1 survey) with photographs and GPS coordinates. Level 2 surveys can be added from the Web to update the status. Each data is Geotagged at a village/ward level. There are 33 Annexures such as Human Death, Animal Loss, Road Damage etc. These annexures are presented on the website & mobile App as survey forms are filled and submitted. The schematic diagram of data and information communication technology is given in Fig. 2.

2.5 Mobile Interface for Data Collection and Updation

The user can upload and submit the information directly from the field and update information periodically. For example, this module can submit periodic progress if a building is added and under construction. The periodic data survey is generated as per the definition in web admin - upon 100 surveys with 100 fields are provisioned for the periodic data survey.

The mobile interface to the KSDMIS has three types of privileges for the users.

1. *Location Restriction:* This allows the user to be locked to a location at the District level/Taluk level/Town Level/Panchayat level/Village level. The user can only submit data for the location assigned. This provision acts as a Geo-fencing for collecting authentic data from the field by an authorised field officer within his jurisdiction or administrative boundary.
2. *Department Restriction:* The user to collect data pertinent to a particular department only. The department, in turn, can set surveys for data collection and periodic updates.

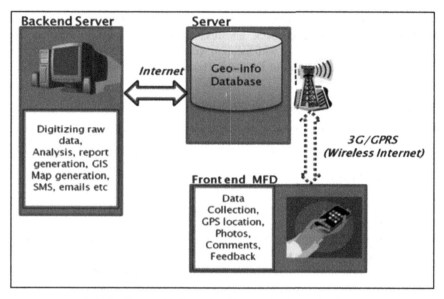

Fig. 2. Data and Information Communication technology

If the department is assigned to a user, only the surveys/periodic data defined and collected in the department can be accessed by the individual user.

3. *Surveys and Periodic Data:* This privilege supersedes department privilege and sets the surveys/periodic data to access or submit.

2.6 Web Interface to the KSDMIS Application Software

The web interface to the KSDMIS has the following features for data collection, updating.

- The web interface enables the user for periodic data submissions for each survey.
- It has provisions for collecting or updating 100 periodic data types, each having 100 data fields.
- Import periodic data definition using excel format (defining each field type and assigning the reference survey). Field type can be photo, Signature, selfie, text number, drop down, date, time etc.
- Sync between Web and Mobile for data definition and uploads.
- Define and assign surveys/systematic data collection to each department.
- Views to see periodic data submitted by the user.

2.7 Adopting Geospatial Technology in KSDMIS

The user will adopt the KSDMIS application at State, District, Taluk and Village level to survey and collect data, assess the loss and damages incurred during a disaster, geotag the validated data and auto-generate a memorandum as an end component. The data so achieved shall be uploaded and verified by taluk and village administration, followed by district level approval. The village-level field staff performs all data collection, survey, monitoring, authentication, feedback, and disaster response activities. The surveyed data is geotagged to the interface with location wise information collected at the disaster affected location. The flowchart of KSDMIS Technology adopted is given in Fig. 3.

2.7.1 KSDMIS Report Generation Mechanism

KSDMIS document engine has two parts viz. Static data is entered as a one-time exercise, and dynamic data is collated from field data entered by various districts using a Web or mobile interface.

The type of data entered into the system is classified as

a. Manually entered using a doc link interface which facilitates easy entering and formatting of data
b. data is obtained dynamically from an API link or URL, and such data is inserted into the document using unique tags specially architected for the purpose. Such an interface facilitated integration with external data from other departments.
c. Architected special tags can be translated to Database hooks. Such database hooks can be of a single value or even a table with images, geo-stamped photos, links etc. They also introduce the opening of GPS navigation by scanning QR codes. Such QR codes are dynamically created and inserted into the document. This enables viewing detailed information from a printed document.
d. Complex Mathematical Expressions can be added to the document based on the database tags. Such expressions can be used to evaluate dynamically - the sum of a list of tags (values), the sum of columns, rows of tables or evaluating a formula dynamically.
e. When a block is marked as a loop, it will inject the block values loop for all districts and value-translated pages into the document. For example, when marked as a loop block, the standard expenditure sheet for each district will be evaluated, and pages will be injected for all districts in the document.

Memorandum has Four parts, namely, Static Information (common objectives, definitions, SOPs, checklists) Meta Information (State or District or Taluk Specific Static Content), Statistical (Dynamic) and Detailed Survey Information (Dynamic).

2.7.2 Approval Flow - There is a Strict Three-Step Approval Process in the System to Improve Accountability and Quality of Data

(1) The field level of users (Uploaders) submit information from the field at a village level and review their submissions. If there is an error in the submission, the system allows a re-submission.
(2) The next level of users (Verifiers) can verify individual submissions made with their Taluk/Block. The verifiers can mark each submission as Approved/Rejected/To be corrected. The uploaders take action to correct any items which verifiers mark.
(3) The third level users (Approvers) review the data, report and summaries at a district level and approve/reject surveys.

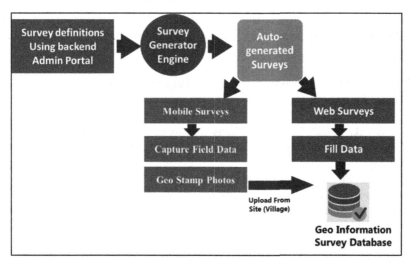

Fig. 3. Flowchart of KSDMIS technology adopted

The reports and memorandum are generated only for the approved entries. Once an item is marked as approved, the uploader cannot resubmit/alter the submission unless marked for correction by the verifier.

3   Geospatial Enabled - District Disaster Management Plan – GEDDMP System

Geospatial-DDMP is a state-of-the-art disaster management technology with real-time wireless infrastructure to collect, store, analyse, communicate, coordinate & present authentic information, geo-stamped with GPS location & time, using a web-based geo-information database/framework. Geospatial Enabled DDMP auto-generates a District Disaster Management Plan (DDMP) using field resource and personnel information with maps of geo-mapped resources. It uses GPS enabled handheld Mobile to capture geo-stamped location and time details with photo/audio/hand-written notes. To & fro data communication is possible wirelessly from the geo-information database to the handheld device using a mobile network.

The conventional disaster management system has limitations like limited access to real-time, authentic, quantifiable information leading to communication gaps or even miscommunication, Lack of information and infrastructure for preparation & communication and difficulties to connect Standard Operating Procedures (SOPs) with the ground reality.

Whereas the Geospatial Enabled DDMP helps to overcome the above limitations with

- Accurate, tamper-proof data authenticated through GPS location and time
- Real-time information transfer wirelessly with a feedback mechanism to the provide updated, relevant data/strategies to field

- Generating and disseminating Instant messages
- Real-time event capture including photo, voice, hand-written notes, forms, status
- Auto-generation of analysis reports, statistics saving manual labour, human errors, paper trails
- Monitoring of reconstruction, restoration and compensation
- Database Archive for future disaster mitigation, accountability, traceability

Since Karnataka is India's IT hub, it leads the way to leverage the latest technology to effectively and efficiently manage Emergencies and Disasters to minimise losses to life and property.

Geospatial Enabled DDMP system given in Fig. 4 will enable the stakeholders to effectively map all the essential resources and associated resource personnel during "peacetime" so that disaster response is predictable, planned, and planned executed with accurate and up to date information.

GEOSPATIAL ENABLED DDMP system facilitates the execution of the disaster management cycle by interfacing each aspect of disaster management with a geo-information database and a real-time data communication infrastructure. During preparation, the data is stored in the geo-information database, and data is used for response and recovery.

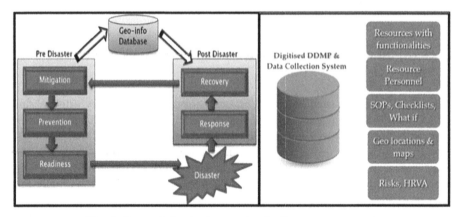

Fig. 4. Geospatial technology system in disaster management

3.1 Operation Strategy

Field data collection is continuously performed by the field officer by collecting activity details through form filling. The teams use existing radio wireless Communication if the mobile network fails to operate. However, status update & data collection is continued on the Mobile. The data is stored on the Mobile and gets synchronised with the server whenever the Mobile gets back in the network range. The operation strategy and what if analysis are given in Fig. 5 and 6.

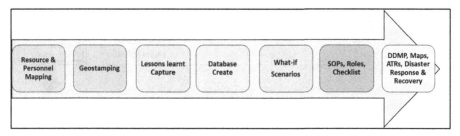

Fig. 5. Operation strategy

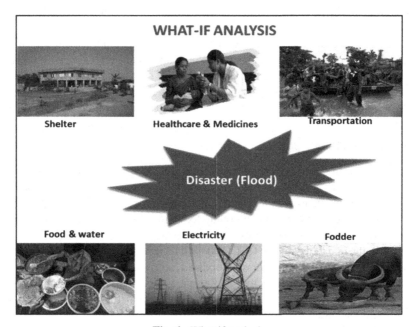

Fig. 6. What if analysis

Resource data is analysed, reviewed and tagged into the roles and responsibilities of departments/officers. Based on the officer's role and the associated activity, the appropriate field resource information will be presented (with the real-time status), enabling a better judgment call during the disaster.

Login ID	Officer Name	Disaster type	Role ID	Description	Resource Info
9012	Shyam P	Flood	RL5467	Take victims to nearest PHC	**Click to view Resources**

Resource ID	Area	PHC Type	No. of Doctors	No. of Beds	Contact
PHC123	Sindgi	24/7	2	5	+919087265342
PHC124	Sindgi	Normal	1	0	+919087388383

According to the role, associating the resource information to the Role ID provides up-to-date field information to the officer. A similar process takes place for checklist generation, through auto-mode from the database, for each department/authority to cross-check and verify preparedness. As soon as a disaster strikes, relevant geo-information data is made available to the field staff. The field staff execute the activities and update the server with the status using the handheld device. The controller or backend officer reviews the status and provides feedback or follow-up issues with other departments.

3.2 Continuous Data Updation

Roles and Responsibilities would be assigned to designated personnel in each department to keep the database up-to-date. Periodic reminders are sent to check and update the system with relevant changes in the data. If no change is required during an incremental update cycle, an explicit sign-off mentioning 'No Update Required' would be expected to ensure that the system is consciously kept updated.

Based on the updated data, the GEDDMP will be revised periodically. The enhanced GEDDMP would contain the sections for updated information on District Profile, Disaster Vulnerability, Telephone Directory of Resource Personnel, Directory of Resources, Duties and Responsibilities, Disaster types, Resource Maps, FAQ, Dos & Don'ts and Checklist & Annexures.

3.3 Benefits of Geospatial Enabled-DDMP System

Simplified Procedures: The manual process of preparing the GEDDMP where all information needed to be revalidated year on year, updating the telephone numbers, and capturing resources were very cumbersome. However, with the GEDDMP, pre-disaster management data collection is structured and standardised by dynamically updating a web portal where departments can add or modify information and click a button. Additional features like generating the roles and responsibilities of various stakeholders, Resource maps, faster communication, alerts and warnings to authorities, departments and local people who are likely to be affected are simplified to a great extent.

Increased Efficiency of Outputs/Processes and Effectiveness of Outcomes: Automated generation of GEDDMP decreased human intervention: saves time, effort, cost, Accurate and up-to-date information, defining clear roles and responsibilities, achieving real-time information from the field eases data collection process which makes instant update possible, automatic generation of MIS reports from the digital database and identify gaps in procedures, provision to incorporate lessons learnt for continuous improvement and continuous updation of information ensures repeatability.

Sustainability of the Initiative: The significant role of Geospatial technology in the deployment, making the initiative repeatable with minimum human intervention. Low cost of sustaining and operating the technology, as the initiative is modelled for comprehensive and holistic disaster management and can be adopted by other states Continuous updating of information and feedback loop with lessons learnt will provide means to improve the system continuously.

Improvement in Delivery Time of Services: Periodically updation/maintenance of GEDDMP during peacetime. A centralised database provides scope for improved communication and more precise role definition across various departments. Automatic generation of GEDDMP, Maps, and MIS reports for disaster management from the digital database at the click of a button. Geospatial-DDMP is truly a next-generation disaster management technology system and overall aims to minimise the loss of life and property with tools & means to holistically and comprehensively manage disasters.

Better Beneficiary/Citizens' Feedback: The Geospatial Enabled DDMP will be available on the Web for all beneficiaries to download and use. The User-friendly data updations by various stakeholders and auto-generation of GEDDMP is a good feature.

3.4 Geospatial Technology for Different Phases of Disaster Management

Geospatial Technology provides accurate spatial data and insights to disaster response strategies and visualises critical vulnerabilities and damage.

A disaster management plan would be more efficient when integrating Preparedness and Planning with Geospatial Technology. Adopting GIS into all the phases of disaster management planning presents an opportunity to prepare and act better during relief efforts through greater efficiency.

Geospatial data helps users to understand the impact of potential damage and further anticipate resource utilisation during an emergency. The line departments access real-time information with GIS-based dashboards and live maps to make informed decisions. We can foster risk analysis, situational planning, recovery operations, and enhanced collaboration with GIS technology. The Schematic diagram depicting pre-disaster and response phase based on Geo-Spatial DDMP given in Fig. 7 and 8 (Fig. 9).

3.5 Geospatial Enabled DDMP Application Software Structure

Geospatial-DDMP System Has Three Technology Components

- Handheld GPS mobile which can capture field information such as
- Forms/questionnaires, photo/video/audio and Signatures on a touch screen and automatically transfer the same to a Geo-information database wirelessly through 3G/GPRS

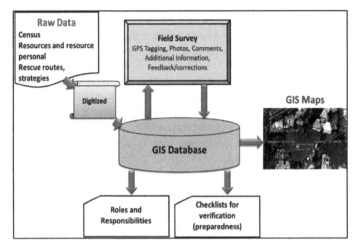

Fig. 7. Geospatial Enabled DDMP - pre-disaster phase

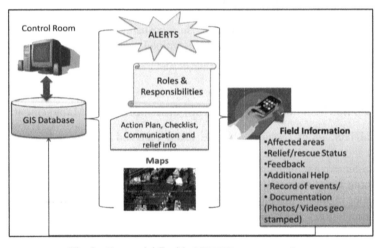

Fig. 8. Geospatial Enabled DDMP - response phase

- Geo-information Database which can store field data or existing digitised data as layers
- Backend system which interprets data from geo-information database and
- Auto-classifies resources
- Auto-assigns resources to roles/responsibilities of Resource Personnel
- Generates DDMP, reports, maps
- Communicate actions, activities, reports to all concerned via the Internet

The field staff performs all the data collection, survey, monitoring, authentication, feedback, and disaster response activities using the login protected handheld mobile device. The data in the geo-information database are stored as layers that can be used for access,

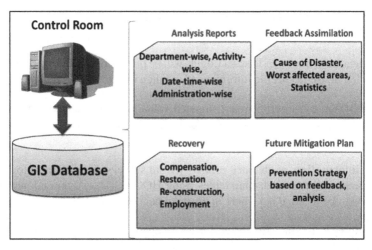

Fig. 9. Geospatial Enabled DDMP - post disaster phase

further analyse or present various combinations and interpretations. The data is finally presented as a webpage through the backend interface or periodically auto-generated documents (DDMP). The Data and Information Communication system are given in Fig. 10.

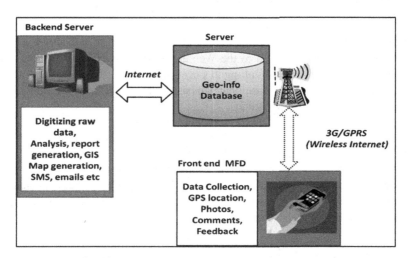

Fig. 10. Data and Information Communication system

3.6   Core Technology of Geospatial-DDMP Application Software

The DDMP has four parts. A user-friendly admin panel will help define various headings and subheadings, Formatting text, inserting tables, links etc. Central Admin Team will fill in DDMP Static Information. Images can be directly inserted into the textbook and formatted.

DDMP Meta Information: District Logins will be provided for entering this Metadata. The users log in, fill in specific information, and then insert HOOKs into the document.

DDMP HOOKs can insert Single computed value, multiple values in the form of a table, Loop a section for each district, fetch data and insert tables or single values, Evaluate expressions & formulas dynamically.

Dynamic information is obtained primarily from surveys. The survey information is used to create statistics or display tables using HOOKs. The system allows dynamic information to be inserted anywhere in the document using HOOKs.

DDMP Surveys: Logins are created for each department in each district, the district user logs in and fills the surveys, the surveys are restricted based on the department and district, and the survey database is used to generate the DDMP by using HOOKs.

3.7 Workflow

1. The admin personnel defines surveys as a one-time activity. Surveys can be Hospital, Ambulance, Vehicle, School,Building, Shelter homes, Material list etc.
2. The surveys are translated into software forms using the DDMP Survey engine, which translates the surveys to dropdowns, text & number boxes, date-time fields, photo upload, signature entry etc.
3. The survey forms are synced to the Web and mobile interface to facilitate users logging in, filling in, and submitting to a central server.
4. The data is stored in a geo-positional database with survey forms tagged with GPS coordinates, photos and signatures.
5. The admin also defines a DDMP template using the backend web portal, which specifies the META data (static), checklists, dos & don'ts and a template for the dynamic portion using DDMP HOOKs.
6. The DDMP generator reads the DDMP templates and survey form data from the geo-positional database to generate a real-time & live DDMP by looping the generator specific to each district. Along with DDMP, resource maps, resource directories, and associated statistics are also auto-generated.

The Workflow of Geospatial Enabled DDMP is given in Fig. 11.

3.8 Features of Survey Template HOOKs

Using the Template Definition module of Geospatial-DDMP, admin personnel can define multiple templates for DDMPs, including static and dynamic content.

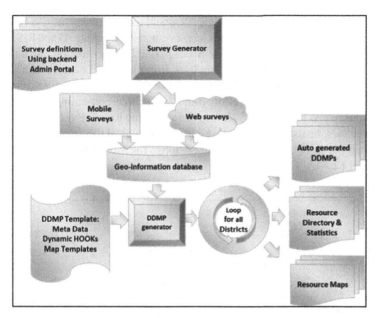

Fig. 11. Workflow of Geospatial Enabled DDMP

The type of information may be

- **Manually** entered using a doc link interface (WYSIWYG) which facilitates easy entering and formatting of data and facilitates.
- **Using API:** data is obtained dynamically from an API link or URL, and such data is inserted into the document using unique tags specially architected for the purpose. Such an interface facilitated integration with external data from other departments.
- **Using Database:** Architected unique tags (HOOKs) which can translate to database hooks. Such database hooks can be of a single value or even a table with images, geo-stamped photos, links etc. Also introduced was the opening of GPS navigation by scanning QR codes. Such QR codes are created dynamically and inserted into the document. This enables information from a printed document; details such as - enlarged photos, user info, date & time, navigation to the GPS location.
- **Expressions:** Complex mathematical expressions can also be added to the document based on the database tags. Such expressions can be used to evaluate dynamically - a sum of a list of tags (values), a sum of columns, rows of tables or evaluating a formula dynamically.
- **Loops:** If a block is marked as a loop, the block values will be looped for all districts, and value-translated pages will be injected into the document. This is useful when deriving state DDMP by consolidating existing district information.

3.9 Roadmap and Futuristic View

While the immediate focus of Geospatial-DDMP is to automate DDMP generation in "peacetime", it lays a foundation to add and expand the platform to further innovative and artificially intelligent (AI) technologies. It would focus on using the geo-information database, historical data, images, lessons learnt systems to integrate AI and IoT technologies to elevate the technology platforms. Some possibilities are explored to automate or use machine learning methods to integrate Bots, Robots and IOT devices with actionable plans. AI has made good progress in predictive analytics which can be lifesaving as data is often too immense for human effort (time & resource consuming). Often rescuers become victims, and they put their lives in danger, trying to save lives. Intelligent robots or AI-driven cars, boats, JCBs etc., can be lifesaving and, at the same time, will not put more human life at risk during rescue operations. The workflow of AI Technology is given in Fig. 12.

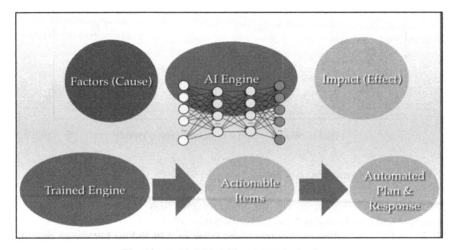

Fig. 12. Artificial intelligent (AI) technology

Historical records of cause and effect are fed into a deep learning AI system that can learn how disasters affect the people/environment based on the (input) conditions and predict future possibilities and probabilities of disasters in even unforeseen circumstances, making it very human-like logical thinking. Internet of Things (IoT) with sensors continuously collecting various data points like seismic readings, water levels, pollution, satellite imagery, social media messages, CCTV, photos and temperature sensors can feed into the AI system with real-time data for real-time planning, real-time decision making and real-time response and rescue.

References

1. Adeniran, T.S.: Disaster risk reduction and management using geospatial data (2014)
2. Westlund, S.: The use of geospatial technology in disaster management. Image **1**, 17–30 (2010). https://doi.org/10.4018/jagr.2010070102
3. Vu, T.T.: The role of geospatial technologies in disaster emergency responses. J. Geol. Geosci. **1**, e101 (2012). https://doi.org/10.4172/2329-6755.1000e101

4. GIS Technology for Disasters and Emergency Management by Russ Johnson An ESRI White Paper, May 2000
5. Emergency Management – A Geospatial Approach V. Bhanumurthy*, G Srinivasa Rao, Harish C Karnatak, S. Mamatha, Ps Roy, K Radhakrishnan National Remote Sensing Agency, Dept. Of Space, Govt. India, Hyderabad-500 037
6. Manfré, L.A., et al.: An analysis of geospatial technologies for risk and natural disaster management. ISPRS Int. J. Geo-Inf. **1**, 166–185 (2012). https://doi.org/10.3390/ijgi1020166
7. Sakurai, M., Murayama, Y.: Information technologies and disaster management – Benefits and issues. https://doi.org/10.1016/j.pdisas.2019.100012
8. Mukhopadhyay, B., Bhattacherjee, B.: Use of information technology in emergency and disaster management. Am. J. Environ. Protect. **4**(2), 101–104 (2015). https://doi.org/10.11648/j. ajep.20150402.15

Information Technologies for Assessing the Effectiveness of the Quarantine Measures

Igor Grebennik[✉], Yevhen Hubarenko, and Maksym Ananiev

Kharkiv National University of Radio Electronics, Kharkiv, Ukraine
{igor.grebennik,evgen.gubarenko,maksym.ananiev}@nure.ua

Abstract. The paper proposes to use information technology for modeling and assessing the effectiveness of alternative quarantine measures to prevent the spread of viral infections (for example, COVID 19). A software tool was developed to simulate the spread of a virus infection, the protection effectiveness and quarantine measures based on the Unity3D engine. The modeling process is accompanied by a visual display of the interaction of observation objects. Statistics are displayed dynamically and are presented both a statistical data and a graph. The simulation system is flexible and adaptive, allowing you to customize a number of parameters. Among which should be noted the following: observation parameters (up to 1000 elements, with an increase at startup on computers with high performance); selection of protection means with a percentage of the number of objects that use the protection type; behavioral scenarios of observed objects. This allows you to check the effectiveness of quarantine measures, to assess the effectiveness of protecting the population from viral infections. The paper also demonstrates a comparison of the obtained simulation results.

Keywords: Information technologies · Modeling · Quarantine measures · Evaluation · Efficiency · Viral infections · COVID-19

1 Importance of Quarantine Measures

Applying restrictive measures helps to slow down the spread of viral infections and to win valuable time to prepare hospitals and medical staff for the increased number of hospital admissions. This is the stance taken by the WHO [1].

Restrictive measures, quarantine measures or quarantine is a set of restrictive and regular anti-epidemic measures aimed at limiting contact with an infected or supposedly infected person, animal, good, product, vehicle, locality, territory, district, region, etc. In some cases, quarantine implies a complete isolation of the outbreak area with the use of armed forces [2]. One of the primary objectives of quarantine is breaking the mechanism of transmission and localising outbreaks of the disease.

Pandemics have occurred regularly throughout history and have resulted in enormous casualties. Some of the most illustrative examples list [3–7]: the Antonine Plague (165–180 AD) with the death toll reaching about 5 million people; the Justinianic Plague (541–542 AD) – 30–50 million; the smallpox epidemic in Japan (735–737 AD) – 1 million;

J. Sasaki et al. (Eds.): ITDRR 2021, IFIP AICT 638, pp. 160–175, 2022.
https://doi.org/10.1007/978-3-031-04170-9_11

the Black Death (bubonic plague) (1347–1351) – 200 million; smallpox (1520) – 56 million; plague pandemic in Europe (seventeenth century) – 3 million; plague pandemic in Europe (eighteenth century) – 600,000; 6 cholera pandemics (1817–1923) – 1 million; plague pandemic in Europe (1855) – 12 million; yellow fever (late 1800) – 100–150 thousand; Spanish flu (1918–1919) – 40–50 million; Russian flu – 1 million 1889–1890 (despite their names, both Spanish and Russian flu outbreaks originated outside these countries); Asian flu (1957–1958) – 1,1 million; Hong Kong flu (1968–1970) – 1 million; Swine flu (2009–2010) – 200,000; Ebola (2014–2016) – 1,000; COVID-19 infections, 2019-present.

The world community with the help of international organisations such as the WHO puts in enormous effort to prevent the spread of diseases, introduces population vaccination policies, etc. However, despite some obvious success, the risk of global pandemic outbreaks remains high enough, the situation with COVID-19 is a good example of it.

It is important to understand that pandemics are usually accompanied by panic and aggression among the population. Restrictive measures (quarantine) are meant not only to protect healthy people and hold back the spread of the disease, but also to protect infected or supposedly infected people from possible outbreaks of physical harm or violence against them.

Isolation of the infected people as well as observation of those who have been in contact with them are both an integral part of quarantine measures. The duration of contact is considered one maximum incubation period of the given disease since the last contact with the infected person or since exiting the epidemic area [2]. Furthermore, quarantine measures also include protection of the state territory from external infectious diseases.

Colloquially, the word "quarantine" may be used to describe restrictive, isolating and observational anti-epidemic measures in childcare institutions and hospitals taken against rapidly spreading infectious diseases such as chickenpox, scarlet fever, diphtheria, influenza, etc. In these cases, however, it is rarely spoken of the full range of measures predefined by a quarantine.

On 10 March 2020 the World Health Organization announced that the COVID-19 virus epidemic, which was first recorded in Wuhan, China, in December 2019, had reached pandemic levels [8]. Having emphasised the "alarming levels of spread and severity" the WHO urged the countries to take immediate and decisive measures to stop the spread of the Coronavirus disease.

2   Variety of Quarantine Measures

Restrictive measures are actions that prescribe special behaviour procedures for a group of people restricting their movement with the aim of the epidemiological protection of the population. There are three different categories of restrictive measures that vary in scope and severity: intensified medical surveillance, observation and quarantine.

Medical surveillance aims at active identification of the infected individuals among the population as well as their consequent isolation and hospitalisation. It is as a rule carried out by means of questioning the complaints, physical examination, thermometry and laboratory analyses.

Observation encompasses intensified medical supervision, as well as restriction of movements, however, it allows for a minimal interaction with the society. At the same time, contacts between those, who are under observation and those, who are not under observation, are not allowed.

Quarantine entails a complete isolation assured by special guards. Interaction with the society takes place only via representatives of medical services who usually use special protective equipment and have to undergo certain cleaning procedures after visiting quarantine areas.

Anti-epidemic measures are normally carried out by specialists from healthcare and treatment facilities. Specialist teams are formed to provide isolation, treatment, disinfection, laboratory and vaccination services.

The following restrictive measures should also be mentioned: self-isolation – is a modern term used to describe a set of measures taken by the population itself in order to organise the quarantine, this term spread out during the COVID-19 pandemic; face mask regime, which means the compulsory wearing of hygiene masks and other respiratory protection items.

3 Application of Restrictive Measures and the Need to Assess Their Efficiency

International human rights norms guarantee every individual the right to the highest attainable standard of health. Consequently, states are obliged to take measures to prevent the threats to public health and to provide medical assistance to those who need it. International human rights standards also permit limitation of certain rights and freedoms in situations of serious threats to public health and emergencies that threaten the life of a nation. Such limitations shall be lawful, limited in time and respectful of human dignity, subject to control and proportionate to the aim pursued.

The scale and severity of the COVID-19 pandemic is clearly reaching such a level of public health threat that it may justify restriction of certain rights and freedoms, as, for instance, restriction of the freedom of movement under the conditions of quarantine or isolation.

Any quarantine measures may result in restriction of human rights, it is, however, a compulsory measure aimed at protecting the health of citizens and, in some cases, their survival. The extent and severity of the restrictive measures, as well as their duration, have to be proved by medical and epidemiological experts on the basis of modelling results, analysis of statistical data and clinical analyses. As can be seen, model synthesis, as well as further modelling and their trials help to assess various developmental scenarios related to the spread of infection. This also helps to answer the question of the effectiveness of certain measures under certain environmental influences.

The unjustified imposition of restrictive measures may cause the destruction of economic relations, resulting in famine and other disasters. On the other hand, an overly liberal approach may lead to the uncontrolled spread of infections, the collapse of the health system and death of numerous people. As can be seen, decisions that are made may have drastic consequences both for a separate region and for the country as a whole. That is why it is utterly important to conduct scientific research, collect statistical data and carry out modelling of the consequences of various restrictive measures. Rarely do researchers have sufficient data in order to conduct a holistic mathematical modelling, instead they often apply simulation modelling.

4   Selection of Modelling Approach for Quarantine Measure Efficiency

Mathematical models are traditionally divided into analytical and simulation models [9–11].

Analytical models are equations or systems of equations written in the form of algebraic, integral, differential, finite-difference and other relations and logical conditions. An analytical model is usually static. The analytical representation is only suitable for very simple and highly idealised tasks and objects, which as a rule have little in common with the real (complicated) world but are highly generalised. This type of model is usually used to describe fundamental properties of objects.

Complicated objects are rarely described analytically. Simulation models (dynamic) are an alternative to analytical models. Simulation models, in contrast to analytical ones, presuppose the construction of an algorithm representing the sequence of processes within the analyzed object. Then the behaviour of the given object is 'played' on a computer. Simulation models are used when the modelling object is so complex that it is impossible or highly difficult to adequately describe its behaviour with mathematical equations.

Simulation modelling allows a large model to be divided into parts (objects, "pieces"), which can be used separately, creating other, simpler or, conversely, more complex models. Thus, the main advantage of simulation modelling in comparison to analytical modelling is the opportunity to solve more complex problems. Simulation models can be gradually made more sophisticated without losing their efficiency. This reproduces the functioning algorithm of the system over time – the behaviour of the system, thereby imitating the elementary phenomena that make up the process, retaining their logical structure and sequence. This allows the initial data to provide information on the current state of the process at certain points in time, making it possible to estimate the characteristics of the system. Simulation models make it relatively easy to take such factors into account as the presence of discrete and continuous elements, non-linear characteristics of system elements, multiple random interactions, etc. which often cause difficulties in analytical analyses [12].

Simulation modelling is close to an object-oriented representation, which describes the natural way of objects, their state, behaviour, and interactions between these objects. Simulation modelling is currently the most efficient method of system analysis, it is often the only practically available method of obtaining information on system behaviour, especially at its design stage. A simulation model, unlike an analytical model, is not a complete system of equations, but a carefully defined scheme with a detailed description of the structure and behaviour of the analysed object. Simulation modelling is characterised by the reproduction of the phenomena described by the model, while maintaining their logical structure, sequence of alternation in time, the interconnection between the parameters and variables of the analysed system.

A large variety of mathematical methods can be used in analytical models, often resulting in an optimal solution and sometimes enabling a sensitivity analysis. Unfortunately, however, analytical solutions do not always exist, whereas the existing ones are not always easy to find. As far as simulation models are concerned, the optimality of the solution is not guaranteed, and it is often difficult to obtain a solution that is at least somewhat close to optimal. Sometimes numerous simulation model trails are required in order to obtain an acceptable confidence in the "goodness" of any solution. Still, simulation modelling can be used to gather the data that is difficult or impossible to obtain with the help of analytical models. For instance, determining the influence of model parameters variability, or determining the behaviour of the model before it reaches a steady state, etc.

Simulation models are considered among the most promising when managing the economic objects. Generally speaking, for complex problems where time and dynamics are important, simulation models are considered one of the most popular and useful methods for quantitative analysis [13].

As a result, some peculiarities of the analytical modelling and simulation which are base of the selection of modelling approach may be formulated.

Specifics of Analytical Modelling:

1. Analytical models may be used to determine an optimal solution.
2. Analytical models tend to be difficult to formalise and formulate, sometimes they are impossible to formulate at all. Any analytical model has its own "complicating" factors, which depend on the specifics of the given model.
3. Analytical models usually offer average or stationary (long-term) solutions. In practice, it is often the non-stationary behaviour of the system or its characteristics over a short period of time that are important, making it impossible to obtain 'average' values.

Specifics of Stimulation Modelling:

1. Simulation modelling requires a large number of trials.
2. It requires assessment of a large number of possible alternative solutions.
3. It allows for multiple alteration of the model parameters.
4. It gives an opportunity to analyse complex behaviour scenarios of the system.
5. Simulation modelling can be run on a wide range of software specifically developed for it.

Having analysed the requirements, possibilities, advantages and disadvantages of both analytical and simulation modelling, one may conclude that it is the simulation modelling that should be used in order to assess the efficiency of applying restrictive measures. This approach enables one to collect the data given different specific conditions and varying restrictive measures.

5   Overview of Epidemiology Models

Many scientists have tackled the task of modelling the spread of epidemics. One of the first references to the construction of mathematical models goes back to the publication titled 'Mathematical Methods for Evaluating the Effectiveness of Smallpox Vaccination Methods' by D. Bernoulli in 1760 [14]. However, the most active development of mathematical models of epidemic spread took place in the twentieth century. The following works are worth mentioning: Brownlee (1906) [15] – he applied a statistical approach to predict the immune protection: epidemic theory (Pearson's distribution)); W.O. Kermack, A.G. McKendrick (1927) [16] – the 'law of mass action' was applied for the first time, according to it, the number of new infections within the population is directly proportional to the product of the current number of the susceptible and infected individuals. Elaboration of the differential SIR model (Susceptible - Infected - Recovered); L. Reed, W.H. Frost (1931) [17] – used chains of binomial distributions to describe the number of infected individuals at each time interval. Noble (1974), Bailey (1975), Murray, Staley and Brown (1986) worked on spatial SIR model [14].

Unfortunately, the twenty-first century did not see the victory over diseases and epidemics, so consequently, numerous research carried on: model of the spread of tuberculosis – A. A. Romanjuha (2004), model of the outbreak of the Severe Acute Respiratory Syndrome (SARS) in China in 2003– J. Zhang (2005) [18], mathematical model of the spread of COVID-19 coronavirus from the source of infection (bats) to humans in Wuhan Province – J. Chen (01.2020) [19]. Modelling is often based on machine learning approach. [20].

6   Model Description and Development of Software

Simulation software architecture may be presented in the form of four separate modules (Fig. 1).

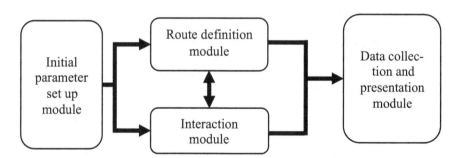

Fig. 1. Scheme of a software modular architecture.

Initial parameter set up module – is an interface element enabling the user to specify parameters and ensuring a flexible and user-friendly tool to manage route defining models, setting up the principles and nature of virus spread, and the availability of defence mechanisms. Unfortunately, at the moment, the software tool is still under development, therefore, its interface allows one to specify the size of the test group, to select the available personal protective measures, including the percentage of the test group members who will be using it, to select the simulation scenario, and to specify whether the place is forbidden to visit. Most of the route definition parameters, maintenance of social distancing or viral infection behaviour have to be set in the programming code;

Route definition module – a wide range of strategies may be implemented thanks to route definition methods. For example, defining a route to visit an accommodation (a private house or a multi-storey building), an office, a shop, a school, a mass event. Moreover, the test group will not be homogeneous, its members will stick to the behavioural strategy given to them at the beginning of the simulation. For instance, 10% should head towards a school facility, hence 10% of the test group will try to enter a facility associated with the school. A visit schedule can also be specified, but there is no differentiation between classroom distribution. In the school facility itself, members of the test group move chaotically, if current facility is forbidden to visit, they will move evenly around the allowed facilities or walk around the city;

Interaction module – specific interactions between the members of the test group as well as with the source of infection. This module manages the principles of infection and consequently patterns of the viral disease spread. Furthermore, the software scripts may contain the principles of immunity build up, characteristics of the nature of the disease, availability of protective measures and their effectiveness, presented in terms of the likelihood of infection;

Data collection and presentation module – is used to gather and visualise the information on the process of simulation.

7   Model Description and Software Development

Main chain algorithm may be described as follows:

Step 1. Setting up the parameters of simulation, namely type of protection measures, size of the test group, type of scenario, location, route definition algorithms for the test group, parameters of interaction and infection spread;

Step 2. Note the information on simulation in the databank;

Step 3. Placing the test group onto the location;

Step 4. Moving the test group around the location according to the scenario;

Step 5. Fulfilling the requirements for the "Encounter" script launch. If there are no members of the test group within the infected area, go to Step 4, otherwise, go to Step 6;

Step 6. If the first member of the test group is infected, go to Step 9, otherwise, go to Step 7;

Step 7. If there are more members of the test group infected, go to Step 11, otherwise, go to Step 8;

Step 8. Running the "Encounter of the Healthy" script, move to Step 15;

Step 9. If there are more infected members of the test group, go to Step 10, otherwise, go to Step 11;

Step 10. Running the "Encounter of the Infected" script, move to Step 15;

Step 11. Calculation of the infection parameters. The probability of infection is determined according to the set up parameters and the availability of personal protective measures;

Step 12. If members of the test group are infected, go to Step 13, otherwise, go to Step 15;

Step 13. Running the "Infection" script, move to Step 15;

Step 14. Running the script "Suspected Infection", go to Step 15;

Step 15. Collection, processing and saving the statistical data, creating diagrams;

Step 16. If conditions for simulation continuation are met, it means that there are still some infected members of the test group, go to Step 4, otherwise, go to Step 17;

Step 17. End of simulation.

The simulation tool implies the possibility of using various models, however, the current version of the tool is based on the main probabilistic characteristics of the viral infection spread and the course of the disease taken from the WHO publications, as well as the article "Clinical characteristics of 1007 intensive care unit patients with SARS-CoV-2 pneumonia" by Glybochko P, Fomin V, Avdeev S, et al. [21].

The software tool is developed in the Unity environment, which enables visualisation of objects' movements, selection of varying route definition algorithms and setting up rules for viral infection behaviour with the help of scripts. Furthermore, it makes it possible to select special algorithms for route definition and influence the likelihood of infection by introducing individual protection equipment. Altogether this enables simulation under varying conditions. Figure 2 illustrates the development environment with the elaborated tool.

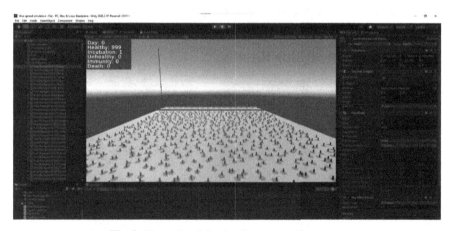

Fig. 2. Example of the development environment.

In order to start the simulation, one has to select and set up a range of initial data (Fig. 3):

– Select Mask Types – availability and type of individual protection equipment (masks and respirators);

– Select Population – sets up the size of the test group for the simulation;
– Select Scene – sets up the simulation scenario

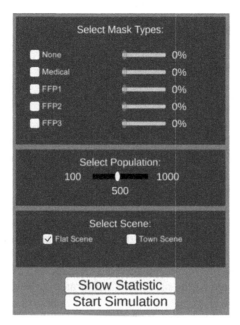

Fig. 3. Example of setting the initial conditions for the simulation.

8 Discussion of Modelling Results

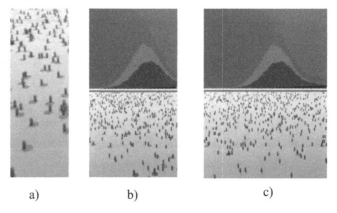

Fig. 4. Simulation results.

A number of computational experiments with the elaborated tool were realized.
Figure 4 shows: a) start of the simulation with the test group interacting in the open

air, b) and c) the simulation process at different stages. As can be seen, the software illustrates the process of simulation and presents the results and dynamics of statistical data collection. The full simulation process can be seen on https://www.youtube.com/watch?v=abU-YzpcrsQ.

Additionally, at the end of simulation one may obtain various numerical data, Fig. 5.

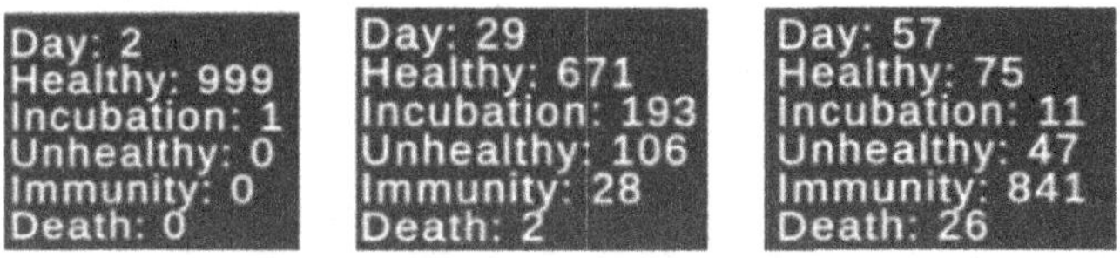

Day: 2
Healthy: 999
Incubation: 1
Unhealthy: 0
Immunity: 0
Death: 0
Day: 29
Healthy: 671
Incubation: 193
Unhealthy: 106
Immunity: 28
Death: 2
Day: 57
Healthy: 75
Incubation: 11
Unhealthy: 47
Immunity: 841
Death: 26

Fig. 5. Example of obtaining numerical data at different simulation stages.

Day: 15
Healthy: 123
Incubation: 198
Unhealthy: 173
Immunity: 5
Death: 1
MALL
School
Theatre

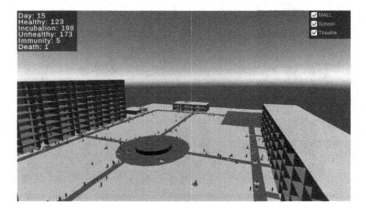

Fig. 6. Example of a Town Scene.

Town Scene simulation (Fig. 6). In the top right corner one can allow or block access to objects, simulating the introduction of restrictive measures, the results of access allowance or denial are shown in Figs. 7 and 8.

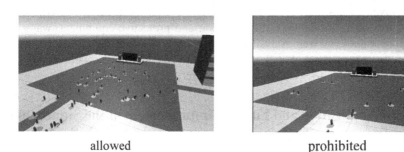

allowed prohibited

Fig. 7. Example of ban on access to public events.

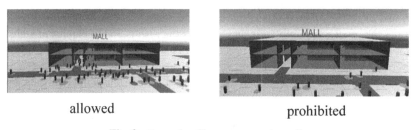

allowed   prohibited

Fig. 8. Example of ban on access to mall.

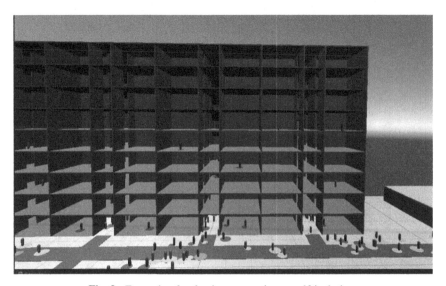

Fig. 9. Example of enforcing quarantine or self-isolation.

Once a person has had contact with an infected individual, there is a certain likelihood that he or she will head 'home' (Fig. 9). 'Home' is considered a multi-storey structure with numerous flats; the person occupies the nearest vacant flat and stays in it for the anticipated period of illness. Given a certain simplification, this behaviour algorithm can be perceived as hospitalisation. In this case, however, such factors as type and intensity of treatment, availability of medication and protective equipment, ways of patients transportation, as well as availability of a certain part of the test group, who will take on the role of medical staff, etc. all have to be taken into account. It will be implemented in the extended version of the software.

9   Scope of Application and Further Improvement of the Simulation Tool

Simulation results allows to compare different alternatives of the decision-making in order to choose the most efficient one. Furthermore, simulation results may be used to elaborate anti-epidemic measures, given the availability of the dynamics of the number of the infected and those who need medical assistance, it is possible to prepare the infrastructure and reduce the negative impact on the region, population and economy in general.

Apart from the described application opportunities, the current version of the simulation model has a range of restrictions, which could be addressed by creating special scenarios. Namely, by introducing certain route definition algorithms for the test group and by adding the scripts that enable specification of a wide number of characteristics for every element of the test group:

- other parameters leading to changes in population are disregarded (natural death, effects of other diseases, migration, relocation, etc.);
- lack of age and sex differentiation;
- possibility of vaccination;
- availability of infrastructure objects and transportation hubs;
- hospitalisation;
- duration of stay in the area with the risk of infection.

The main restriction of the tool remains its performance. The software requires a lot of computing power given a large size of the test group (more than 10,000), especially in complex scenarios where it is necessary to run collision and route definition scripts for each item.

In closed rooms such as shops or schools, the number of test persons should not exceed 1,000. In addition, congestions in closed rooms are also not uncommon, this is due to the fact that the elements cannot pass through each other and have to keep social distancing.

The modeling process for human behavior inside buildings is described in «Distributed Simulation of Crowds with Groups in CrowdSim» [22].

Furthermore, simulation models have to take social and economic factors of the region into account [23]. Simulation results may be used for development of strategies to manage disasters [24, 25], elaboration of infrastructure objects operation plan [26], reengineering and modernisation of public utility systems, including power sector [27].

10 Comparison of Modeling Results

In order to compare the ability of the application to achieve acceptable modelling results, we have implemented the same model in the NetLogo environment and using the GPSS language. A part of the results is shown in Table 1.

In Table 1, column A is the result of the simulation with developed application, column B contains the NetLogo simulation results, and column C is the GPSS simulation result. As can be seen, the simulation results are quite similar, as confirmed by the graphs, which illustrate the dynamics of the simulation. The following graphs (Figs. 10, 11 and 12) illustrate the dynamics of "Unhealthy". Despite the slight local differences, the general dynamic is the same.

Table 1. Comparing the results of the modelling.

Day	0			25			40			70		
	A	B	C	A	B	C	A	B	C	A	B	C
Healthy	999	999	999	819	824	819	179	174	173	74	71	67
Incubation	1	1	1	101	99	100	203	204	182	0	0	0
Unhealthy	0	0	0	69	68	70	327	329	329	1	0	1
Immunity	0	0	0	10	8	10	283	285	308	894	899	901
Death	0	0	0	1	1	1	8	8	8	31	30	31

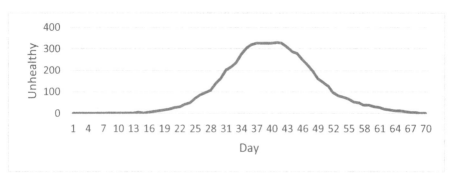

Fig. 10. Dynamics of the unhealthy parameter when modelling in the developed application.

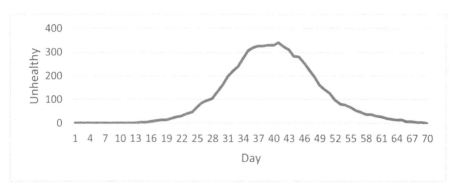

Fig. 11. Dynamics of the unhealthy parameter when modelling in NetLogo.

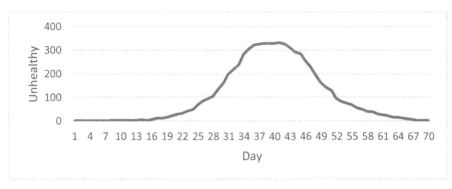

Fig. 12. Dynamics of the unhealthy parameter when modelling using GPSS

11 Conclusions

A software tool, enabling by means of simulation modelling to analyse the effectiveness of restrictive measures as well as the application of personal protective equipment, has been developed. The software was created in the Unity environment. The software allows the setting of the size of the test group, availability and type of individual protection equipment as well as varying simulation scenarios. As a result of the simulation, there is data available on the statistics and dynamics of the number of the infected, healthy, immunised and dead. Due to the possibility of creating scripts in the Unity environment, it is possible to recreate unique situations during the simulation and to evaluate the effectiveness of restrictive measures. The opportunity to simulate and evaluate the effectiveness of restrictive measures helps to justify the appropriateness of such restrictions and to choose the most efficient solution. This will minimise losses, both in terms of human casualties and economic indicators. The results of simulations carried out in different environments turned out similar. The dynamics of changes in key parameters differ by less than 3% on average and do not exceed 5% at each iteration step. Such modelling results suggest that the proposed simulation tool provides correct results and may be used for research, forecasting and decision-making.

References

1. World Health Organization: Considerations for quarantine of individuals in the context of containment for coronavirus disease (COVID-19). 19 March 2020. World Health Organization, Geneva (2020). https://apps.who.int/iris/bitstream/handle/10665/331497/WHO-2019-nCoV-IHR_Quarantine-2020.2-eng.pdf?sequence=1&isAllowed=y. Accessed 24 Sept 2021
2. Rothstein, M.A., Alcalde, M.G., Elster, N.R., Majumder, M.A., et al.: Quarantine and isolation: lessons learned from SARS, a report to the Centers for Disease Control and Prevention, pp. 1–160. Institute for Bioethics Health Policy and Law, University of Louisville School of Medicine, Louisville (KY) (2013)
3. Tognotti, E.: Lessons from the history of quarantine, from plague to influenza A. Emerg. Infect. Dis. **19**(2), 254–259 (2013). https://doi.org/10.3201/eid1902.120312
4. Cohen, D.: The Black Death, pp. 1347–1351. Franklin Watts, New York (1974)

5. Barua, D.: History of cholera. In: Barua, D., Greenough, W.B. III (eds.) Cholera. Plenum Medical Book Co., New York (1992)
6. Mafart, B., Perret, J.L.: History of the concept of quarantine. Med. Trop (Mars). **58**, 14–20 (1998). (in French)
7. Tognotti, E.: Scientific triumphalism and learning from facts: bacteriology and the "Spanish flu" challenge of 1918. Soc. Hist. Med. **16**, 97–110 (2003). https://doi.org/10.1093/shm/16.1.97
8. World Health Organization: Key messages and actions for COVID-19 prevention and control in schools. World Health Organization, Geneva. https://www.who.int/docs/default-source/coronaviruse/key-messages-and-actions-for-covid-19-prevention-and-control-in-schools-march-2020.pdf. Accessed 24 Sept 2021
9. Liu, W., Hethcote, H.W., Levin, S.A.: Dynamical behavior of epidemiological models with nonlinear incidence rates. J. Math. Biol. **25**(4), 359–380 (1987)
10. Wang, P., Zheng, X., Ai, G., Liu, D., Zhu, B.: Time series prediction for the epidemic trends of COVID-19 using the improved LSTM deep learning method: case studies in Russia, Peru, and Iran. Chaos Solit. Fract. **140**, 110214, 1–8 (2020). https://doi.org/10.1016/j.chaos.2020.110214
11. Ng, K.Y., Gui, M.M.: COVID-19: development of a robust mathematical model and simulation package with consideration for ageing population and time delay for control action and resusceptibility. Phys. D. **411**, 132599 (2020). https://doi.org/10.1016/j.physd.2020.132599
12. Schruben, L.: Analytical simulation modeling. In: 2008 Winter Simulation Conference, pp. 113–121 (2008). https://doi.org/10.1109/WSC.2008.4736061
13. Yanbo, P., Takahiro, Y., Kota, T., Takehiro, K., Sekimoto, Y.: Development of a people mass movement simulation framework based on reinforcement learning. Transp. Res. Part C Emerg. Technol. **117**, 1–16 (2020)
14. Daley, D.J.: Epidemic Modelling: An Introduction. Cambridge University Press, Cambridge (2008)
15. Fine, P.E.M.: John Brownlee and the measurement of infectiousness: an historical study in epidemic theory. J. R. Stat. Soc. Ser. A (General) **142**, 347–362 (1979). https://doi.org/10.2307/2982487
16. Kermack, W.O., McKendrick, A.G.: A contribution to the mathematical theory of epidemics. Proc. R. Soc. A **115**, 700–721 (1927). https://doi.org/10.1098/rspa.1927.0118
17. Engelmann, L.: A box, a trough and marbles: how the reed-frost epidemic theory shaped epidemiological reasoning in the 20th century. Hist. Philos. Life Sci. **43**(3), 1–24 (2021). https://doi.org/10.1007/s40656-021-00445-z
18. Zhang, J., Jin, Z., Sun, G.-Q., Sun, X.-D., Ruan, S.: Spatial spread of rabies in China. J. Comput. Anal. Appl. **2**, 111–126 (2012)
19. Chen, J., Zou, L., Jin, Z., Ruan, S.: Modeling the geographic spread of rabies in China. PLoS Negl. Trop. Dis. **9**(5), 1–18 (2015)
20. Chumachenko, D., Chumachenko, T., Meniailov, I., Pyrohov, P., Kuzin, I., Rodyna, R.: On-line data processing, simulation and forecasting of the coronavirus disease (COVID-19) propagation in Ukraine based on machine learning approach. In: Babichev, S., Peleshko, D., Vynokurova, O. (eds.) DSMP 2020. CCIS, vol. 1158, pp. 372–382. Springer, Cham (2020). https://doi.org/10.1007/978-3-030-61656-4_25
21. Glybochko, P., Fomin, V., Avdeev, S., et al.: Clinical characteristics of 1007 intensive care unit patients with SARS-CoV-2 pneumonia. Klinicheskaya farmakologiya i terapiya. Clin. Pharmacol. Ther. **29**(2), 21–29 (2020). https://doi.org/10.32756/0869-5490-2020-2-21-29
22. Abadeer, M., Gorlatch, S.: Distributed simulation of crowds with groups in CrowdSim. DS-RT 2019: In: Proceedings of the 23rd IEEE/ACM International Symposium on Distributed Simulation and Real Time Applications. pp. 128–135 (2019)

23. Grebennik, I., Semenets, V., Hubarenko, Y.: Information technologies for assessing the impact of climate change and natural disasters in socio-economic systems. In: Murayama, Y., Velev, D., Zlateva, P. (eds.) ITDRR 2019. IAICT, vol. 575, pp. 21–30. Springer, Cham (2020). https://doi.org/10.1007/978-3-030-48939-7_3
24. Grebennik, I., Khriapkin, O., Ovezgeldyyev, A., Pisklakova, V., Urniaieva, I.: The concept of a regional information-analytical system for emergency situations. In: Murayama, Y., Velev, D., Zlateva, P. (eds.) ITDRR 2017. IAICT, vol. 516, pp. 55–66. Springer, Cham (2019). https://doi.org/10.1007/978-3-030-18293-9_6
25. Grebennik, I., Reshetnik, V., Ovezgeldyyev, A., Ivanov, V., Urniaieva, I.: Strategy of effective decision-making in planning and elimination of consequences of emergency situations In: Murayama, Y., Velev, D., Zlateva, P. (eds.) Information technology in disaster risk reduction, ITDRR 2018, vol. 550, pp. 66–75. IFIP Advances in Information and Communication Technology (2019)
26. Grebennik, I., Semenets, V., Hubarenko, Y., Hubarenko, M., Spasybin, M.: Creating a list of works on reconstruction of infrastructure elements in natural disasters based on information technologies. In: Murayama, Y., Velev, D., Zlateva, P. (eds.) ITDRR 2020. IAICT, vol. 622, pp. 144–159. Springer, Cham (2021). https://doi.org/10.1007/978-3-030-81469-4_12
27. Grebennik, I., Ovezgeldyyev, A., Hubarenko, Y., Hubarenko, M.: Information technology reengineering of the electricity generation system in post-disaster recovery. In: Murayama, Y., Velev, D., Zlateva, P. (eds.) ITDRR 2019. IAICT, vol. 575, pp. 9–20. Springer, Cham (2020). https://doi.org/10.1007/978-3-030-48939-7_2

Author Index

Printed in the United States
by Baker & Taylor Publisher Services